THE REVIEW

OF

ANCIENT AND MODERN

SPIRITUALISM.

L. SOLENTIA.

IN TWO VOLUMES.

VOL. I.

REVIEW OF

NATURES DIVINE·REVELATIONS,

AND

A. J. DAVIS ON SPIRITUALISM.

NEW YORK:
O. W. SCOTT & A. G. MARTIN, PUBLISHERS.
1862.

CONTENTS.

NOTES TO CONTENTS OF VOL. I.

I. The object of the Prelude is to discover the locality of this age in the moral sphere of the race. To this end the signs of the times are considered ; error is, without apology, called by its true name. False professions, and not the true church are opposed. And while the untrue and unfaithful are exposed, the truth and its lovers are revered. The Church of Christ is sought and the true christian defended.

II. Being — its state, is the philosophy of Religion and man's religious nature epitomized. This forms a key to succeeding subjects.

III. The "Review of A. J. Davis," exhibits the emptiness of Pantheism : and "Nature's Divine Revelations" is selected because it comprehends the fundamental arguments of the philosophy opposed to christianity.

IV. This volume is the first step in our expose of false metaphysics and the defence of Christianity ; as such it is the base of the Ant-Pantheist.

INTRODUCTION.

So urgent is the "spirit of the age" upon improvement, and novel subjects for the display of genius, that the mind has an aversion to what *has been* adopted; and like a ship loosing from its native shore, is launching into unknown seas. The triumph of the arts and sciences has so exalted man in his own estimation, that many, forgetting their utter dependence, feel shielded by their own mightiness. Casting off fear, they restrain prayer before God, and, as if the first born, and made before the hills, boast of *their reason;* assume the judgment seat, seek to adjust universal balances, and determine the ways of the Almighty; pass judgment upon Bible religion, pronouncing it mythological, unreasonable, and doomed to fall before the spirit of improvement. The world, they affirm, "needs a philosophy which Jesus did not furnish; a revelation to *reason* which the Bible does not contain."

Since the Patriarchal age, the doctrine of Divine Inspiration has never been more boldly assailed than now. And no country bears a more luxuriant harvest of Deism than America.

The land sought by the Puritans for the unobstructed growth of Bible Religion, has become the nursery of as rank infidelity as ever blinded the eyes and benumbed the sense of man. And the proud foe of God rocks the continent, lulling man's conscience with *Circean melody,* while he is shorn of his strength, and deprived of his vision.

Science is declared at variance with the Scriptures, and unfolding law, with the christian faith; and Modern Spiritualism, as "God's interpreter," urges its bewildering tide upon the world, gathering thousands into its necromatic current.

This volume is devoted to the discussion of those claims which have been and are being urged as more rational and useful to the race than christianity—which are denominated by the advocates, "The Religion of Reason;" and no one familiar with the modern mind and the tendency of the age, can fail to have discovered that the Rationalists have done much to weaken the faith of many in the doctrines of a revealed Religion. This is not only manifest by the common mind, but men of high professions and no ordinary influence have been either metamosphosed or greatly swerved in their religious belief, by this power of anti-Christ. And while the secret workings of Infidel principles have been moulding the mind, too few, by far, of professed Christians, have labored to qualify themselves to properly oppose the anti-Christian tide, and compete with the influence of those who have been laboring to undermine the Church of Jesus.

In these volumes the author has endeavored to provide the reader with the leading propositions and arguments now urged against the Christian Religion, and also, with their analysis, and in a manner to disclose their unsoundness, inconsistency, and utter incapacity to meet the wants of the soul, or commend themselves to the sense of well balanced, uncharmed and unbewildered minds.

The surface tide of Modern Mesmerism, Psychology, and Spiritualism, having subsided, it is often asked, "Why agitate the subject? Why not let the fanaticism die by neglect?" As well might the household seek to extinguish the smouldering fire in their dwelling by neglect, or a community seek to sleep down a pestilence. For this moral malaria arising from the decayed ruins of ancient Pantheism, is infusing its religious bane throughout the enlightened world, and those of sensitive natures are receiving the elements as secretly as an enemy sows tares by night. And since the novelty of the newly garbed materialism of the ancients has passed, the mind effected is cleaveing to the writings of A. J. Davis, the real founder and oracle of the modern manifestations, hence the greater danger, for in a silent and unobtrusive manner the unlearned and pleasure-loving are being indoctrinated. And thus, a secret enemy is wielding a moral and religious influence unnoticed and unmolested by the multitudes. For this reason, the Author has selected and reviewed the first work of Mr. Davis, a work which, in fact, is the text book of his Hommorialism, and which contains the germs of the issues promulgated by modern opposers of Christianity, and advocates of Spiritualism. This work, entitled "Nature's Divine Revelations, or a voice to Mankind," is chosen, for the following reasons:

1. Because it purports to be the speech of Nature, her own address in behalf of her true character, and her self-exoneration from false charges brought by the Theocratic system, which has been offered to man as "Divine

Revelation," the "Word of God," the "Revelations" inspired by the Holy Spirit, which this "Speech of Nature" claims as false, and a burlesque.

2. Because it is perhaps the most complete work among those in which the subject is systematized.

3. Because it is admitted as a great literary production, even by many who do not credit its purported authenticity.

4. Because it was produced under the most favorable circumstances, those calculated to render it as perfect a system as can be developed upon the subject.

5. Because it was developed in this age—an age well adapted to the defence of a natural religion.

6. Because it blends the Pantheism of the past with the Deistic Spiritualism of the present.

7. Because it spiritualizes those theories that have been laid down as the foundation of material philosophy and the religion of Nature.

8. Because it emerged from the mesmeric fountain as the head tide of Modern Spiritualism, and suggests the system of doctrines promulgated by modern spiritualists.

9. Because its strength is the congregation of those principles arrayed against the Bible, by those who oppose the Christian religion.

10. And finally, we introduce "Nature's Divine Revelations," with our analysis of it, because its sophistry, the magnetic spirit with which it is infused, its high-toned transcendentalism and bewildering influences, have led and are leading, by the charm of novelty, many to reject the doctrines of christianity and trust in it as a

better system of religion. And because its influence upon the mind of believers tends to weaken their sense of Divine rights and to deify man; and because it started from their moorings, those who have been most prominent in the promulgation of anti-biblical sentiments, under the title of "the Harmonialism Philosophy," and Modern Spiritualism.

In our analysis, we have, in two instances, contrasted the philosophy of this book with the statements of the Bible, upon the same subjects, in order thereby to reveal their disparity.

In opening the discussion, we have, under the title of "The Prelude," glanced at the signs of the times, and addressed a class of modern religionists whom we denominate "Nominal Christians, the modern Jerusalems," a class who make *faith* and *religion* dependent upon intellectual attainments, compromizing spiritual and humble devotion, while their piety and worship is addressed to the *taste* of the fastidious rather than the soul and to the God and object of true religious devotions. *Such, and such only, are those addressed in the Prelude, and not the true church of the living God, the members of which seek to draw near the Throne, and to worship in Spirit and in Truth, and who are laboring for the world's redemption, through Divine Agency.*

The volume concludes with a summary review of the position and arguments of A. J. Davis, with regard to Modern Spiritualism. In this Review we have no disposition to judge the motives or sincerity of any—principles and not men, are, therefore, analyzed and criticised.

There are many quite indisposed to examine modern

phenomena, or read arguments against the anti-Christian philosophy of this age. But every believer in the Christian Religion should be prepared to answer the arguments of the opposer; if not for themselves, they should be qualified to shield others, and sustain the weak. To this end the present work is offered to the public. For, if the Christian may not himself be tempted into infidelity, he should understand the sophistry of his opposers, sufficiently to to defeat his purpose upon uncultivated minds.

PROSPECT SUMMIT, SCOTT, N. Y.

L. SOLENTIA.

April 25, 1862.

PRELUDE.

THE Nineteenth Century! Age unequalled! age of wonders! In this are blending the inspiring elements of antecedent ages.

This especial period—the *middle* of the nine teenth century—by many of the best informed and clearest minds has been considered the period, which above all others, would result in fearful and momentous consequences. And indeed, so strange and startling are present events, that men of profound research, deem this the closing epoch foretold in the Scriptures, and understood as "*the end of the world.*"

These are comparing the movements of men, and the phenomena of nature, with the prophecies, to determine if the time is not at hand when the Sun of the Millennial year shall arise, and shed the glory of its peaceful reign upon the world. And who, from a critical examination of the "signs of the times," can fail to realize the foreshadowing of some great event?

Accumulating facts admonish us that our age is one of unprecedented interest; one of strange developments and of universal restlessness.

New discoveries in the principles and procedures of nature, and the rapid advance of scientific improvements, indicate augmented labor, in the great human sensory of the analytical and constructive laws of mind; and that these laws, urging their inspiring currents along the channels of genius, are especially active in the development of principles; and from the conception of design prompting speedy ultimation.

Man therefore, with apparent supernatural perception and unlimited wisdom, scans the manifestations of nature around him, traces minutely the movements of her mysterious laws, and, by reason of his superior attainments, directs them at will, and in their mightitude they obey him.

Subservient then to man, earth unveils her long concealed treasures, and lavishly pours at his feet her exhaustless stores. The aqueous element, also, obedient to his mandate, transformed, arises, and propelling his massive and complicated machinery, bears him over land and sea; and thus increasing his commercial facilities, enables him to bestow upon inland dwellers, from maritime marts, the productions of every clime and the wealth of every sea.

The lightning too, whose destructive bolt shivers the massive oak, and whose majesty utters terrific thunders, controlled by man, courses the magnetic wire—courier of National decrees, or bearer of kindly messages to absent friends.

By these means, the hitherto severed and distracted tribes and nations of the Earth, members of one common race, are fraternally linked, and with ties as enduring as those of a domestic brotherhood.

But these advantages do not meet the wants of man, nor bear him to the goal of his marvelous expectancy. He will not be satisfied though he can hie him o'er the Continent with the fleetness of the wind, and chase the wild tempest with his rattling car; can rush his floating palace through storm and wave, or take the lightning in his hand, bidding it, more faithful than the carrier dove and with the velocity of thought, convey his message to a distant clime. Or, from his observatory, resolve the heavenly spheres, pursue the flaming comet in its boundless wanderings, and with mathematical precision determine the transits of revolving orbs.

Not capable, with these grand achievements, of meeting the wants of his ambitious spirit, man indulges bright hopes of still higher attainments; and thus inspired, fixes his earnest gaze upon objects yet in the distance; pleads with nature for unequalled developments, and smiles at surrounding mysteries as things of trifling merit. A presentiment of approaching wonders fires his being, prompting him to wild adventures, and he proceeds to displace whatever impedes his progress, and to change the order of things, as may best conserve his interest. He therefore proceeds to level mountains and exalt valleys; he lays his hand upon Royal Brows, and plucks Diadems from Kingly Heads; bids Monarchs abdicate their Thrones, and crushes Nations with his iron grasp.

Shall we not deem these manifestations important, and this the age of wonders foretold by the spirit of prophecy? "Behold," saith the Spirit, "The shield of His mighty men shall be made red, the valiant men are in scarlet: the chariots shall be with flaming torches in the day of his preparation, and the fir trees shall be terribly shaken. The chariots shall rage in the streets, they shall jostle one against another in the broad ways: they shall seem like torches, they shall run like the lightnings. The gates of the rivers shall be opened and the palace shall be dissolved." Naham ch. 2.

And again: "Ye shall hear of wars and rumors of wars. Nation shall rise up against nation, and kingdom against kingdom, and there shall be famine and pestilence; and upon earth distress of nations with perplexity; men's hearts failing them for fear and for looking after those things which are coming upon the earth; for the powers of heaven shall be shaken. And then shall ye see the signs of the Son of Man coming in the clouds. And when ye begin to see these things come to pass, then lift up your heads, for your redemption draweth nigh."

Another and by no means inferior indication that the old world is passing away, is manifested in that undefinable mingling of man's spiritual nature with his efforts for freedom, and which prospectively blends the present with the consequences of a portentious future. This is revealed by the revolutions now razing the governments of men from their foundations.

Some of the most prominent actors in this great political drama now moving before the amazed world, although professedly prompted by the spirit of an improved governmental policy, seem inspired by some strange influences.

Some seem urged forth by a desire of ecclesiastical supremacy, as instanced in the disruption of kingdoms in the eastern world; some are professing holy *dictum* from the spirits of fallen heroes, others from the Eternal Spirit.

Leading statesmen in every Kingdom and Government, are predicting events pregnant with new born policy, which shall effect significant changes in the jurisprudence of men and nations—and their predictions are borne in haste over every sea, and chase each other along the telegraphic wires of every land. And thus the world is agitated, monarchs are untiring in their efforts to confirm their power, while appears an almost universal desire with the populace to arise out of the present and to assume new forms of government.

And our own Nation, a nation hitherto, crowned with honor and bearer of the ensign of peace, is aroused from its peaceful repose, and war is devastating the land. Brother is armed against brother, and father against son, so that in truth "a man's foes are those of his own house."

The world feels the commotion of this far-famed and hitherto much honored Republic—and nations stand aghast while witnessing the awful conflict, and as is recorded of a fallen city,—

"The merchants of the earth stand afar off saying alas, that great city, which was clothed in fine linen, and decked with gold! For in an hour so great riches has come to naught, and every ship-master, and all the company in ships, and sailors, and as many as trade by sea stood afar off, and cried, when they saw the smoke of her burning, alas, alas, that city wherein were made rich all that had ships in the sea by reason of her costliness! for in one hour she is made desolate."*

Terror has seized the hearts of Americans, and widows and orphans mourn for their loved ones

*Rev. 18.

slain in the conflicts—in that land hitherto deemed a nation of hope, the world's asylum.

Combattants are invoking the arm of Jehovah to aid in their struggle, while the hand of war clutches the government with its bloody grasp. The pious are before the throne, while the profane vent their spirit of revenge.

Learned divines, throughout Christendome, are scrutinizing the phenomena of the day to determine their relation to the events which, according to the prophets, are immediately to precede the millenial reign; and the press is uttering their deductions in every civilized land.

As we emerge from these exciting scenes we meet another wild wave of the great maelstrom which is bearing the past to its gloomy sepulchre. And here are gyrating the prophets of unnumbered modern "isms," who are announcing their mission to what they term a church-enthralled race. These, while seeking to annul the Bible, denouncing it as the tool of cunning priestcraft, aver that *they* are commissioned to reveal the laws and counsels of "Superior Spheres," and therefore laws which, if obeyed—and they affirm they must be sooner or later—will result in freedom from the bonds of biblical religion, which is the object of their mission.

From these whirling elements, therefore, arises

a strange form; one of gigantic dimensions, on whose frantic brow is inscribed "*Harmonial Spiritualism*," and controlling the senses of these modern prophets, poets and seers, it moves its multitudinous tongue and we hear, as the utterances of ten thousand voices, "*Manes*," "*Manes*." Self-redeemed Nature arises supernal. *All is well*."

These prophets and advocates of *harmonial spiritualism* assay to compete with Bible miracles by the display of their strange powers, and numbering their forces as the stars of heaven, shout *their* triumph, and the overthrow of the Christian Religion.

Some, however,

> Less bold by far and courteous too

Sing of Jesus, as

> The Man Divine:

But denying human depravity, the reason why men need the Savior, they make void his Mission, and by flattering unsound and pleasure-loving churchmen, wheedle them into stepping stones to the tympanum of a capricious public, where perched these proud Euphuists

> Warble forth enchanting Strains
> Of senseless melody.

These authors of spiritual vagaries, poetic fancies, and transcendental dreamings, by charming, render enthusiastic the unstable and excitable members of community. Hence originate conflicting and vague interpretations of Nature and Revelation, which are proffered as more perfect means of redemption than God has revealed in his Holy Word. From this cause arises confirmed opposition to all who believe in the Lord Jesus as the Savior of Sinners.

Prayer is ridiculed as the height of religious delusion; the Bible represented as an imperfect, compend of the notions of undeveloped and half civilized men,—the imperfect sketches of semi-barbarous spiritualists, or a book of unchaste legends, unworthy of confidence in this age of superior light and revelation.

Denying the Divinity of Jesus Christ, it is affirmed that nature, and modern clairvoyant and necromantic teachings, afford ample means for intellectual and spiritual improvement; and that all former knowledge is the mere semblance of truth. Therefore, past Revelations compared to the present, are as the falling husks from the substantial kernel, or the separation of diseased bodies from the pure spirit.

Does not this opposition to the Christian Religion confirm the truth of the Bible, the very Word opposed, and also fulfill those Scriptures which refer to the latter day? saying, "There were false prophets also among the people, as there shall be false teachers among you, who shall privily bring in damnable heresies even denying the Lord that bought them, and bring upon themselves swift destruction, and many shall follow their pernicious ways, by reason of which the way of truth shall be evil spoken of. For the spirit speaketh expressly that in the latter times some shall depart from the faith, giving heed to seducing spirits and doctrines of devils; speaking lies in hypocrisy, having their consciences seared as with a hot iron. And then shall that wicked be revealed, whose coming is after the working of Satan, with all power, and signs, and lying wonders, and in all deceitfulness and uurighteousness in them that perish.

Could prophecy have been more explicit in the delineation of that power which is now making war with the Bible?

The relation which many sustain to the events of the day indicates the predicted trial. For, while infidelity is bearing the youthful mind by the mysterious agencies, which seem as urgent as unconquerable monsoons, through the channels of religious skepticism to the vortex of death, nominal professors of Christianity are shrinking from the bold declarations of Truth, and error is fostered and substituted for the teachings of the Bible. And no marvel if by the side of the indifferent and their misguided followers the sword of the Spirit should hang in the scabbard of popular applause, or the Gospel banner droop by the cross, while over the chasm existing between Truth and Error, such are bending to place their lips to those of infidels; or that truth should suffer and faith decline, while beneath these inclining forms the masses are allured from the Gospel by the sophistry of false ethics. Woe to the city when her watchmen join hands with besiegers.

Such teachers do not proceed with the keen scalpel of Truth to trace the living nerve, and with a resolute hand to sever the fibres of diseased parts and accumulating fungus? Neither with a sense of the responsibility of an heavenly embassador, and with the earnestness of divine unction, proclaim the unadulterated and living Oracles of God? Nor by removing the mystic garb obscuring the end of evil, reveals the hideous form of unbelief, and with the pencil of Truth portray the awful abode of the perverted soul in the gloomy regions of the dead—the sphere outwrought by a life of transgression.

Are such built upon the foundation of the prophets and apostles, Jesus Christ being the chief corner stone? Or do their works liken them to the Israelites, who condemned the meek Nazerene to the cross? and whose fate indicates the final subjugation of all like ecclesiastic polity.

Let those who deem the reference foreign or

unjust, unite with us while we raise the fallen curtain which conceals from modern vision the scenes of olden times, and trace the calendar of the past to the memorable day when Jesus of Nazareth preached the kingdom of God with men. In the land of Judea let us pause beneath the shadow of the house of Israel, that we may the more perfectly determine the analogy. And in the gorgeous synagogue and religious parade of the Sanhedrim, let the proud and the vain of the Nineteenth Century behold their image; and in the hollow worship, the emptiness of their religious show. Or, with the opulent, from their arched terraces observe that strange form moving with the gathering crowd; that personage whose coat, without a seam, does not display the pride of life, the fashion or taste of the worldly wise, whose sandals the dust of the streets cannot harm, who gives audience to the poorest of the sons of men, and with whom there is no respect of persons.

His movements are slow and solemn. His calm demeanor betokens his holy dignity. His regard for the afflicted, who pray "O, thou Son of David, have mercy on us," reveals the emotion of his overflowing soul. And who is this? Echo, from the proud Sanhedrim, answers, "The Nazarene—the carpenter's son—Jesus, the impostor;" while a voice from heaven utters,

"THIS IS MY BELOVED SON." And the Scriptures answer, "*Amen,*" *His works say,* "*Amen;*" and the Church Militant, in her humility, from the rack and burning fagot, responds, "Amen." "Jesus of Nazareth is our Saviour, our Life, our hope, and source of everlasting joy. God manifest in the flesh. The King of kings and Lord of lords."

Thus is revealed—and sad to realize—by the Author of Redemption and his professed Israel, the infinite contrast eternally existing between the Spirit of Jesus and Christianity, and the religion of perverted men: and how great the contrast!

The proud Pharisees beneath the emblazoned arch, with mocking mien scorn the humble Nazarene, moving with the masses below.

They, by their polished profession, are as whited sepulchres; while Jesus, unpretending and lamb-like, bends over prostrate humanity, wipes tears from weeping eyes, soothes the troubled spirit, and bids the mourner go in peace. He, the King of Israel—"God with us"—pities and forgives the guilty, while they cast off and contemn the innocent.

They, receive honor of men and despise the poor; He, the Shepherd, takes the lambs in his arms, protects them from devouring wolves and chilling blasts. They listen to idle flattery, and are satisfied; He hears the suppliant's prayer, and, blessing, receives as his reward, the tears of gladness, and the homage of contrite hearts. Great the contrast!

They, lead to altars of vain show, and prompt religious mockery. He, inspires the sacrifice of pure praise and exalts to mansions in heaven, purchased by his own blood. They, dwell with the rich and feast in royal palaces. He, frequents the abodes of the poor and eats with publicans and sinners, saying, "The foxes have holes and the birds of the air have nests; but the Son of Man hath not where to lay his head."

Finally, in death, they recline upon silken couches, and the populace in mournful measures, chant their solemn requiem.

But He, by the world unpitied and condemned, bleeds for transgressors upon the cross, while the frantic multitude vociferate, "Crucify him, crucify him." INFINITE THE CONTRAST!

This distinction is clearly illustrated in the parable of the Pharisee and the Publican. The Pharisee stood and prayed thus with himself: "God I thank thee that I am not as other men, extortioners, unjust, adulterers, or even as this publican. I fast twice in the week, and give tithes of all I possess." But the publican, standing afar off, would not lift up so much as his eyes unto heaven, but smote upon his breast, saying,

"God be merciful to me a sinner." "Every one that exalteth himself shall be abased; and he that humbleth himself shall be exalted."

Blinded by their conceit, and clad in self-righteousness, the pompous Jews rested secure; nor could they be aroused to a sense of the ruin that awaited their hierarchical dominion.

Have nominal professors. eyes, and cannot see; ears, and cannot hear? And, in view of the vain service and final fall of the haughty Jews, will they trifle with sacred rites and mimic the spirit of divine ordinances? Then may they read their destiny in the doom of that ancient city, whose policy, having no divine protection, yielded to the strong arm of the besieger.

Bow down and worship, thou modern Jerusalem; in deep humility call upon thy God; if peradventure thy doom may be averted. Or hast thou parted with thy birthright, and for a morsel bartered thy inheritance! Shall thy fate be like that of ancient Israel, whose prayer was unavailing when the smoke of her torments lowered the heavens above and the elements frowned upon her; when famine and pestilence reigned within the walls of the great city, and mothers, mad with hunger, fed upon the flesh of their own babes!

The Jewish priest called upon Israel's God, and there was no answer; but the heavens became as brass above, while the earth gave way beneath them. Proud Israel fell!

Will your priests, in the day of trial offer in vain their oblation; and, drinking the cup of your fornication, will ye plunge into the fearful abyss?

Did afflicted Jerusalem regard Jehovah unmerciful, that he did not hear; and unrighteous in the measure of their afflictions?

They might have read in the gleaming cloud of the fierce tempest, the cause of their unmitigated woe.

Did they remember the despised Nazarene? Had they forgotten the declaration of his mission of love to them; and that when rejected, in tears and solemn lamentation, he cried, "O Jerusalem, Jerusalem, thou that killest the prophets and stonest them which are sent unto thee, how often would I have gathered thy children unto me as a hen gathereth her brood under her wings; but ye would not!"

"In vain gifts have been bestowed upon you; in vain the oxen and fatling have been killed; and in vain Mercy pleads at your door. As ye make light of the King and his offering, thus provoking the fearful retribution which awaits you, heaven repeats the irrevocable law, and unveils before you the dread consequences of its violation. Could more be done for your peace? Ye have had line upon line, and precept upon precept. But when they came to you with the King's embassy, ye have wantonly slain his servants, and wasted his goods in your riotings. Ye also seek the life of his only Son, while mercifully pleading with you. Behold, your house is left unto you desolate!

"Oh, Jerusalem! House of Israel! I have plead with you until the day is spent, and until my locks are wet with the drops of the night. Ye will not rise from your bed of myrrh! ye will not hearken!

"Henceforth the vineyard shall not flourish, until the hedge thereof shall be taken away and the walls thereof be trodden down: but there shall come up briers and thorns, and the clouds, by command, shall not rain upon it.

"Ye who are wise in your own eyes, and prudent in your own sight, and who say to the voice of God that bringeth these tidings, 'Let him make speed, and hasten his work, that we may see it: and let his counsel who would have us regard him as the Holy One of Israel, draw nigh, and let him come in the display of his power, that we may know it!'

"Wo unto you who call evil good, and good evil, which justify the wicked for reward, and take away the righteousness of the righteous from him. As the fire devoureth the stubble, and the flame consumeth the chaff, so your root shall be as rottenness, and the blossom of your doings shall go up as dust; because ye have cast away the law of the Lord of hosts, and despised the Word of the Holy One of Israel. Isa. 5.

"And now I go to him that sent me. Ye shall seek me and shall not find me. Henceforth ye shall not see me until ye shall say, 'Blessed is he that cometh in the name of the Lord.' Did Israel still remember that solemn message? Was not the image of the suffering Son before them; and did not the echo of his solemn valedictory still dwell in the quivering atmosphere; and had not each word of that awful prophesy assumed living form, and pursued them like ghostly spectres? Or, as immortal entities, did they not repeat: "Behold your house is left unto you desolate; and I go to him that sent me. Ye shall seek me and shall not find me?"

No marvel, then, that the abased Sanhedrim should, in the day of trial, afflict their souls in vain; should put on sackcloth, and mourn in dust and ashes without avail. Or that the Priests should multiply their sacrifices and burnt offerings upon golden altars, unanswered by the Shekinah.

They had offered the Great Sacrifice, though in malice, when they hung upon the Cross their

King. Thus rejecting the True Light, darkness encompassed them.

When Jesus expired, the vail of the Temple was rent, and the Life and Power thereof departed. And as they despised the only name in heaven, or given among men, by which Salvation cometh, why offer the oblation,—pleading the Lord to avert the impending judgment,—since Jesus, finally cast off by them, uttered, "Behold, your house is left unto you desolate!" There was no hope! Jerusalem *fell!*"

To the Christian of the Nineteenth Century we solemnly appeal, and of him enquire, if, according to the Scriptures, he is looking for the consummation of the Gospel of Jesus. Does he not expect the Judgment; and must *it* not begin at the house of God?

When the Refiner appeareth, the gold must be purified; and when He maketh up His jewels, they that fear God and work righteousness will be spared, as a man spareth his own son that serveth him. Israel of old departed from God, and in her trial failed, and the storm swept her away like a house built upon the sand. Yet a remnant was saved, who bore the Spiritual Ark and Covenant to the Gentiles. And when the fullness of time is come, they too shall be judged, and in that judgment the faithful and obedient shall be spared, and encompassed as with a shield of fire; but the faithless and unbelieving, the hypocrite and profane, shall be swept away as with the besom of destruction.

From the foregoing we conclude—

1. That the strange phenomena moving mind and matter, the conflict of Nations, the peculiar manifestations of man's religious nature; modern prophets, and the strange excitement known as spiritualism, indicate some important crisis at hand.

2. From the determinate and unprecedented opposition to the Christian religion, we conclude, according to the Scriptures, that Antichrist has arisen.

3. We judge that nominal Christians, omitting the weightier matters of the law, Justice, Mercy and Faith, and seeking fellowship with Mammon and her worshipers, are fulfilling, in themselves, the prophets, and affording evidence of the approaching Consummation.

4. Having reference to the history of the Jews —their ignorance of the presence of the Messiah, although in their midst, his final rejection by them, together with their fall; by analogy, we infer that nominal christians of this day, who manifest so little of the true spirit of Christ, are imitating the example of ancient Israel, and thus provoking upon themselves like consequences —the consequences that await the apostate church in the last day. Thus in the events of

this age, the Word of God is maintained and fulfilled, and signs are afforded of the second coming of the Son of Man.

That these conclusions are legitimate, we appeal to the history of the past; the scenes of the present, the hope of the child of God, and finally, to the WORD, in which God has covenanted in Jesus, by whom he is reconciling the world to himself, to restore all things.

Then wo to the rebellious, the hypocrite and unbeliever, to the lords and potentates of the earth: for a day of terror awaits the ungodly. But joy, peace and salvation unto those who love the Lord Jesus, and like the wise virgins, are patiently waiting the coming of the Bridegroom, for they shall enter through the gates into the holy City.

And, to the slumbering watchman, it may be said, "Sleep on: the Day of the Lord has come. Ye taught it and believed it not'"

BEING—ITS STATE.

It is of the utmost importance that we understand the intrinsic qualities of our primary being, together with the extrinsic influences to which it is liable. This knowledge is especially essential when considered in the light of our immortality. To obtain it should engage our first thoughts.

Man, in his constitution unites those principles and forces which qualify him a receptacle of the laws and attributes of the physical and spiritual realm, both of which blend in his composition. A truer statement of man, originally, cannot be made—a more perfect philosophy of his being, and of its creation, cannot be adduced, than is recorded in Gen., chap. 2. "The Lord God formed man of the dust of the ground, and breathed into his nostrils the breath of life, and he became a living soul."

Volumes have been written as exponents of man, of his origin and constitution, but all do not say more. The profoundest thought cannot fathom its depths, the widest range does not approach its boundary, nor the most lofty flight ascend its exalted dome.

The quality and proportion uniting in man's existence, from the natural and spiritual realms of which he partakes, determine the character of his essential being; that which matures him, determines the condition of his futurity.

If the immediate sphere from which he is propagated, and the realm through which he arises into maturity, shall have been, from any cause, rendered discordant and unhealthy, it follows, as a natural sequence, that he will be but a type of their imperfections. Again, as growth is the reproduction, and in a special form, of the inherent, incorporated, modified, and unfolded properties surrounding and involving life, man, natively, can only obtain a changed or higher mode of the principles engaging his being; and that mode must tend to the natural *ultum* of the preponderating qualities, inherent or obtained. If, therefore, his being incline to, and absorb, predominantly, the material or outer sphere of his existence, it follows that the baser propension will obtain to a disproportion, the inclinations will be debased, and the spirit robbed of those diviner attainments intended in his creation.

And if his sphere be deranged and misdirected, how indispensable to man, for his present and future good, is a knowledge of himself and the nature of the laws and principles affecting him, together with the means of his restoration.

To diminish the life-sources of the body renders it more impotent; a want of proper mental exercise encourages mental imbecility, and spiritual depression deprives the soul of its vitality.

The laws and necessities of the body, duly regarded, and properly supplied, sustain and accelerate the energies of the mind. And a proper blending of the movements of body and mind inspire spiritual activity; thence the influence of the Divine Spirit reveals man's necessities, and prepares him for the reception of the spirit of Grace, which, from God the Life, seeks his redemption and exaltation from his imperfect state. And since man's spiritual nature is that which qualifies him for the reception of heavenly influx, and constitutes the life-sphere of his immortality, that Divine injunction, "Seek first the Kingdom of God and his righteousness," is founded in immutable law, the violation of which involves the highest interest of the soul.

Man's ever failing effort to erect with his own hands a heaven-reaching tower, reveals his native ignorance of the means adapted to his spiritual attainments, hence the laws and conditions of his spiritual being: and, also, his incapacity to overcome his insufficiency, and to secure the end of his hope. To this end, however, extensive schemes have been multiplied and exhausted, but without avail; and to obtain "*the life elixir*," millions have been sacrificed; but to no effect. Man remains the same, and age upon age only repeats the mode and end of his useless toil.

The Bible, a true criterion, is given to the world, by which the laws and conditions affecting man may be determined; and its salutary influence upon the character of those who accept it as the sure guide, an unerring Counselor, proves its fitness to his necessities, and commends it as a rule of action adequate to his wants.

Other books are offered as more sure and ample means of light to conduct man from his forlorn and bewildered state; but from which can be derived as clear, faithful and unsophisticated statements as the Bible affords? statements that awaken the deepest sense of the soul to the unsatisfying nature of this world, and the realities of that which is to come?

Every soul of man should hail with acclamations of joy any additional light upon subjects so important, but because multitudes appear before the public, laden with new revelations, it is not, therefore, evident that they originate in higher truths and devise means of salvation, superior to what have been previously revealed. But facts rather indicate that this fleet now cruising the sea of time, prepared from olden wrecks and newly manned, have weighed anchor and put out to sea without proper ballast, rudder, compass, or even a skillful mariner. Then wo to the passengers that crowd the saloons of these creaking crafts, for a storm seems gathering in the heavens. So indicates the Bible, which, time and test shall prove, is the true spiritual barometer.

What but a wreck could be hoped from those who institute for themselves such extraordinary claims, and deny them to others? who, while making *sacred their* productions, denounce the Bible, and treat with contumely those who revere it.? What real merit they possess should be regarded; for whatever is true, whatever is just, pure, and useful, should be received, whether from the pen of the sage, poet, or the lips of the stammerer; from the trembling leaf, roaring deep, or belching crater; from the crawling insect, or the glory crowned angel; from *any* source *truth* should be cherished, nor should it or its advocates be rejected. For "a word fitly spoken is like apples of gold in pictures of silver, and more to be desired than jewels of fine gold. It cannot be compared with the precious onyx or the sapphire. No name shall be made of it, for the price of it is above rubies, and all things that may be desired."

But before we indorse that which would intercept former Revelations, although denominated the revelations of an advanced age, and the product of *reason* just from the school of "the progressed," should we not examine the causes which produce them, and from their character consider their determinations?

Faith in a system brings its likeness and inspires us with its motive; therefore too deep an interest cannot be awakened in the mind, relative to the examination and adoption of principles and theories which would lead us into new fields of thought and action, and thereby transform our character. "Prove all things, hold fast that which is good." Bible.

PANTHEISM.

Pantheism, a species of philosophical idolatry connected with Atheism, is of very ancient date. It was, however, revived in the sixteenth century, and its crudeness somewhat modified and tempered to that age, by Benedict Spinoza, a citizen of Amsterdam and a Jew. Since then it has been more properly known as "*Spinozism*," until very recently, having passed another modifying transition by means of A. J. Davis, a magnetised subject, it has assumed the form of "Harmonialism," or the "Harmonial philosophy." And blending with modern *Pantheistic spiritualism*, has settled into an "*ism*" known as "*Harmonial Spiritualism.*" Andrew Jackson Davis, the vehicle of its modern development and notoriety, was an unpretending youth, residing in Poughkeepsie, N. Y., at the time of his introduction into the mesmeric state, through the ordinary mode of manipulations, otherwise animal magnetism. In his abnormal, or mesmeric state, Mr. Davis evinced some striking peculiarities. The most important, however, in his incipiency, consisted in his remarkable pathological powers, manifested in the diagnosis of disease, and his therapeutic aptness. By these he was enabled, in many instances, when clairvoyant, to determine the cause, type and malignancy of diseases, and to apply from a sort of eclectic pharmacy, the recuperative remedies.

Then, at a time when this law was little understood, it was by no means difficult to obtain notoriety. And from the novelty of the subject, and the high claims instituted for him, Mr. Davis attracted to himself many of the scientific. Henceforth his companions were mostly of the learned, whose atmosphere he breathed, and from whose literary and scientific spheres his mental being received constant nutriment.

Those familiar with the science of Anthropology, especially those departments which display the laws of cranioscopy, pathetism, and psycometry, can readily trace this remarkable psycological vein to its source, and thence comprehend the results as the effects of a sort of mental-in-spiritual *consensual movement* operating through Mr. Davis' organism from the mental cerebra of the combined entities composing his coterie, or the sphere affecting him.

The student in mental philosophy knows full well, that unless intercepted or suppressed, any suggestion received into the human sensory, by the ever active and reproductive laws of mind, must ultimate in the revelation of a sentiment or theory, partially at least, matured; and that this will epitomize the united characters of the blending causes, and their renewing agents. Those conversant with the phenomena of mental quickening by means of animal magnetism, understand that the subject under mesmeric influence exalts and renders more lucid or transcendental, than he would normally, the subject-matter of his discourse. And although he may only reproduce the principles of the inductive agents, he will from his position exalt them, if not to a plane superior to that of the causes, to one above his own personally attainable apex. But if he be a proper medium by the union of the constituents he will evolve their combined elements materially sublimated. Therefore the maximum may appear to the unlearned or superficial observer *as a* REVELATION!

Without at this time considering the justice of the superior claims of clairvoyance, with these prefatory remarks, we proceed to trace more distinctly the vein of that psycological phenomenon immediately connected with Mr. Davis; since he is the "medium" of the "Pantheistic Harmonialism" reflected upon this age.

Mr. Davis was first mesmerized late in the autumn of 1843, by Mr. Livingston, a resident of Poughkeepsie, N. Y. Thence commenced the display of his pathological ability, which at that time, attracted so much attention. This power has since, however, lost much of its marvel by a profligate use of its remarkable claims, and Mr. Davis, leaving the masses to revel in the glory of that attainment, has assumed a superior plane of action.

The following March, (1844) he is said, without the aid of his magnetizer to have fallen into a strange abnormal state, whence he received his impression that he was to become the shepherd of man; and that it was his mission to lead the forlorn race from their "unprogressed," or semi-developed state, into the prolific planes of *reason*, and thence to HARMONIALISM "*the heaven of the senses*." In 1845 Mr. Davis in his abnormal state selected L. S. Lyon, M. D., for his manipulater, and the Rev. Wm. Fishbough, who possesses rare scientific and philosophic ability, for his scribe.

These gentlemen were to serve him while delivering a course of lectures: Dr. Lyon to magnetize him, and the Rev. Mr. Fishbough to write and *prepare for the press*, his discourses delivered in the magnetic state.

On the evening of Nov. 29, 1845, he commenced those lectures, and Jan. 25, 1847, closed them. They were, according to his choice, compiled by Mr. Fishbough, who, with Dr. Lyon, published them in a book of 782 octavo pages, entitled, "THE PRINCIPLES OF NATURE, HER DIVINE

REVELATIONS, AND A VOICE TO MANKIND," otherwise, "NATURE'S DIVINE REVELATIONS. BY A. J. DAVIS, THE POUGHKEEPSIE SEER."

The literary merit of this work is what would be expected from the pen of Mr. Fishbough. But its metaphysics are so incomplete and sophistical, and withal based upon fundamental assumption, as will hereafter be shown, that whatever merit it may possess is involved in inexplicable complications. It claims omnipercipience; overlooking the vista of past duration; of time so illimitable as to annihilate the idea of time, and to behold the very beginning of that which is so eternal as not to have had beginning.

Lest the reader should consider this statement too sweeping, and to illustrate our position, the following extracts are introduced, from "Nature's Divine Revelation," page 121:

"In the BEGINNING, the Univercœlum was one boundless, undefinable, and unimaginable ocean of LIQUID FIRE! There was one vast expanse of liquid substance. It was without bounds—inconceivable,—with qualities and essences incomprehensible. This was the original condition of MATTER. It was without form; for it was but *one* form. It had not motion; but it was an eternity of motion. It was without parts; for it was a Whole. Particles did not exist; but the whole was *one* Particle. There were not Suns, but it was one Eternal Sun. It had no beginning; and it was without end. It had not length; for it was a vortex of one Eternity. It had not circles; for it was one infinite Circle. It had not disconnected power; but it was the very essence of all Power. Its inconceivable magnitude and constitution were such as not to develop forces, but Omnipotent Power! Matter and power were existing as a whole, inseparable. The *matter* contained the substance to produce all suns, all worlds, etc. The *Power* contained Wisdom and Goodness,—Justice, Mercy, and Truth. It contained the original and essential Principle that is displayed throughout immensity of space, controlling worlds and systems of worlds, and producing Motion, Life, Sensation, and Intelligence, to be impartially disseminated upon their surfaces as their Ultimates!

"This great Centre of worlds—this Great Power of Intelligence—this Great Germ of all existences—was *One World!* * * * * "This Matter and motion are co-eternal Principles, established by virtue of their own nature." * * * "This great Mass of Matter abounded with heat and fire immense, insomuch that each seeming particle was in reality not such, but the whole was a mass of liquid lava. * * * The power contained in this vortex was the *Great Positive Mind!*" (that is, Deity!) "and its development was *Eternal Motion!* and so Matter and Motion constituted the original condition of all things! * * * The Great First cause, or the vortex of pure Intelligence, was a *First*, or Cause Internal. Matter, with its properties and inconceivable combinations, was an accompaniment or counterpart that may be termed a *Second* or Effect. And the external or countervailing force developed by the action of the Internal, was a *Third* or *Ultimate*. Thus was established the Law of universal and eternal MOTION."

Here, according to his theory, is the *beginning* of what had no beginning. For, he affirms, that Matter and Motion constituted the original condition of all things, and that this *First* Ocean of *Liquid Fire* was an eternity of Motion, and *The power contained in this* Great Vortex, was, the *Great Positive Mind*, and its development was *Eternal* Motion; therefore, the only legitimate conclusion is, that the "Seer" claims to have comprehended, and in "the work" to have revealed, the beginning of that which, being eternal, had not beginning.

Yet the advocates of this complicated and never-to-be-defined theory of "Creation and her Author," indulge profound pity for the Christian who believes in the "tri-unity" of God, that is, "God manifest as Creator, Redeemer, and a quickening Spirit"

The omnipercipient assumption of the foregoing, fully accords with the "Seer's" claims of "Superior condition." For in "N. D. Revelations," page 120, he says, "To reveal the Second Sphere, I progress or ascend to the *Third;* thence to the Fourth; thence upward and upward to the Fifth, Sixth, and finally, as an ultimate, to the *Seventh*—in which sphere I shall be able to comprehend all others." And there, enthroned within the crowning ultimates of Nature and her Author, the "Seer" proceeds to analyze and define the evolution of spheres along vast molten vortices, which issue, or are thrown off, from the boundless Univercœlum, or ocean of liquid fire, through illimitable space and unnumbered metamorphic transitions, until Universes revolve as satelites around each *terminus*, or centre Sun; each of which is of inconceivable magnitude. And ensconsed within his super-celestial observatory, he makes the Almighty and his Works as familiar as household words.

Thus seated, he attempts to work out the deep problems of Nature, and adjust the conceptions of terrestrial formations from their immense vortices, through an infinite variety of evolutions, until our globe appears. Thence, scanning its sphere, he essays to pursue its igneous material while borne in the arms of its inherent laws—a lesser deity emanated from the "*great vortex* or

Positive Mind"—throughout the varied stratified incrustations; thence through the mineral, vegetable and animal kingdoms, to Man, the climax, or ultimate of the attributes and forces of its original Nebula. And again, by his theory of progression, he prospectively ascends with man, along the self-projected octaves of his nature, until the Universe of sublimated and spiritualized matter and its inherent deity, attains to the realms of the Original *First Cause;* the *Great Positive Mind;* the *Vortex* of liquid lava—of pure Intelligence; whence it *was;* and from which, according to his theory, it could never depart. Thus, organized and exalted it completes his grand equilibrium of Spirit. In this realm the "Seer" leaves the Great "Positive Mind" and the Ultimates of its Omnipotent and Proceeding Power—a universe of Spirit-Entities, so equipoised and harmonious as to perfect "*One great whole.*"

Such are the fundamental principles of "Nature's Divine Revelations, by A. J. Davis, the Poughkeepsie Seer;" and such the character of that work which is considered by thousands the "Book of books," the Light of Reason, the reflected substance of universal Truths; whose theory is man's hope and salvation, and whose Author is considered as the "*Man*" of ages, and compend of universal Law; a living Automaton.

Lest those unacquainted with the work should deem our criticisms unjust, and our conclusions unreasonable, we will introduce the "Seer's" own language upon this subject. N. D. R. page 672. "From the position now occupied I can perceive, and in a degree comprehend, the *Seventh Sphere*, or the Infinite Vortex of Love and Wisdom, and the great Spiritual Sun of the Divine Mind that illuminates all the Spirit worlds."

And again, although in one department he informs us that the Great Centre Vortex disseminated from itself through immensity of space material for unfolding an infinite number of systems of inconceivable magnitude, on page 121 he informs us that "In the beginning the Univercœlum was one boundless ocean of liquid fire. It had no beginning, and it was without end. It had not length; for it was a vortex of eternity. It had not circles; for it was one infinite circle." Such being the all-pervading and all-encompassing nature of this first-cause vortex, what could emanate from it" and by an infinite procedure "unfold ultimate and return to it." But in support of the evolution of Matter along its immense channels *from* the First-Cause Vortex, and its final spiritualization and *ascension whence it came*, he remarks, page 50, "It is the law of *Matter* to produce its ultimate Mind. It is the law of mind to produce its corresponding *Spirit.*"

And finally, page 149, "Thus all matter will pass the multifarious forms and stages that are existing, and all will ultimately be resolved into the *unparticled* state, and will ascend to associate with higher and more glorious spheres—of *spiritual* composition. Then the Great Positive Mind, around whose Centre exists this exhaustless fountain of materials, will be *Positive* to the great *Negative* formed by the perfections of all things else in being. And then *Deity* and *Spirit* will be existing only."

Thus, through the marvelous interposition of this strange phenomenon, we have revealed to us as a *First*, or *Cause* of all things, an illimitable and eternal ocean of *Liquid Fire;* and that, from Fire proceeds Matter, from Matter Mind, from Mind Spirit; or, Fire unfolds into Nature, Nature into Spirit; and this Spirit or Ultimate finally arises, a *Negative* to the First Great Positive Cause, "and thence between the two will emanate new worlds—an epoch of another *Beginning*. Page 149, N. D. R.

Such are some of the claims of this Pantheistic Bible of the Nineteenth Century. And from these extracts the reader is in a degree apprised of the ceaseless involutions, by which it conducts the mind of its devotee into a bewildering amazement, thence along its imaginary spheres to its material heaven.

CHAPTER II.

PANTHEISTIC THEORY OF THE FIRST CAUSE, AND THE ORDER OF CREATION.

Father, from whom all life descends,
  By whom all forms and beings are;
To thee my soul in prayer ascends—
  For wealth of thought my mind prepare.
Thine is the Life, and thine the Word,
  Perfection dwells with thee alone:
Inspire each thought, thou sovereign Lord,
  And make that perfect thou'st begun.

In vain we toil and urge the mind,
  Or seek divinity to scan;
In every effort, Lord, we find
  The inefficiency of in man.
Then move this heart, and guide this pen,
  Nor let a human thought prevail—
Truths, unperceived by finite ken,
  Can only in this cause avail.

"NATURE'S Divine Revelations, by A. J. Davis," cursorily reviewed in the foregoing chapter maintains the "Harmonial Theory," and may properly be denominated the "Text Book" of Infidelity, since it contains the principles of that system which has ever opposed Christianity. In this work the "Seer" attempts to impart universal knowledge, and to inform the world upon every question of import. To this end he bequeaths to the race his labored theory of the First Cause, and his elaborate scheme of "progression." These he proffers as the *Wisdom of Nature*, her "Divine Revelations;" and for purity of style harmonic perfection, light of Truth, historic accuracy, perspicuity and sublimity of narration, scientific sense, metaphysical correctness, spirit of life, and divine conception, as more perfect and rational, by far, than the *Inspired Word.*

The spirit of this Work is antagonistic to that of the Scriptures. It therefore repudiates them, denies their divine authenticity, and the existence of the Supreme Being. It affects to overwhelm the Bible, with a tide of rhapsodical reasoning, and to bear it with precursory waves into the desolate regions of oblivion. Fancying by these means to have overcome the principles of the Christian religion, the main impediment to its progress, and deeming therefore the foundation of human ignorance and oppression removed, Sampson-like it feels for the pillars of the Church; and grasping a phantom, exerts its energies, awaits the impending crash, and thence the dawn of earth's long sought day of peace, the glory of material divinity. The entire metaphysics of this work depend upon two fundamental principles, that is,

1. The pre-existence of an original and illimitable ocean of LIQUID FIRE, composed of a co-existent and co-eternal mass of primitive matter pervaded by co-efficient and co-eternal Motion, and capable of developing Infinite, Eternal and Omnipotent power: otherwise, an unbounded *univercœlum*, or *vortex* of *Electro-Mentalized* essence pervading an *Abyss of Flaming Substance* possessing all the qualities and attributes of God and Nature; and which was subsequently self-wrought into form and being and disseminated throughout space, and,

2. It is dependent upon the reliability and capability of Animal Magnetism, its means of revelation, and thence the fitness of the magnetizee for its cosmical and metaphysical revealments. Its doctrines are multifarious, laboring to embrace the cause, principles and means of the development of universal nature. All of which, agreeable to the "Revelations" were not only "*begotten*" by virtue of their own inherent laws and properties—those of the original Univercœlum; but had absolute "*pre-existence*," moreover *were* the *constituents* of the first ocean of liquid fire, the vortex of pure intelligence.

These two conflicting statements, the "*pre-existence*" and also the "*begetting*" of the principles of nature, are abundantly sustained in the WORK; but a brief extract upon each will be sufficient for our present purpose. To elucidate the *first position*, see N. D. R. p. 122—"This Great Power of Intelligence—this Great Germ of all Existence—was One World!—corresponding to a globe visible; for it was *but* One—containing the *materials* and *power* to produce all others. So the whole of these were joined into one vast *vortex* of *Pure Intelligence.* "Thus," continues the Seer, "matter and motion are co-eternal principles, established by virtue of their own nature, and they were the germ, containing all properties, all essences, all principles, to produce all other forms and spheres that are now known to be existing." "This great original mass was a substance, containing within itself the embryo of its own perfection." But the "Seer," in a *second statement*, informs us that "It" (the original mass, or univercœlum,) "became impregnated by virtue of its own laws, and controlled, guided, and perfected by virtue of its own Omnipotent Power." "It contained the power of progression, but had not progressed."

These statements reveal the univercœlum, although composed of, yet engendering germinal principles, suitable for universal distribution and metamorphosis, and equal to the necessities of space and duration. Thus Creation was begun, and this is the first degree.

In further illustration of this theory, the

"Seer" remarks, N. D. R., p. 121, etc., "matter and motion constitute the original condition of all things," and "matter and motion reigned throughout the regions of boundless infinitude.—There were no other forms and no other attributes evolved from power, for they all existed undeveloped." Yet, notwithstanding the above, it is also revealed that the "Inconceivable magnitude and constitution of the univercœlum were not such as to develope force, but Omnipotent Power!" And again—"The whole was flaming with internal heat, which evolved, as an effect, the principle of light—so matter, heat, and light constituted the primitive condition of the *material, eternal substance.* Possessing all these essential qualities, characteristics, and compounds, it was suitable to produce all things which have been produced, and to be the cause and effect to produce interminable ultimates." "Matter contained all the attributes, characteristics, essential qualities, and peculiar combinations, which the whole univercœlum manifests. Its ultimate purification would necessarily produce the peculiar essences of animal life and intelligence." Also, page 154, N. D. R., "Every particle in being is constantly passing through *forms*, and *orders*, and *degrees.* This is the universal law of matter."

But again: "In order that *this matter* might

assume form, the action of the great Positive Power was neçessary to impel it to higher states of progression."

These statements confirm the foregoing conflicting propositions, and also maintain that, "Matter contained all the attributes, characteristics, essential qualities, and peculiar combinations which the univercœlum manifests," and must therefore, of itself, have constitued, and yet evolved, as actor and agent, all substance, essence, life, motion, power, wisdom, goodness, justice, mercy, mind, spirit, affection, cause, purpose, ultimatés, and deity.

This diagram of Nature presents the universe as an immensurable anatomy; the soul and body of the Almighty, whose elements are self-begotten and self-modified to conditions; that these several conditions assume forms, and these forms, although many and various, are separate organs of one body, and so properly adjusted as to prefigure an enormous and universal *Creature.* The universe of Mind and Matter, Power and Motion, is, then, agreeable to this theory, and, which accords with that of Ancient Pantheism, an animal of illimitable dimensions: a leviathan, vast in proportions, endued with Omnipotent Might; whose uncreated motion engendered its eternal motion; whose infinite power created its own omnipotent power; whose life breathed forth its eternal vitality, and, hence, whose vast and original vortex evolved itself into universal being: that is, the universe, although eternal, is represented as self-originated, self-formed, and self-disseminated throughout the illimitable *vacuum*—thence, is *floating in space!*

These deductions are abundantly sustained by the "Seer" throughout his expatiations, as he breathes forth his profuse declarations relative to the Eternity, Power, Wisdom, Goodness, Justice, Mercy, and Truth of the original Vortex. And also his majestic scheme of Nature's *birth*, or the *birth* of the *unbegotten Univercœlum*, as especially unfolded in his lofty utterance, N. D. R., page 673.

"Of the body and constitution of the material sun the univercœlum was born into being, caressed, nourished, illuminated, and perfected in universal order and harmony." . . "This displays the order and harmony of the Divine Mind, and this is one body of one Immortal Soul."!! *

If this system of Creation represents Nature, then Nature is the perfection of chaos, and can-

*NOTE —A marginal note on the page from which the above is taken, informs us that the discovery and revelation of this last august statement, for the time being at least, well nigh cost the "Seer" his mental equilibrium, since, to obtain it, "He was elevated to such close proximity to the sphere of the spiritual sun that the light was beyond endurance."

not as yet have obtained to any very worthy end by her long and wearied routine of progressive unfoldings. She still greatly stammers in her utterance, and has not approached her youthful maturity: or learned the order of speech. She slumbers in her swadlings and is cradled in nonentity.

Such conclusions inevitably force themselves upon the mind while perusing "N. D. Revelations." Indeed it seems impossible that it should be otherwise, unless the sense becomes so psychologized by its transcendental display, and bewildered by its involutions as to accept discord as harmony and assumptions for causes: imaginary movements for magnificent procedures of Nature, and glaring illusions as her grand results.

But the scale of Nature as revealed by Mr. Davis, is not yet complete, since his discovery and comprehension of the beginning and of the works of Nature manifest throughout all pre-existing time, only indicates a more grand result. And therefore, his Omnipercipient vision must penetrate the unfathomable and mysterious future. Hence, he overspans that duration of whose infinity no finite mind has any power or means to conceive, and determines the results of whatever has been, is, or is to be, in this eternity. And in that great day which witnesseth the sublimation, mentalization and spiritualization of all the materials of the First Univercœlum, and the present existing Universe, also whatever shall henceforth unfold from it, he pauses, takes a precursory review of its incomprehensible, inconceivable and eternalized conditions: defines and arranges them in the Sanctum of his intellectual Tabernacle, and thence epitomizes on this wise. "And by immutable and eternal laws originally established, it" (the Univercœlum) "will continue to reproduce and recreate new worlds of supreme excellence and exalted states of material perfection, until every particle that composes every sun and every system of suns and Worlds of worlds, extending infinitely beyond the power of human thought, and infinitely beyond all that has been yet produced and organized—until *these* and *all their particles* become the *very essence* of *vegetable* and *animal existence!* And the latter, with the active energies inherently accompanying it, not only will pass to the perfection of *spiritual* essence, but will work its mighty influence upon every thing below it, until all things arrive at an exalted state of spiritual and celestial perfection!" "And then *Deity* and *Spirit* will be existing *only!*" "Thus all Matter and Motion will *finally* become what they originally were" (!) "will be resolved into one grand and glorious SUN, more refined and perfected, more excellent in all its qualities and compositions, that *it* may again bring forth a *new* system of suns, and an infinite *corresponding* creation throughout space! And as there is in *all* things a constant evolving and emanation, development and progression, from the centre, of refined essences which dispose themselves in concentric circles, this is a representation of the great circles that surround the *infinite* sun—and of the great Circle of development from the beginning of time (or of the present formation) to the final arrival of every particle at the Great Center and Parent from which they all emanated! This may be termed the *beginning* and *end* of ONE TIME." * * * "And the final resolution of the present creations in infinite space, will be the consummation of the glorious End contemplated. And then the Great Sun, becoming more perfected, will breathe forth new and more refined elements, and roll into space successively a corresponding, yet more, far more perfect Univercœlum!" Thence the "Seer" does not proceed to "*unfold.*" He is not "impressed" to bestow upon us the priceless *gems* that shall cluster in the crystal groves of that Immortal Age. Sufficient for our sphere is the delineation of this pre-eternity of our existence. Boundless enough the region already explored for the range of our awaking undeveloped intellects. Scope, quite adequate to the wants of our dull apprehensions, and glory fully equal to the capacity of our dormant senses and slumbering spirits, are bestowed in this Proem to Nature's eternal SPEECH. Indeed, such is the spirit and the character of "Nature's Divine Revelation," that from its *ipse dixit* there is admitted no appeal. Its conclusions are, therefore, imperative. No speech could be more authoritative; no language more egotistic and presumptuous, and no effort to sustain assumed positions, could be more labored. In fact, the Work depends upon fundamental assumptions, whose sentiments are elaborated into extensive and complicated theories. Such as the followlowing, constitute the "axioms" of the scheme. "I am impressed," "I perceive," "From my illumined condition," "From the position I now occupy," "In the Beginning the Univercœlum was, etc.," "It is the law of Matter to produce its ultimate Mind," "It is the law of mind to produce its corresponding *Spirit*," "And then *Deity* and *Spirit* will be existing only," "And thence between the two will emanate new worlds —an epoch of another *Beginning*," "And then the Great Sun, will roll into space, a far more perfect Univercœlum." While reviewing this Work, which appears but the rehearsal of ideas obtained from the "Magic Panorama" which passed before the Magnetic Vision of the "Seer," the Bible's *rationale* of man's bewildered state, enforces its important truths upon us. If this mental effusion is the essence, yea the Wisdom of Nature, as it purports, its inconsistent statements and bold contradictions reveal her inefficiency, and deepen the conviction of man's moral weakness, spiritual blindness, mental imbecility, and therefore of his *depravity.* Sadly the Work proves that "All have gonè out of the way" and forcibly illustrates these solemn truths uttered by the Psalmist, "The fool hath said in his heart, there is no God." "God looked down upon the children of men, to see if there were *any* that did understand, that did seek God. Every one of them is gone back."

If this work be a faithful representation of Nature, Nature is deplorably at fault; but if Nature be harmonious and efficient, then the WORK is not her production, and man, its proximate cause, is bewildered and effeminate.

The reasoning throughout, is so cloudy and sophistic; the absurdities are so palpable and glaring; the propositions so contradictory, dreamy, and inexplicable, that they convey no definite idea of a First Cause, or of any existing Design in the mechanism of Nature. And the multifarious motor-forces are so diversely constructed and applied, that one "Function" is forced to compete with another, until the complicated aggregate presents Nature's grand periphery as wild and hazy, and her intermedium vague and mystic. The propositions, inductions, and conclusions, whirl so deliriously as to render the Universe of Matter and Mind, they seek to represent, absolutely chaotic, the manifestation of impulsive imbecility.

One "portraiture" represents Nature as the acme of perfection; another, as an illimitable abyss of igneous surging elements, which by their own might are developing Omnipotent Power; and still another, as a sea of molten glass, most transparent, which reflects the august contour of the Great Positive Mind,—all-pervading and all-encompassing. This is succeeded by a scene which reveals the Great Positive Mind as a Vortex of Pure Intelligence, and as ingathering the abyss of flaming substance into his vast thorax; thence arises in form of an Infinite God-Head, Love, Will, Wisdom, Justice, Mercy, and Truth. As this scene merges into another, the being last revealed resolves himself into the primitive Univercœlum, or Sea of Lava, whose boundless and undefinable realm extends throughout infinite *space*, that which has been eternally pervaded by its matchless perfection. Thence a sudden contraction seizes the immeasurable Univercœlum, and a vortex of flaming elements appears exerting its internal powers to re-expel itself into space. Again emerge vast molten billows, impelled from the Great Centre Vortex. These have scarcely obtained their orbits, and assumed their spherical forms, ere, as though seized with Omnipotent convulsions, each struggles to impel its elements into a system of subordinate orbs, and, lo, innumerable currents diverge from these centre vortices, and space is traversed by their fiery combinations. Old night awakens from her eternal slumbers, and the expansive void presents the appearance of a Universe in flames. "This," echoes "Nature's Divine Revelations," "is one Body of one immortal Soul." "This is Deity!" and lo! the knell of their mortality sounds, and the *orbs*, the *seas*, flaming substance, and the Centre Vortex—the constituents, parent and dwelling-place of the Great Positive Mind, disappear.

Withdrawing from the illusive reverie, behold! Nature is proceeding in her accustomed order, proving the "Work."

But the dream of a magnetized dreamer:

Nevertheless this is the true character and the substance of the Harmonial Philosophy—the vitality of the magnificent scheme set forth in "Nature's Divine Revelations;" the Soul of Infidel Spiritualism; the Breath of anti-Christ; and the Pantheism of Orpheus, Bruno, Descartes, and Spinoza; and the principal tenets of these several systems are the same, however much their modes of theorizing may vary.

"Bruno supposed God to be the soul of the Universe; others seem to have discovered an original *substance*, in which all contradictions cease, and all subjects of finite thought disappear; by which they understood that which has an independent existence, and which is incapable of creating anything material or intellectual, for all matter and mind are comprehended in itself. Its attributes are infinite thought and infinite extension. God, this all-embracing being, can act only in accordance with the established order, for otherwise we must suppose him capable of a change of nature, or that there exists a nature different from his own. Thought and extension, spirit and matter, the finite and the infinite, motion and repose, good and evil, causes and effects, are attributes of this sole substance, which produces nothing but modifications of itself. All that exists is only a necessary succession of modes of being in substance for ever the same. The morality of this system is founded mainly on force and utility."—[Enc. Am., vol. xi. p. 596.

Buck in his Theological Dictionary, somewhat enlarging upon the above, remarks: "*Pantheism*, a philosophical species of idolatry, leading to Atheism, in which the universe was considered as the Supreme God. Who was the inventor of this absurd system is, perhaps, not known; but it was of early origin, and differently modified by different philosophers. Some held the universe to be one immense animal, of which the incorporeal soul was properly their God, and the heavens and the earth the body of that God; whilst others held but one substance, partly active and partly passive, and therefore looked upon the visible universe as the only *Numen*.—The earliest Grecian Pantheist of whom we read was Orpheus, who called the world the *body of God*, and its several parts his members, making the whole universe one *divine animal*. According to Cudworth, Orpheus and his followers believed in the immaterial soul of the world, therein agreeing with Aristotle, who certainly held that God and matter are co-eternal, and that there is some such union between them as subsists between the souls and bodies of men. An institution, imbibing sentiments nearly of this kind, was set on foot about eighty or ninety years ago in this kingdom, (Great Britain,) by a society of philosophical idolators, who called themselves *Pantheists*, because they professed the worship of all Nature as their deity. Their liturgy was in Latin; an English translation was published in 1751, from which the following sentiments are extracted: "The etherial fire environs all things, and is a revivifying fire; it rules all things; it disposes all things." (How like Mr. Davis' "Great Positive Mind.") "In it is soul, mind, prudence," (from which Mr. Davis borrowed his "Love, Will, Wisdom.") "This fire is Horace's particle of divine breath, and Virgil's *inwardly* nourishing spirit. All things are comprised in an intelligent Nature." This force they call the soul of the world, as also a mind of perfect wisdom, and, consequently, God. Vanini, the Italian philosopher, was nearly of this opinion; his God was Nature. Spinoza taught that there is but one substance in Nature, and that this only substance is endued with an infinite variety of attributes, among which are extension and cogitation; that all the bodies in the universe are modifications of this substance, extended; and that all the souls of men are modifications of the same substance, considered as cogitative: that God is a necessary and infinitely perfect being, and is the cause of all things that exist, but not a different being from them; that there is but one Being and one Nature, and that this Nature produces within itself, by an immanent act, all those which we call creatures; and that this Being is, at the same time, both agent and patient, efficient cause and subject, but that he produces nothing but modifications of himself. Thus is the Deity made the sole agent as well as patient, in all evil, both physical and moral. If this impious doctrine (continues Mr. Buck) be not Atheism, (or, as it is sometimes called, Pantheism,) I know not what it is."

Although it may be denied by the friends of Harmonialism that its philosophy is Pantheistic, and that "N. D. Revelations" are predicated upon Pantheistic principles long since promulgated, still the nature of a doctrine depends upon what is understood by the First Cause, and what relation existing things are considered to sustain to him. And any religion is Pantheistic in so far as it takes for granted *a fate* or a *power of Nature* which determines every thing. And who, in any degree acquainted with the Harmonial philosophy, as set forth by Mr. Davis in "Nature's Divine Revelations," "The Great Harmonial," etc. or any of the text books of that system, will for a moment deny that the doctrine of *fate* constitutes its leading principles?

Upon this subject, Mr. Davis remarks, in N. D. R. p 326. "These laws of Nature are known to be unchangeable; and these are merely the expressions of divine Thought. These laws, therefore, are emanations from the universal Cause, and by resting upon their *immutable* and *harmonious* results, we would be resting our interior affections upon the Thoughts of an all-pervading infinitely perfect, and Omnipotent Mind." It should be remembered, however, that "these laws of Nature" are innate in matter, are the active principles in its composition, "And so matter and motion constituted the original condition of all things" is the language employed on this subject, N. D. R., p 122. This law of Motion, therefore, is the Great Positive Power, whose reflections are the Thoughts of the Divine Mind, of which the Work treats so extensively. But on page 314, Ibid., we are more specifically informed of the eternity of fate connected with Nature. "Each form and peculiar organization in Nature," says the "Seer," while enforcing this law, "is determined by the existing, controlling circumstances, which are the causes of such form's creation. It follows, then, that Physical, Mental, Moral and Spiritual formations and their several conditions are encompassed within the controlling influences of this immutable law, which is that of force, and which determines all things. Thence every mode of existence, every action, whether of physical or spiritual nature, together with all ultimates and consequences, are the result of necessity: *and this is Pantheism.*

Thus we determine, and from good authority, that the doctrines which are so rapidly obtaining and which apparently owe their birth to Nature's Divine Revelations, are not the especial production of this developed age; that they are not the brilliant result, and at this favored period of that immutable and eternally progressive law, which throughout all time has been laboring to evolve this grand system as Nature's infinite speech—her Divine Revelations, and which could not have been previously unfolded from the great Vortex of Intelligence, for want of a proper agent of communication, and an age of developed minds suitable for its reception; that it is not a New Revelation as the unlearned accept it: but the echo of what for ages past, has been uttered by the spirit of material sense, and offered to Man as *the* Religion of Reason, a religion in harmony with Nature, the only source of true intelligence, of true enjoyment, and the only means of heavenly attainments. Verily, this is the system which has ever opposed the doctrine of the Inspired Word. And shall we deem it a more *sure word?* and seek to satisfy our reason with its philosophy? and our spiritual wants with the vitality it imparts? For its vague and dreamy statements, shall we relinquish our faith in the God of Nature, revealed in the Scriptures? yield our hope of that Heaven which the Supreme Spirit illumines with His Divine Presence? and cleaving to "Nature's Divine Revelations," or any Pantheistic Creed, as a source of Divine Wisdom and Heavenly Beatitudes—

Shall we conceive the Almighty Lord
  As matter only vitalized—
The sense and soul atoms afford—
  But inert Nature deitized?
That orbs themselves assume their forms,
  Outwrought from molten seas of yore?
The wondrous work Nature performs
  Restores her whence she was, before
Her might proceeded to awake
  Her unbegotten energies?
Or ere arose to undertake
  To manifest what Nature is?

4

CHAPTER III.

BIBLICAL DOCTRINES OF GOD AND NATURE OPPOSED TO PANTHEISM.

The Lord is light, and he alone
  Illumes the universe etern.
Life, Lord, Creator, God, are one;
  Immensity the Spirit's Urn.
The atoms in the vast domain
  By Him have form, by Him exist;
All Nature by His laws obtain,
  In Him all worlds, all heavens subsist.
God is the Life, and God the Word—
  Atoms, obedient to His Will
Conducted by the Sovereign Lord,
  Proceed His purpose to fulfill.

To Nature's Divine Revelations, and all forms of Pantheism, we oppose the INSPIRED WORD, and urge its supremacy, 1. Because its metaphysics (as the analysis will determine,) accord more perfectly with the *facts* of mundane existence, with corporeal nature as allied to man, with human propensions, with physical, spiritual and moral frailties, with mental contradictions, and all known results within the sphere of human sense. 2. Because the Nature, Eternity of Existence, and Infinite Attributes of the Supreme Being, as revealed in the Scriptures, more rationally commend him as God, Creator, and Divine Benefactor, than the "*fire god*" of Pantheism—the igneous and surging "Intelligence-Vortex" of Nature's Divine Revelations; and 3. Because the ethics of the Sacred Text are more wisely adapted to the social, moral and spiritual necessities of man, than the law of magnetic attraction of Harmonialism. The Inspired Word does not come to us as the result of human magnetism, but as the revealed WILL of Heaven, in accordance with the laws of Theopneusty—by the Inspiration of God, creating truthful conceptions of Divine Law and Wisdom, in the vital consciousness of Heaven's elected agents—the Patriarchs, Prophets and Apostles; by the Divine Logos, and by the ministration of angels, who were of God appointed holy Embassadors to those chosen from among men as external enunciators of Divine Truths.

Having, in the foregoing chapter, stated the leading principles of Pantheism, respecting Deity, or rather, Nature and her mode of unfolding, we shall now introduce the doctrines of the Scriptures upon the subject of Creation and her Author, that the two systems may appear in their proper light, and so proximate to each other as to reveal their contrast; thence the truth of the one and the error of the other.

That we may properly present this subject, it is necessary to inquire,

I. The effect these systems have upon the sense of those who have been the media of their external expression.

II. In what light they viewed the Creator.

Thus we may discover, in a degree, the characters of the inspiring principles, for these agents must, of necessity, reflect, in part at least, the nature of the revealing cause, and the burden of their utterance will accord with the character of whatever quickens their sense, enlarges their conceptions, and guides their speech.

The heart of the men of old, who wrote as moved by the Holy Ghost, is revealed by the Psalmist when he said, "Oh, come, let us worship, let us kneel before the Lord our Maker." How much more befitting finite man, when contemplating Infinity, was the sense of David's inspired soul, as conveyed in this meek expression, than the presumptuous arrogance betrayed by the Poughkeepsie "Seer" when he uttered the following: "To reveal the second sphere" (the region of eternity proximate to earth,) "I shall progress or ascend to the third," (the region of eternity still above or more remote from earth than the second sphere); "thence to the fourth; thence upward and upward to the fifth, sixth, and finally, as an ultimate, to the seventh," (the highest heaven, that of infinite perfection,) "in which I shall be able to comprehend all others."—N. D. R. p. 120. This the modern philosophy calls rational, in the first degree. In harmony with the above, it is written, page 672 ibid: "From the position now occupied I can perceive, and in a degree comprehend, the *Seventh Sphere*, or the Infinite *Vortex* of Love and Wisdom," (Deity,) "and the great Spiritual Sun of the Divine Mind that illumines all the Spirit worlds." *Whose* province is it to overlook, span, and, in a degree, comprehend the *Almighty*? *Could* the mightiest Angel, whose glory would veil the sun in night? the reflections of whose capacious mind are incomprehensible to man? whose journeyings number the stars as points of local distances? and before whose vision the unnumbered orbs are as pebbles in the distant landscape! Nay, as he turned his almost omnipercipient eye from the boundless realms of material nature, and glanced along the angelic heavens; as his thoughts arose toward the infinite Architect, *he* would exclaim, "O, the wisdom and goodness of God, how unsearchable, and his ways past finding out." But the Poughkeepsie "Seer," by a few human manipulations, ascends at once to the sphere of infinite perfection, fully capacitated to comprehend all others, and, in a degree, the sphere of the Spiritual Sun, or *Infinite* Vortex of the Divine *Mind*. Surely, *this is* an age of Progression! With this statement as a text, the advocates of N. D. Revelations, as well as the "Seer," denounce the *Bible* as a book of absurdities—the doctrine of the Incarnation as contrary to reason; a violation of law! That is, the Lord cannot come to earth, but "*our prophet*" could, while but a novice, Mahomet-like, ascend to the seventh heaven; approach, and, "in a degree, comprehend the Almighty;" and there, in the Audience-Chamber of the infinite "Intelligence-Vortex," obtain the Biography of the "Great Positive Mind," and the *modus operandi* of his works; compile the Harmonial Philosophy, and a Catechism for the religion of the senses.

Thus the Revelations of this Oracle of the Nineteenth Century assume; and how unlike the meek spirit manifested by the Prophets of old! They, veiled and bowed before high Heaven, with the profoundest reverence, and a solemn sense of the glory of the Shekinah, softly uttered the *name* of the Supreme Being. Thus, in the spirit of true devotion, they acknowledged Him whom the spirit revealed as Jehovah, to be the self-existing Lord Almighty, the I AM, *whose* Throne is Eternity, and whose Glory and Being are incomprehensible, undefinable: from everlasting to everlasting, God over all, and blessed forevermore.

While the Poughkeepsie "Seer" scans the original infinitude of might, intelligence, and the eternity of substance, the Prophets of the Lord, in view of his works, exclaim, "Canst thou by searching, find out God! How unsearchable are his judgements, and his ways past finding out. Who hath known the mind of the Lord? who hath seen his countenance? or who hath been his counselor? For of him, through him, and to him are all things; to him be glory forever Amen."

"Who hath directed the spirit of the Lord? or being his counsellor, hath taught him? Behold, the Nations are as the drop of the bucket, and are considered as the small dust of the balance. *To whom will ye liken God, or what likeness will ye compare unto him.* The heavens declare his glory, and the firmament showeth forth his handiwork. Lift up your eyes on high, behold who hath created these things, that bringeth out their hosts by numbers." Who hath formed nature that unfoldeth into such inconceivable varieties and in such perfection. Whose evolutions as immortal notes ascend the universal octave of diviner harmonies. "Oh Lord God thou art clothed with honor and might, who coverest thyself with light as with a garment; who spreadest out the heavens as a curtain; who maketh his angels spirits; his ministers a flaming fire."

Thus did the holy men of old, who spake as moved by the Holy Ghost, conceive of God; thus make known, to a slumbering world, his Being, Glory, and Omnipotence. And this is the God of the Bible, even the Lord, whom Christians adore. With Him, therefore, and the "Lava-god" of Nature's Divine Revelations, there can be no comparison. Of the eternity of God's existence, the Prophets conceived him an infinite spirit, who before the mountains were brought forth, or the earth was formed, was God; whose throne was established of old; who remaineth for ever, and to whose years there is no end. Of his Creative Power, they conceived him, "The Lord God Omnipotent, infinite in his attributes; who formed the light; who made the earth by his power, and established the world by his wisdom." This is the Creator, by whose Spirit the Prophets wrote; this is the El-Shaddai, or God All-Sufficient, of the Inspired Word. And, need we enquire, which is the most *rational* doctrine of the First Cause, this, or that of the Poughkeepsie Seer?

There is an eloquence in simplicity, a divinity in meekness, a wisdom in an humble acknowledgement of incapacity, where it self-evidently exists; an irrefutable argment for truth in conceding its divinity, and the utter inability of mind to comprehend its mightiness, when its character is such as to impress the soul with its infinitude. The infinite greatness of the Creator is stamped upon all things; not an atom in being but reveals the Omnipotence of God; not one organic form or movement in Nature, no quickning procedure or living thing, but bespeaks the unsearchableness of his wisdom; not one throb in the universal sensation, but leads to the incomprehensibility of his life-giving power; not one thought in the universe of mind but baffles the sense of man, and utters the awfulness of that intellectual capacity forever unknown to created beings. And how shall frail humanity, since so easily and universally baffled in wisdom, presume to comprehend unnumbered spheres, and determine the measure of the Almighty? 'Tis folly to attempt it, especially since man cannot comprehend himself. This, the crawling worm, sweeping elements, and the wheeling orbs declare. Who, then, is wise? He that affects to face the realms of unendurable light, and measure the movement of eternal law, and in a degree comprehend the Almighty CAUSE? or that soul, that realizes the majesty of Jehovah, while witnessing the glory and wonder of his works, and seeks of God wisdom to guide to the source of true knowledge and the fountain of everlasting peace?

'Tis not the "Seer" we especially regard in this review of Nature's Divine Revelation, but that system which, in these modern times, bears his name; that system which seems to obtain with many, and to find earnest, and, no doubt, honest advocates; which has won to its cause many, who, for the want of a proper understanding of its character, have, for its teachings, abandoned the Christian religion, and are seeking heaven by other means than through the Lord our Redeemer; that system which involves the mind in the meshes of its sophistry, and charms the sense with its fascinating magnetism; controlls the affections, and thence the will, by its psychological powers: that system which seeks the child of God in his closet, domestic circle, and in the public assembly; yea, that, which benumbs, if possible, his religious sense, and induces him from the Courts of the Lord, and to the necromantic circles, where the sayings of mesmerized subjects are taken for heavenly truths, and the impulsive dictations of sensitive media are received as the speech of angels!

Such is the system whose errors we seek to expose, and the fallacy of whose reasoning we seek to unveil. Flattering, indeed, when superficially observed, are its ingeniously-wrought inducements, and with great subtlety presented to affect our choice. Like one of old, who proffered Jesus the kingdoms of the world if he would bow before him, this *ism* lavishly tenders to its faithful subjects, by virtue of unremitting fate, not only earth but the heavens, and even the nature and attributes of deities. Let the race admit its philosophy, (of which especial mention shall be made in a more appropriate portion of this work,) and they are promised *progression* from the ignorance now encompassing them, the thraldom of Bible religion, and the consequent woes that attend them on every hand. They shall dwell upon the lovely banks of beauteous streams; shall recline beneath the shady groves that garland the rivers of pleasure, and gather ripe clusters of knowledge from the depending boughs that droop o'er earth from the superior spheres. They shall also gambol along the gorgeous avenues of affinity, and sip from the sparkly cups of bliss, that shall touch each willing lip; and bathe henceforth in the ever flowing fountains of harmonial peace.—"Glorious day! long sought day of light and reason!" in lively accents, therefore, glides along the quivering atmosphere. And the burden of their prayer, who move in the harmonial element, is, that Christianity may speedily slumber in the cold sepulchre of the Past; that the temples of religious worship, where the glory of the Cross has shown, may resound with the merry song; and the dome of heaven reflect the divine harmonies of passional attraction.

Such is the sentiment and the spirit of that inflated system under consideration, and by such manifestations the author of N. D. Revelations and his followers hope to control the world! How unlike that spirit which the Inspired Penman revealed? Who can refrain, in the light of both causes, from a deep sense of the inconsistency and finiteness of the one, and the infinitude and divine harmony of the other?

While Mr. Davis beholds God and Nature combined in the unbounded sea of fire, the Patriarchs, Prophets, and Apostles, as already shown, conceived the sublime doctrine of the Infinite, Eternal, Omnipotent, Omnific, and absolutely Holy Being of the Supreme Spirit.

The Pantheistic notion of the fiery materiality of the First Cause, forces the theory of its self-emanation into the present existing universe. But the doctrines of the Inspired Word, maintaining the almightiness and the self-existence of Jehovah, establish that rational premise which accounts for the magnificent manifestations of Nature upon the pre-existence of an intelligent and Omnific Cause. And thus, as well as by Inspiration, reasoning *a priori*, Moses assuming the only legitimate conclusion, born of facts, introduced the Sacred History in this graphic and appropriate language: "In the beginning God created the heaven and the earth." Not as Mr. Davis revealed—"From the position now occupied I can, in a degree, comprehend the great Spiritual Sun of the Divine Mind that illumines all the Spiritual worlds." "*In the Beginning* the Univercœlum was one boundless, undefinable, and unimaginable ocean of liquid fire." "This great centre of worlds, this great Power of Intelligence, had wisdom, goodness, justice, mercy, lenity, forbearance. It contained truth eternalized like its own nature. So the whole of these principles were joined in one vast *Vortex of Pure Intelligence!*" "The Power contained in this great Vortex was the Great Positive Mind; and its development was eternal motion." "The essence it contained would inevitably breathe forth the amazing and indescribable qualities that characterize all the organic kingdoms." And now, according to the "Seer," Nature begins to throw off from itself other vortices, worlds, etc., and thus creation was begun. But the Sacred Writer, meek and unassuming, conceded his incapacity to comprehend even Nature, or to encounter with his weak intellect the might of those laws which move the massive members of the Universe. Not inclined to ærial flights, to spin out romantic worlds, or to construct fairy heavens and people them with blooming sylphs; and, without attempting to define infinitude, from his inspired soul he acknowledged the Author of creation, the eternal, uncreated Supreme Being. Thence, through him, of those works which rolled forth from eternity at God's command, the spirit of Inspiration uttered, "In the Beginning God created the heaven and the earth." And this is all that could be said of *the Beginning* to the understanding of mortals, or by finite speech. Whoever attempts more beggars his cause and mocks divinity. What but insanity could induce a mere mortal, whose breath is in his nostrils, and whose life trembles in its shattered vase of clay, to presume to comprehend the Almighty? or to define his pre-eternal movements who peopled space with super-stellar orbs; whose pavilion is the effulgence of his divinity; and from whose breath of Life the universe of immortal entities derives animation?—When man can rotate and retrospect the heavens as the philosopher does his planetarium; when he can say to the *deep*, thus far shalt thou go and no farther; can arise omnipotent above disintegral elements; chain death forever, that his withering hand shall no more touch material combinations; can take down the temple of Nature, remodel and exalt it;—when man can thus devise and execute, then he may assert his might and God-like wisdom: but, until then, man's greater wisdom is manifested in the humble acknowledgement of the existence of a Supreme Being, and rendering obedience to that divine law immediately affecting him. Thus he doubtless will more nearly fulfill the purposes of this life, and be better prepared for the realities of a disembodied spirit, than to dream his mortal hours away in vain speculations, only to awake at death a novice in the rudiments of real existence.

Such seems to have been the impressions formed in the mind of MOSES when called to record, for man's instruction, the Wisdom of Inspiration; and such seems to accord with what Divine Truth would impart to novitiate man.—Even man, when in exalted stations, does not unfold his design, only as it may conserve his purpose, or the interest of his subjects; and especially when the plebian *could* not comprehend him or his laws. The Monarch only imparts that knowledge adapted to the condition of each province of his kingdom—and he is but a man. Shall *Deity* exert omnipotent strength to incorporate infinite thought into the frail sense of finite man? Would he commission his angels to inform erring mortals on subjects of whose character a seraph could not conceive? Verily, that man should solve the Almighty, as the student does a mathematical problem, is a strange order of reasoning!

It is not thus, however, with the Inspired *Word*, which first announces God as the I AM— Almighty in Power, Wisdom, and Goodness; by whom all things have being; and that in the beginning God formed the heavens, which are spread out as a curtain; made the sun, moon, and the stars; and when the earth was without form, and void, and darkness was upon the face of the deep, the Divine Proceeding Energy moved upon the face of the elements: that is, this God, who is Life Eternal, Power Omnipotent, and Wisdom Infinite, said, "Let there be light," and the creative energy unfolded light; and as this light unrolled, the purpose of God revealed a firmament; and the illumined expanse appeared; and thence proceeded that Divine Power which formed the Earth; and God said, "Let the waters under the heaven be gathered together into one place, and let the *dry land* appear. And it was so." Thus declared the Spirit. Can man say more? Even though he ascend his chariot of human magnetism, thence retrace the winds of the morning, and witness the birth of time, can he add? yea, even though he enter the sanctum of an atom, and return with it whence it came, will he not ejaculate at last, "O thou inconceivable eternity, thy infinity knows no bounds; incomprehensible, indeed, are thy ways, O, thou eternal Cause!" To this conclusion the Atheist is forced, and this the Poughkeepsie "Seer," for all his pretensions, acknowledges in N. D. R., p. 673. "For speech is vain, and all that might be said of the incomprehensibility, the magnitude, and the infinitude of the truth centred in the Spiritual Sun, would consist only of words," (rational conclusion,) "and these it would be useless to speak and impress upon the human mind." (Yet he declares to have, himself, in a degree comprehended that Sun of the Divine Mind.) "Neither would it be proper to speak of the essences, qualities, and attributes dwelling within the vortex from which rolled forth the Universe, inasmuch as each possible atom comprehends more than the human mind is able to grasp." "This much only can be said: it is an inexhaustible Vortex of Life and Light, which are Love, and Order of Form, which are Wisdom—which flow not only into Heaven, but into the material Universe, and everything is thereby breathed into being. And the Great Centre and Spiritual Sun is the habitation and throne of the Divine Mind, the Great Positive, Central Power of the Universe, and of all eternal movement! And it is a Fountain in which nothing exists but what is pure, divine, everlasting, and infinite." Here, then, he is, despite of all his effort, where the Bible begins, save that his conclusion is clogged with materiality, and therefore, vague. Nevertheless, while laboring his own theory, he glides into the Bible account; and sheltered within its strong-hold, he acknowledges all attempts to delineate the First Cause, or to comprehend an "atom," in vain. (More the Scriptures do not claim, or the Christian believe.) Well he may thus avow, since nothing but weakness could induce an effort to say more of Deity, or of the origin and first principles of matter, than, "God is, and *by him nature appears.*" When more is attempted by finite intellect, thought ends where it begins, and speech rebounds upon itself, the empty echo of hollow sound. Fully then, the "Seer," after having so earnestly toiled to overthrow the Sacred Text; to set the world right upon the philosophy of creation; and to say *something new* and *strange* of the First Cause; concedes the doctrine of the Inspired Word. "How are the mighty fallen!" He who seemed to understand what to say of the lineage of original vortices; of the movement of eternal Motion; the development of Omnipotent Power; the birth of the illimitable Univercœlum, and of the Power of Intelligence; awed and humbled by the magnitude of an atom, bends before it, exclaiming: "Each possible atom comprehends more than the human mind can grasp! Yea, lost in its domain, his marvelous disclosures of God and Nature, seem to have escaped his memory; and he, to have so far forgotten his denunciations of the Bible and the Christian Religion, as now, in the presence of this "particle," to yield to that Truth which sustains the Scriptures!

Mr. Davis thus admits his highest thoughts borrowed from the Inspired Word, and therefore the incompleteness of his system. Where then is the strong hold of this Harmonial theory! Lo it yields at its base and the fabric crumbles to dust dissolved by the "Seer's" own avowal. The scheme evaporates, touched by the wand of his own declaration. What farther need we? By admitting the existence of that Eternity, whose glory is unapproachable; whose capacity is undefinable; and whose dominion is the Throne of the Lord of Hosts; the Christian's God is acknowledged and thence the Divinity of the Word. May we not here rest the review of the first principles of N. D. Revelations? Since the author of that work, virtually affirms that no more can be known of the *beginning*, or of that Divine Being who said of himself, "I AM THAT I AM," than Moses wrote?

Why should the Christian wander in his thoughts! *Reason, Facts,* and even the *Enemies* of our holy religion, bear testimony to the truth of *Inspiration*. And should not the humble follower of our Lord and Redeemer, constantly abide in that spirit of confidence which begets obedience to Heaven's requirements? Should he not indulge that living faith in God, which bears the peaceful fruits of righteousness? and that firm hope which as an anchor to the soul, is both sure and steadfast, and which entereth into that within the vail, whither Jesus, the forerunner, is for us entered?

To God alone due homage pay:
  To him let ceaseless praise be given,
"Whose years are one eternal day,"
  Whose glory crowns the highest heaven.
At his command all worlds appear,
  By him all heavenly orders rise.
Deep in his soul, let man revere
  Th' Almighty Maker of the skies.
He is the Lord, who gives the sun
  Power to shed material rays—
The glory of the eternal One;
  Man's hope of heaven's diviner lays.
This God, upholds created things;
  Formed man of clay and bade him live;
His Mercy every blessing brings—
  To him eternal honors give.
Not as a God whose ocean-wave,
  Rolling along unending space,
From molten surges, thenceforth gave
  Its god, will, wisdom, love and grace.

CHAPTER IV.

PANTHEISTIC THEORY OF MAN.

Spirit Divine, let not my speech betray
The cause of Jesus, by its human frailty.

THE subject now approached; is the constitution of man; the cause and design of his being; the means by which his physical nature obtained its peculiar type: by which his life and constitution are made to differ so widely from other forms of animated nature; by which his propensions are so peculiarly inclined; by which the texture of his physiology is so exalted; by which his attitude is so absolutely distinct, and his physiognomy so majestic;—the means by which his mode of thought, action, expression and communication, are so radically one, and beyond the power of imitation by any other order of mundane existence; by which he changes the mode of material manifestation around him; conquers other members of creation; controls even the elements; and by which he is capable of devising and executing;—the means by which he conceives of moral quality, and hopes for futurity; by which he aspires to supermundane existence, knowledge, and attainments; and his contemplations, as antennæ, seek to know the measure of infinity;—finally, by which, with such extatic delight, he bids adieu to earthly forms, and launches forth into the boundless and unknown realms of spiritual life. These considerations, these realities, and the truths thereof, are all embraced in that metaphysical question, the solution of which, Mr. Davis attempts in this subject: and upon the truth of which depend the vitality of all metaphysical and ethical sciences. Involved within the limits of this capacious theme, is that truth for which the philosopher, sage, poet, prophet, and saint, have sighed. The pearl hidden in the field of material treasure; buried beneath the avalanche of human error; o'erhung by the dark and heavy cloud of sensual passions; lost to the eye of human reason; and unperceived by material sense. Of its locality, the deist, atheist, pantheist, and infidel, have contended; of its nature and use, the christian and sensualist have ever varied. This is the question, the all-important question, introduced into this chapter. It is the object of our labor; the desire of our heart, and the burden of our prayer.

In view of the importance of this subject, our extracts and references will be liberal, that the sentiments entertained by pantheists, materialists, and harmonial spiritualists, may appear in their proper light.

Truth, especially upon a question of this magnitude, should be the object of all research and discussion, and therefore no effort should be spared, or earthly consideration regarded, while laboring to secure it.

Pursuing the order of Creation, according to N. D. Revelations, we learn: After the original mass had been duly prepared to unfold its principles, it caused to emerge vast billows of native element; and after these were resolved into sun systems, and suns had evolved nebular spheres, and these by integral laws had determined their spheroidal forms, and thence obtained stratified surfaces; then, mineral motion, vegetable life, animal sensation, and human instinct or reason appeared.

As the "Seer" approaches the plane of animal existence upon this orb, he thus comments:

"The earth, when comprehended as an entire whole, is a *stomach*, an organ of imperceptible but ceaseless digestion—of which the mineral substances constitute the ultimate and excrement." "And thus the minerals are the polygastric bodies by which the vegetable kingdom receives existence and life, and the vegetable kingdom is a universe of polygastric parts, by which a higher creation is breathed into being." N. D. R. p. 309.

This proposition it is well to note. Earth is

here represented as a stomach, whose ultimate and excrement, constitute the mineral substances; the minerals digest vegetables; vegetables, according to the theory, animals; animals, men.

Having announced the polygastric constitution of earth, he pursues the mineral and vegetable kingdom until the inferior orders of animal life manifest themselves. Whence through the various forms of radiata, articulata, molusca and the vertebrata, he traces the native elements of human beings, until arising somewhat superior to the Saurian and Mammalia tribes, they merge into the Quadrumana, where he dilates upon the subject as follows:

"I come now to a stage of creation in which the lower types of *Mankind* are distinctly exemplified. And of these I am impressed to speak particularly, and to trace them connectedly and with rather more minuteness than the other degrees of creation have been traced. And this will be done in order to impress the understanding with the important truth displayed in the first ascension of interior principles to the individualization of the inner man. * * * Before speaking of the type of anatomy that exemplifies partially the form of man, it is well to remark that Nature is like the human brain—and is incessantly producing *forms*, as the brain is thoughts. And each form and peculiar organization in Nature is determined by the existing, controlling circumstances, which were the cause of such form's creation. It is therefore impossible for any order of animals to remain for many periods the same as its original: for they are changed in accordance with the existing surrounding circumstances. * * * At the present period of creation, which is the first part of the sixth day, the *quadrumana* that existed were very differently formed from those *now* existing, and their stature and strength exceeded those of man at the *present* day. They resembled very much those that were described as existing on the planet Saturn. Their body was short and heavy; their limbs disproportionately long, and their heads of a very wide and low form. The spinal column in the early species resembled more nearly that of the fish than that of any other form. The shoulders were of great width, and the neck was very short and full. The whole body was covered with thick, heavy hair, like many of the plantigrades of that period. Some parts of the body of this quadrumana, resembled those of the lower animals, such as the fore limbs, which were used always in walking. The trunk bore some resemblance to those of the lower saurian species, and the head nearly represented a combination of forms that were then existing upon the earth. Some of the fossils of these animals have been discovered, and they have been supposed to belong to a branch of the saurian species—also to some of the marsupial mammalia. This animal was the first type, after many ages of regeneration, which resembled in many particulars the form of man. And the resemblance was in the peculiar form of the shoulders, back, and hips; but it resembled other animals in its extremities and main features. This animal, like the classes previously mentioned, developed the positive and negative forces of the organs, and the proper functions of each organ were developed. * * The muscular system was very powerful, the osseous portions were very gross in composition, and the cerebral portions were such as are connected with an undeveloped mental constitution. It possessed no thoughts that were not caused by the sensations of the body. Thus, though motion, life, and sensation, were all unfolded in this animal's organization, the higher endowments were as yet unknown; for there was no mental organization capable of developing intelligence. I am impressed distinctly that this class of animals" (undeveloped men) "remained on earth nearly nine hundred years, during which time the physical elements experienced many changes, which at length resulted in the production of a higher form of the same class." * * * "The extremities resembled partially those of the bear and partially those of the human being; but they used them all in walking, which made them like the plantigrade in habit, though they were like the bimana in some other respects. This form could not have existed, except as a progressive unfolding of the previous form."

This stage of development, represents the race as having progressed to the superior plane of the mammal-sphere occupied by the Felis Pardus, Canis, and the Ursus, where the superior functions of the Digitigrade, Plantigrade, and the Quadrumana amalgamated. In this sphere, the human principle poised, prepared, by another grand revolution of Nature, to unfold the mongrel and incipient type of the bimana into the superior grade of the ape species. Of this transition, in which Nature is represented to have finished that mighty work, by projecting a creature, (the ape) which, possessing the primary elements of man combined, especially indicated him, and which finally unfolded the inferior order of the human species, the Seer thus reveals:

"After many physical changes had occurred, this same species also gave place to a new form. This, like the other, was a very dark, gigantic, and powerful animal; but it was not so gross as the previous species of the same order. The anatomy was somewhat differently constructed, and was adapted to a new use." "This animal did not develope the forces necessary for the full unfolding of all interior qualities; but inasmuch as its forces had ascended from the primitive species of the same class, so they were adapted to unfold themselves, and to give birth to new and higher forms, such as were subsequently created." "The whole structure of the body manifested an adaptation of parts to new and more perfect uses." "There is now a decrease in the species of the quadrumana, and decrease of forms indicates a composition of more refined materials. Thus the present class has less hair upon the surface of the body." "The little hair that was upon their surfaces indicates, as does their general composition, more refined ingredients. Therefore, the whole body constitutes the first type of a species far below the negro inhabitants of the earth as now existing. Depreciation of this species was a result of subsequent periods, and finally this gave place to a new species. We have now a different type of anatomy, and, in many particulars, a new plan of organization. The head is not so large as in the previous species, but assumes a more oblong shape, and joins very closely the medulla oblongata." "The jaw-bones were of great length, the mouth was large and distended, the cheek-bones were prominent, and the head greatly represented those of several of the feline tribe. The nose was broad and flat, the brows were full, and the eyes were rather inclined to the top of the nose." "This class existed upon the earth nearly seven hundred years, during which time the whole of the animal kingdom assumed imperceptibly a higher degree of refinement. * * "This next class ascends to a degree in the scale of animal formation that may be properly termed an ultimate representation of all living things. In this form the *bimana* organization becomes more distinctly visible. . . Being well formed in its main portions, it is still better calculated to generate active, living forces, and thereby approaches nearer to the capacity of mental perception and intelligence." "And this is the first type by which a true conception is conveyed of the power of the mutual living forces: for it must be discovered that the animal forms, as they become more fully developed, combine more forces within their organization. . . Various species of these animals inhabited Asia and Africa. Being yet animals, they were highly susceptible to the influences of external circumstances; more so, indeed, than any other order of animals. They were of great stature, had great power of will, and possessed strong passions, as owing to the highly susceptible inclinations inherent in their constitutions. . . These animals, to the present inhabitants of the earth, would appear like giants in form and stature; indeed, they were larger than any similar forms now upon any portion of the earth. These were the first that displayed any indication of mental activity. They were so formed that it became convenient for them to use distinct *sounds*, which were significant to the minds of those addressed. . . These animals were distinguished from all others in habit and disposition. They even had a conception of rearing artificial structures wherein they might reside; and they often inhabited caves: but they generally, like the lower species of the same order, dwelt upon the surface of the earth. They did not possess any of the aquatic or amphibious characteristics; therefore it is manifest that they were more refined in form, in degree, and in disposition, than any of the previous classes or orders in the animal kingdom.—These dwelt undisturbed upon the earth nearly one thousand years. The degree of organization which subsequently took their place, was the first form that approached or indicated in the least degree any of the peculiar characteristics of mankind. . . After this, three successive and distinct orders pressed in their stead. The highest of these approached in every particular the more perfect form of the human organization. . And this brings the period of the sixth day of creation to a point three thousand and eight hundred years before the commencement of the race as referred to in the primitive, written record. . . And it was at this time that a new tribe was introduced upon the earth, rising entirely above the undeveloped features of the lower forms. These constituted what may be properly termed a transition from the animal to the man; and these were the first forms that could be properly termed *man*. . . Here, then, we rest satisfied. Man is created, and exerts a power over all creation. . . Now is revealed the whole use of Nature; and now can be perceived the adaptation of every part belonging to the whole mass to produce a more exalted form; which, again, is adapted to the unfolding of far greater and eternal beauties. And all the laws and forces which have been heretofore explained, are now plainly understood as converging to the formation of man. Man, then, represents the universal progressive development, which is an inherent and eternal law of matter; also, he represents a resurrection of every gross material in being."—N. D. R. p. 314, etc.

To this period in the Harmonial theory of man's creation, or rather development from Nature, comments are uncalled for, as there seems no great consequences attached to this story of animal ascension; only as it may be worthy of remark, that Nature, while thus laboring to reveal through her Oracle the method by which she gave birth to man, passes from point to point, in the ascending scale, by statements such as the following: "The first animal forms of the present day (a period early in the history of earth,) are the simplest, like those of the previous periods." "There were many huge animals upon the face of the earth, such as the Mammoth and kindred species. I am impressed with the reason why these higher gigantic animals passed at successive periods from the face of the earth." "I am impressed that many species not known to naturalists, both of this and other orders, were also existing upon the earth, and likewise became extinct." "I am impressed distinctly that this class of animals remained upon the earth nearly nine hundred years, during which time the physical elements experienced many changes, which at length resulted in the production of a higher form of the same class." "There is a law running through this system of comparative anatomy not perceived in a superficial view of the order of creation."— "But if the mind could be carried back to the beginning principles, and then follow each law and order of development through all the successive changes, the connection between the present degree of organization and the lower animated forms, could be distinctly seen." "There is now a decrease in the species of quadrumana." "These constitute what may be properly termed a transition from animal to man." "And as the confluence of all these establishes and constitutes the organization of man, man becomes the perfection and representation of them all." "Nature is the cause; forms are the effects; and man is the ultimate production."

This is the chart, given us in Nature's Divine Revelations, of man's pilgrimage from the mineral, vegetable and animal kingdoms. It assays to pursue and note his meandering pathway, and the circuit of his unnumbered metamorphoses, until he emerges from the ape, in form and character an intellectual being. This system cites us to the crawling and venomous serpent, the sly and skulking panther, the sneaking wolf, the voracious tiger, the swaggering mastodon, moping bear, and filthy ape as our progenitors.

And is this man? And such his cause?
  Are brutes his true nativity?
Saurians formed by equal laws
  Have Moluscs a divinity?
Also the Cete and Corvus
  Marsupial, Digitigrade;
Pachydermata and Urus,
  Rodentia and the Plantigrade?

Did Troglodytes of Simia,
 As saith this pantheistic plan,
Arise from apes to Bimana,
 And thus the creature create *man?*

Admitting this man's ancestry,
 In him all creatures are combined;
And thence to all eternity,
 His spirit is the brute refined!
But *how* such species did unfold;
 Perform their transit into man,
Remains *the secret* yet untold:
 Can Nature know whence we began?

This is the Book Old Nature spake,
 At least the Work informs us so:
But *how* of spirit we partake,
 If from an ape, has failed to show.
And ne'er by her has been explained,
 A *law* by which the monkey race,
The intellect of man obtained;
 And then assumed so fair a face!
And dropped his marked appendage too:
 Declared himself above baboons;
Thence off his native costume threw:
 Assumed the frock and pantaloons!

"Here we rest satisfied," says the Seer, "Man is created. Now is revealed the purposes of Nature."

THE PANTHEISTIC THEORY OF MIND AND SPIRIT constitutes the succeeding degree in this scale of progression, and, therefore, demands consideration in connection with the creation of Man. And as this is the essential part of Nature's great Work, the Oracle proceeds to the discovery of properties and essences in Matter, that shall finally create for this "system" a human soul. And page 50, N. D. R., the subject is thus introduced:

"So, tracing the refinement of matter from vegetable to animal existence (the life or soul of plants being perfected to become animal sensation,) the refinement and perfection of these two, to become the substance of *mind*—and the progression of *its* nature to its second sphere and investiture, you arrive, naturally and reasonably at an idea of the future properties, the positively individualized condition and existence of the Mind in its first ultimate stage of progression." And, p. 74, Ibid. "And as matter contains the essences and properties to produce man, as a progressive ultimate, so motion contains the properties to produce Life and sensation. These together and perfectly organized, develope spirits. But such principles must have an existence eternally — as emanating from the Great Source and Fountain of Intelligence," (The great center Vortex, the ocean of Liquid Lava) "but it could not be individualized and made *manifest* without a vessel like unto man." "For as the human embryo contains an essential pinciple and quality to produce the perfect organization of man, so does the germ of all existence possess the essence and quality to produce its corresponding *Spirit.*"

Again. "The all-pervading Essence contained in Nature is of itself an eternal and immortal principle. Every particle of matter, at some time during the course of ages, passes through and becomes a part of *animal life!* The hardest substance that is existing in the earth; the earth itself, and all things contained in, below, and above it, will ultimately, and at different periods, compose some parts or particles of animal existence." "Forms and entities are mere modifications of original matter." Page 118. "And these," (worlds) "and all their particles, will become the very essence of vegetable and animal existence. And the latter, with the active energies inherently accompanying it, not only will pass to the perfection of spiritual essence, but will work its mighty influence upon everything below it, until all things arrive at an exalted state of spiritual and celestial perfection. Thus all matter will pass through the multifarious forms and stages that are existing, and all will ultimately pass into the *unparticled state*, and will ascend to associate with higher and more glorious spheres—of *spiritual* composition." "In *quality*, the *last* of all things, or spiritual principles, will be like the first of all things, or the Great Positive Mind." Page 149.

"Matter and Motion," according to this theory, as previously shown, "constituted the original condition of all things;" therefore, according to the above, these, ultimate themselves into orbs, into minerals, into vegetables, into animals, into mind and spirit; and into Deity. Mind and spirit are, then, matter and motion, self-evolved and sublimated into thinking principles.

In continuation of this Theory, the "Seer," p. 593, thus enlarges: "I have not spoken particularly of the physical productions and constitutions of man, nor of those peculiar elements, qualities, and essential principles, that elevate him above the animal creation, and that constitute and characterize that animated principle known as the Soul, Spirit or Mind. I find it necessary to generalize then, in order to establish the connection between Nature, with its various lower forms, and Man, and between Man and the higher spheres."

"I have ascended, then, to the important question, *What is Man*, MATERIALLY? And the answer is, He is the wisdom, head and King of all animated forms. He is the perfection of matter. I proceed to prove this proposition by descending to the interior forms and substances that constitute the rudiments of all organic beings, and tracing them connectedly until they ascend and become perfected in the human organism. The first forms or particles that made their appearance after the condensation of the matter composing the earth, were those constituting the *mineral kingdom*." "Meanwhile they make a perfect compound, the whole of which forms the Vegetable Creation. The highest form, which is the ascending circular, becomes the connecting form between the vegetable and animal." . . . . "The highest forms in the animal are the perfected spiritual, which join the animal compound to the material organization of man. Here, then, the spiritual forms introduce the particles to compose the organization of MAN, which, when perfected, developes the *highest* or *celestial* forms in matter. Thus the perfect *spiritual* becomes the *first celestial* forms, the perfection of which establishes the human organization. What I mean by *celestial* forms, are those particles of matter that contain in themselves every species of form in the subordinate kingdoms, and meanwhile become the receptacles of all degrees of spiritual life, which are not only contained in, but developed by them, in such a perfect and corresponding manner, that all the lower forms in the animal, vegetable and mineral worlds are by them governed, mirrored, and vividly represented." "Thus in man are these lower forms fully developed and perfected." "It will be seen by this that the *angular* particles of matter develope the *circular*, which in their turn unfold the rectilinear planes, diameters, axes, and poles, all of which are discovered in the Vegetable World." "The progressive *circulars* unfold the *spirals*. The spiral contains the circular and all its properties; all these are discoverable in the Animal World. Then, again, the successive spiral forms unfold the spiritual, which latter, in like manner, unfold the celestial or perfect forms of rudimental matter. Thus the *angular* developes the *circular*, this the *spiral*, this the *spiritual*, and this the *celestial*—all of which are contained in the perfect forms of the Human World." "Thus man is the highest and most perfect combination of organized matter."

"Thus it is made manifest that the three degrees of creation (which are the Mineral, Vegetable, and Animal,) flow into, and, as it were, spontaneously unfold the whole human creation; and that the three are necessary in order to unfold a complete and symmetrical organization; and this is the Head, Flower, and Lord of Creation, and is called Man." . . . "Man *materially* is the lord and governor of animated nature; *spiritually he is the perfection of motion*, or of the *first great moving princi-*

ples of the Universe." In other words,—"*He is the Wisdom of Love.*"

Finally, the "Seer" thus completes this theory of the creation of man: "Motion, in the three united degrees of this form, became a new principle, which was *life*, and this is the soul of the *vegetable* world. Life is, therefore, a development of motion; this of sensation, and this is the soul of the *animal* world.' "And it is made also clear that Motion, Life, and Sensation, which form one, is included in the latter, progressed to the *spiritual*, and through this into the *perfect* spiritual, which is the *celestial* form. Sensation, becoming thus perfected, constitutes the Soul of man, which is Intelligence." "Thus Motion contained *in germ* all the essential parts and forms which, when ascended and perfected, constitute the Soul of the *Human* World, which is the Wisdom and Intelligence of this whole rudimental system of creations. Thus Motion is the Soul of the Mineral World, Life is the Soul of the Vegetable World, Sensation the Soul of the Animal World, and Intelligence the Soul of the Human World." . . "Intelligence, therefore, is the perfection of the principle of *Motion*, and this answers the question, What is man *spiritually?*" "Thus the human body is a *Universe*, subsisting and existing upon all lower forms of organic life, and is of itself a *whole crea-*

tion, in and by which the labors of Nature, and the ultimate design of the Great Eternal Cause are typified and absolutely fulfilled. And the human form is of all this a clear and living demonstration." "All forms, then, are the established organs by which gross and inferior particles are purified and refined, in order that they may become suitable to enter into, and create, and sustain the highest form of matter, which is Man." "Man is then above all forms in being, and all congregations of forms; for he is the point, centre, and goal to which all other forms flow and are perfected, refined, and made useful to the whole constitution of Nature and the Universe." "From past considerations it is made clear that *man materially is a perfection of all Matter in Nature;* and that *man spiritually is a perfection of all Motion in the Universe*, or of the First Great Principle of Motion, which is the Divine Mind," etc.—[N. D. R. p. 513, 539.

"Ye shall be as gods knowing good and evil," was the language from the *interior*, and through an appropriate external medium, by *one* who in the beginning of man's sorrows flattered the unsuspecting pair into disobedience.—Gen. 3, 5. "Ye are gods," is the ultum of this "marvel" of the nineteenth century. This the foregoing extracts from N. D. R. clearly expresses. In order to sustain this position, which appears to be the purpose of the work, it became necessary to create man by self-moving principles, and, therefore, Pantheism attempts to bring out of *atoms* the human spirit, and to crown and glorify it with the divinity of matter. To accomplish this a trinity of matter is first established, and each member is allotted a denomination suited to the end of the unity. One is styled the angular, another the circular, and the ultimate the spiral. Each of these is endued with vital force, and unfolding ability. By their constitution, the angular develope the circular, the circular the spiral, and the spiral, in which the former blend, develope the spiritual. And now, (for so it is revealed,) having attained to certain degrees of perfection, the spiritual develope the celestial. Thence the human being is formed. Moreover, as saith the theory, motion, which is denominated the soul of the mineral kingdom, unfolds forces, tendencies, and actuating laws. By these, motion unfolds life, or the soul of the vegetable world. The vegetable world unfolds a new principle of life and energy, which constitutes *sensation*, the soul and proceeding principle of the animal world. The animal world was then prepared for a degree still more exalted; and thence motion, life and sensation combining, unfolded the spiritual, and the perfect spiritual unfolded the celestial. And sensation, by this means perfected, unfolded the soul of man, which is Intelligence. Intelligence, therefore, is the perfection of the principle of motion, according to the theory, and this is man Spiritually.

Such is the Pantheistic Theory of Man; a theory which renders him the ultimate of Nature. And whatever may be the effort in these "Revelations," or of the advocates of this system, to sustain the reverse, or to theorize upon the Great First Cause, man is here represented as a perfection of that Moving Principle "which is the Divine Mind." In a former statement the Seer declares man to be the wisdom, head, and king of all animated beings. In other portions of the work he assures us that without a human structure this divine spirit-essence could not have obtained organic form. Without the human anatomy, therefore, this principle of motion is but an undefined and omnipotent motor-force. Nature was originally matter and motion; these evolved principle, order, and organic bodies, the crowning object of which was to unfold intellect, the spirit or soul of man. Man is now unfolded, and is the perfection, etc. Could a theory be more explicit? Man is (thus it is revealed,) the original or First Principle of Nature modified and exalted. Need he look up? To what shall he aspire? Is there any sphere above him? Is he perfection? And where is the Divine mind?

If man is not, is there any Divine Mind?

However much the followers of A. J. Davis may seek to evade this conclusion, and also the proposition that "N. D. Revelations" denies the existence of the Supreme Being—the Christian's God—such are the ultimates of his display of terms and of his theorizing. He and his disciples may use swelling words concerning the Great Positive Mind, Power of Intelligence, Love, Will, Wisdom, etc.; but his entire scheme makes the First Cause but a mass of moving igneous elements, undefined and unorganized, whose motion finally preponderated Universe-ward, and thence the mass disseminated itself into the several sun systems, and these unfolded into beings, spiritual and intellectual, which, as before noticed, are the crowning glory of the Universe, etc. What, then, is man? Again, the system and its devotees teach that to obey the promptings (affinities or passions,) of our beings, is to render obedience to God. Who, then, is God? Is not man? Should he not, then, away with his old theology, his weak and superstitious looking upward for a Supreme Being—a First Cause, as God over all, and blessed forever more? And becoming wise, learn that *he* originally *did exist* as an integral portion of the surging Univercœlum? and that thence, by an omnipotent effort, escaped that illimitable prison house; became floating nebulæ; thence mineral, vegetable, animal, and is now the perfection of his original elements? And, recognizing his *nativity* and *himself*, by wisdom overcome the errors with which his soul has become unconsciously involved?—errors he has amassed by fancying the existence of a God above him, and who requires the affections of his heart, the obedience of his mind, and the adoration of his being? Is this progression? Moreover,—to continue the theory,—man, having thus advanced, will henceforth obey the promptings of his nature, which is rendering obedience to the highest law.—Strange as this may appear, when the Bible is rejected, such reasoning becomes the only alternative; and all who are neglecting the Holy Scriptures, and are devoting their minds to the study of opposing writings, are tending to this result; they MUST, if they pursue the materialistic reasoning, become haters of Bible Religion, and self-worshipers; their inclinations will become their God. Such is the end of N. D. R., which, although much of its labor is devoted to an attempt to reveal, or define the First Cause, concludes in deifying man, rendering him the head of those members whose aggregate is Deity. "One body of one immortal soul," is the definition of Nature by the Seer, and that man is the head thereof.

He also represents Nature as a magnificent Tree, whose trunk is gross matter and of necessity, whose sap is the spirit-essence, the Divine Mind, and man in his incipiency the flowers, in his maturity the ripened fruit. He is, therefore, a combination of all subordinate or original principles. Without him the Tree could not have been complete, or secured the end of its unthinking designer, and of its eternal evolutions. Consequently man is the culmination of its properties and essences. What then is man? Is not the flower the glory? and the fruit the perfection of the Tree? And does it not contain the germ of re-production — of future form and being? Admitting these premises, and this *may* appear very well: man *may* be a perfection of the Divine Mind: but at present he is a horrible manifestation. Again, the symbol indicates the decomposition of the original stalk, after it shall have subserved its purpose. Man, or spirit, then, agreeable to the reasoning will alone exist, since Nature, which is Cause, Means and Ultimates, finally ends or ripens into Spirit. From this view of the subject the "Seer" affirms that the present existing Universe will pass into higher forms — "return whence it came," and that, thence "will emanate new worlds, an epoch of another Beginning." Despite, therefore, of his affirmations, relative to the eternal

Positive Nature of the Great First Cause, and also of the Negativeness of unfolded or created spirit, (which the present reasoning seems to have overlooked,) Nature is here made to ripen into man, and, as there is, according to the system nothing supernatural, the deific nature of matter is deified in him who thus becomes a perfection of the Divine Mind. Than this,there can be no other conclusion. Does man indicate his nature? The unsoundness herein displayed, is too palpable to be concealed by wordy sophistry.

When the subject is considered in all its bearings, there seems, also, other important deficiencies. For the system maintains that *Nature* is to complete one grand circle; that Man is to be the "*key-stone*" to the stupendous Arch. It would, then, appear, that the vast Edifice *must endure;* that the Cause, Means and Ultimates must remain perfect in all their parts. Otherwise, how could it form "an infinite circle"? For, if all nature is resolved into man, (Spirit,) and he is the Key-stone, there can be no arch for the *Key-stone* (obtained) alone remains!

Again, by this figure the boundless Universe is represented. Can the Universe or its primary principles undergo any fundamental change, or cease to be, and the several parts, from the beginning, constitute one eternal and infinitely perfect circle? Shall the life depart and the body remain? Or shall the body, its inseverable and co-eternal counterpart, disappear, and the tree still flourish, the circle continue perfect? How shall the arch support itself in the absence of the keystone? or the keystone retain its position without the arch. How shall the tree exist without its sap or life-current? or the vital essences retain being, and operate separate from the tree, especially if it is composed of and contains within itself the matter, motion and principles of all Nature—is even eternity itself? If it ripen *itself* into fruit, the old shall have passed away, and a new universe appears in the form of organized intelligences.

By this reasoning the Great Positive Mind is depreciated, if not removed, and man supremely exalted. For God is Nature and Nature is God. The figurative tree is the representation of Nature. It yields its virtue to the fruit or seed—"and this is the end of one Time, the Epoch of a New Beginning." So declares the "Seer."

Thus analyzing this theory by whatever method, it is only found self-annihilating, and culminates (if at all,) in the God-hood of man.

A few remarks of the "Seer," taken from other portions of the work, may, perhaps, reflect light upon this subject. On page 72, etc., he thus premises and proceeds to reason: "The two great propositions, then, which it is the object to establish, are the original Cause of all things, and the ultimate of man, which is *Spirit.* The premise is, the co-existence and universal action of matter and motion; This establishes the existence of an *original Cause.*" The reader will especially regard this proposition. The original cause is here declared to be matter and motion. In the quotations heretofore considered, it is *affirmed* that "man materially is a perfection of all matter in Nature, and spiritually is a perfection of all motion in the Universe, or of the first principles of motion, which is the Divine mind." It is clear from these references that the "Seer" maintains the doctrine which declares that *Nature* resolves itself (progresses) into man—therefore deifies him. "It is a familiar truth," says Mr. Davis, p. 76, "universally known, yet but little comprehended, that the germ of the plant contains within itself, though not as perceptible, all the essential qualities of its future being. . . And thus from the germ to the ultimate, exist and are developed the powers originally embodied. Hence, the *germ* was the *cause;* the *form* the *effect;* the *seed* the ultimate individualized. This not only establishes the law of progression, but it proves that there is a *circle* in the progression; for the plant ends precisely where it begins. It only makes *perfect* what the original essence contained *imperfect.*"

What evidence does Nature afford that plants improve their quality at each successive ripening? or that each returning generation arises to a superior plane? Has the *pyrus coronaria* lost its acerbity, and given, by progression, birth to the delicious pome? Are not the *pyrus communis* and the *citrus aurantium* the same as in ages past? What proof, then, does Nature afford that the native principles, unaided by the hand of art, *progress*, and that each successive seed-time ensures a more perfect development? And *especially* if, as the "Seer" sums up, the seed or ultimate ends precisely where it begins? Again, p. 597, ibid: "For the seed of all material compounds is involved in the lowest stage of matter, which germinates and produces the *Mineral World.* This, again, adds to the great Tree of Creation, whose next stage of development is the form of the *Vegetable World.* The next expansion of the body of this great Tree developes the *Animal World.* It now puts forth branches, which bud, and the flower is the *Human World.* Thus it is that the material Tree of Causation has successively yielded new forms, which correspond in every general feature to germ body, branches, buds, and blossoms. . . Thus man is the highest and most perfect combination of matter. . *Man* is to Nature what the *head* is to man."

If we remember that matter, according to the Revelations, is composed of a trinity of particles—the angular, circular, and spiral—and that these contain and finally develope the soul, or intelligence of man, we cannot fail to recognize in the "material Tree" the Cause and Principle of all existence. Matter and Motion constituted the original condition—were co-existent and co-eternal principles—developed Omnipotent Power, etc—hence were the cause, and man is the flower of Nature, a perfection of these principles; and without the human form as a vessel, says the "Seer," *spirit* (*Motion,*) could not have intellectually unfolded. Therefore we again inevitably arrive at the conclusion that Nature is in man Deitized. Or if all things finally become what they originally were, and the plant terminates precisely where it begins, and if man does not retain his entity as the glory and intellectual crown of all, he must be resolved into the original Vortex! What, then, has Nature accomplished by her magnificent display? Words may adorn, but reason disgarbs the facts, revealing the deformity of this magnetic scheme. But as the figure employed is denominated "the Tree of material Causation," "the tree of Creation," etc., and lest an attempt be made to evade these conclusions by affirming that *deeper* in Eternity exists *a cause,* we will repeat some of the fundamental statements of the system upon this point. Page 120, etc., we are informed that "It (the Univercœlum) was one vast expanse of liquid substance, without bounds. This was the original condition of MATTER. It was but one form; was an eternity of *motion;* was a whole; one eternal sun. It had not beginning, and was without end; was a Vortex of Eternity; one infinite Circle; was the very essence of Power. Its inconceivable magnitude and constitution were such as not to develope forces but Omnipotent Power. Matter and motion were existing as a Whole, inseparable. The *Matter* contained the substance to produce all suns, all worlds, and systems of worlds throughout the universe of space, and qualities to produce all things that are existing upon each of these worlds." (This is matter.) "The *Power* contained Wisdom and Goodness, Justice, Mercy, and Truth." Power was developed from motion, for without motion there could be no development. Moreover, Omnipotent Power *was developed.* And besides, matter and motion were co-eternal principles, established by virtue of their own nature; they reigned throughout the regions of boundless infinitude, and constituted the original condition of all things, etc.

Matter and Motion, accordingly, not only em brace, but are absolutely *the* great First Cause

These propositions are laid down as *the premise* of the scheme. They are the foundation and corner-stone of the Edifice: the length, breadth, height and depth of the First, or original Cause. Thence the "Seer" proceeds to his work, and builds his Universe, etc. This Matter and Motion, which he denominates co-eternal principles, and the original constitution of all things, form the body and soul of his Univercœlum; and the body, life, branches, flower and fruit of his figurative Tree. Therefore, the Tree is employed as a representative of Nature. Nature embraces all things, and Matter and Motion enter into the composition of all particles and combinations; constitute all original conditions and terminate in all grand results. Man is a perfection thereof, etc. So the Oracle informs us.

Thus is established, and beyond the power of criticism, the fact, that this "Pantheistic Theory of man," renders him, not only the ultimate of physical manifestation, but absolutely perfects in him the cause and means of Nature; and thus in his being Deifies Matter, worlds without end.

Finally, and in the concluding reflection upon this figurative Tree of Nature, we notice, that a tree has not only branches and body, but roots which serve as a means of life, position and endurance. The inquiry, therefore, naturally arises: Where does this magnificent Tree take root?

Does its caudex spread its massive supporters throughout, and take hold of space? Space, then, is a depending cause, a means of quickening, and immutable. But space is nonenity. Is the Tree a phantom? Does it take root within itself? This would render the figure defective, radically so, as vegetation is incapable of the comparison. It would also indicate that its radicals infold and fix their spongioles in the sub-heart of the immensurable trunk, as perpetual absorbents of its vital essences. And this involves the principles in primary contradictions by rendering the body self-absorbing without adequate resources. The inconsistency of the philosophy is made still more manifest by its progressive claims. These cause the original Tree or Univercœlum to unfold or ripen itself into another, and far superior growth.

And as man is the head, or ultimate, (the fruit) by the figure he falls to the primary condition, becomes the germ, or seed from which is to unfold another Universe. Man, then, becomes the Cause and Creator of the "Seers" second Univercœlum or great centre Sun. In this he is not only deitized, but is absolutely the *Creator* of a Univercœlum far more glorious than the present. This is called rational. It is therefore considered more consistent with *sense* to conceive matter a vast laboratory, self-formed, self-propelled, self-directed, and finally as manufacturing itself into men, (by chance, dark and vague) than to behold Nature as the manifestation or workmanship of a Being infinitely perfect and harmonious in attributes: a Being, who exists independent of Nature, as the Supreme Creator thereof, and also, that man physically the head of physical creation; was quickened spiritually, and formed intellectually, by the breath of his Life, who is God the Life, all quickening and all animating; God the Lord, all controlling and sustaining; God the Holy Procedure all creating; Universes unnumbered and unending.

If it be alleged that this Tree of Nature rests in the principles of the great First Cause, it is only to assert, as heretofore shown, that it inverts its supporters, and derives life and unfolding power from its own vitality. The conclusion, then, of this theory of man, is, that Nature is comparable to a tree of immensurable magnitude, with infolded roots, and that it is situated in space: that its capillaries finally absorb the original stalk, and incorporate it into fruit, thence drops into space precisely where the former commenced. How inconsistent and opposed to every known law of Nature! If it is urged in the support of this self-suspending law of Nature, that the *centrifugal* and *centripetal* laws governing planetary systems account for this inconsistency, let it be borne in mind, that this figurative Tree *embraces all things in universal space or existence.* If reference is had to the law of *gravitation*, the illustration is rendered still more absurd, for it is that law by which parts adhere and converge to one common centre; while the aggregate is sustained by those laws which not only embrace the spheroids, but pervade intermediate realms; laws which move and guide the rolling spheres while traversing the undefinable regions of illimitable space.

If it is claimed that the self-creating, self-supporting and self-unfolding doctrine of Pantheism is a Truth deducible from the inherent life of plants, etc. which spring, self-prompted, into active being; even a superficial view of the workings of nature within the compass of human research and the power of human test reveals the contrary. Every organism, every quickening and every movement of physical manifestation, by its mode confesses its dependence, in a greater or less degree, upon extrinsic laws. Not a plant of the most inferior class or a living thing, but receives aid from foreign agencies and man the boasted head, crown, glory, and perfection of all, is a living and irrefutable argument against the theory. Nature, then, herself denies the charge brought against her, and lifts up her voice to him who is her Cause, Life and means of perpetuation.

But if it is still urged that each body or movement is connected with and therefore the immediate result of nature; that plants, insects and *men* are born of the principles composing this sphere; then it follows that this orb and attending elements are but the fruit of some anterior body from which they derived *their original* properties, form and order of movement. By pursuing this method, we finally, and inevitably arrive at some self-originated, self-prompted and self-unfolding Orb, or Centre. This of course Mr. Davis would denominate his *original Vortex.* But removing *the Beginning* at a distance, however remote, by no means obviates the difficulty. To say that the "Beginning" possessed these qualifications, and begat, by turns, its several qualities and attributes, does not render the proposition true. But this, in accordance with all philosophical propositions, needs demonstration, or at least, some means to test its truth. All the evidence and tangible sequence of Nature, and all frank reasoning bears testimony to the untruthfulness of this Pantheistic assumption. This vital question, therefore, whence and how the Beginning originated, and thence proceeded to material manifestation, is a question the Pantheist can never answer. It is with him mere assumption, whence he proceeds and finally brings forth man. *Assumption* then, is the Pantheist's First Cause. Lead him to *this,* and there is not sufficient vitality to afford one breath of life, and he is left gasping in unparticled and unvitalized space. The christian's Theory is the reverse. From Nature he appeals to Nature's God, in whose eternal Causation he has abundant relief and substantial argument for all abstruse metaphysical propositions.

Apparently conscious that his system is defective in its first principles—is soulless, the "Seer" mystifies by an attempt to so infold, and descend toward some centre, as to fix the mind upon an infinity within an infinity, henceforth and forever. But this seems the perfection of his weakness, since, if he withdraw from the periphery to the intermedium, or descend from the cortex to the pith, there must be a point or radix, beyond which he cannot pass. There is a centre, and there must be a circumference, otherwise his figure and philosophy is utterly at fault. And particularly so, since Matter is the body and Motion the soul of his original Univercœlum, and constitute all primary conditions as well as principles. But it seems a cause unworthy of farther remark, and indeed it would be, only for its bewildering transcendentalism, which in sections, float over the dark vault of human frailty, like so many *ignes fatui* in the deadly miasm of marshy realms. However, in conclusion, we observe that if "*mind-essences*" exist as prominently throughout nature as this Pantheistic Theory maintains; if they constitute the quickening qualities, and refined ultimates of substances, then they must prevail in all embodiments: and if the several kingdoms possess so abundantly these *essential* and *sensitive* essences, cannot nature again unfold human species? If nature produced from sub-elements, the original bimana hath she not like principles in store? and can she not repeat her effort and arrive at equal or superior results? All nature is not reconstructed and thence disqualified for kindred purposes. Are not the faunal kingdoms still available? If primary nature still exists, and her unfolding, progressive, and purifying laws are unceasing; if her polygastric powers have not abated in their labors, why has she not, yea, why does she not often, from the animal races, unfold man, and terminate her gestation as in days of yore? and from Simia why do not men continue to arise? And if there is no depreciation: if her laws move perpetually onward, and her efforts are sure; why has not the beaver changed his nature? the ape given place to a superior race? and man arisen to another and more exalted one?

If nature, by this "Seer," truly reveals her hidden laws, and proposes thus to redeem us from the dogma and oppression of Bible Religion; if she would deliver us from captivity; why not in this day of her special favor, if in no other way, group the simia of earth, and demonstrate her theory by unfolding therefrom *one* human pair? even an *inferior* type of the bimana? Is not the cause a worthy one? Human chemists urge laws, and hasten results. Is not Nature the great original Chemist? Is the suggestion unjust? and not legitimate? If it is maintained that nature having once originated man, has in him accomplished her great object, and thence suspended her laws; we suggest that no such evidence exists in her mundane dominion. The former degrees, and spheres as they have been for ages, still remain. Nor is there evidence that they were originally ephemeral in their procreating nature.

Having now considered the highest claims and strongest arguments afforded by the Pantheists, relative to their theory of the First Cause, the beginning and subsequent manifestation of nature, also, the creation of man, we are, in conclusion, constrained to indulge the following reflections:

First, that a Jewish High Priest, with propriety equal to what this system affords, could instruct the unlearned Hebrew, that Solomon's Temple was a manifestation of artistic nature, self-progressed and self-ultimated. He might from this assumption, speculate upon the great First Cause, and affirm, that, *in the beginning* the materials of the *House* existed in a chaotic state; that they were constituted of atomic substance, pervaded by a subtle vitality, which, by an incomprehensible, inconceivable and co-eternal inclination begot, of itself, motion and power; that thence it expanded its atomic and illimitable body into space; that this substance, as it emanated from the Great Centre, was, by an incomprehensible law, the *Centre emerging from itself*, and therefore possessed all the attributes and qualifications of the original, that by its eternal power and motion, it begot that momentum, which caused it to travel to space's remotest bounds, and there resolve itself into spheroids; that these revolved around the parent Centre as immensurable satellites; and after an inconceivable lapse of time, they created, for themselves, a suite of satellites, or subordinate spheroids, one of which was the planet Earth: that earth proceeded until it formed the mineral kingdom and overlaid the dry land with vegetation. Finally, in the process of time, that it begot men and women, who subsequently needed a House in which to congregate and worship; whereupon, the quarries of earth unfolded, without square or plumet, the polished stone, each of which were self-formed into proportions for their specific use in the building. Moreover, the Cedar, Olive tree, etc. unfolded themselves into every necessary form and dimension and carved with exceeding great skill; and that, finally, the costly stone and the curiously wrought timbers, moved by the unerring law of progression, simultaneously and in perfect order proceeded to their appropriate position in the structure. (*Hence why they came together without the sound of hammer or axe.*) And thus the Temple was built. Also the mines of earth gave up their treasures, which, once evolved, proceeded to overlay the floor of the Temple, the Oracle, Cherubim, etc., with pure gold; and thus the House was adorned!

Or, secondly: The untutored Aborigine, seated with bow and arrow upon some rocky battlement overlooking the blue deep, while beholding the floating palace of civilization, might declare it a self-formed creature, and that by means of self-originated, and self-applied laws, it was forcing its way through Neptune's foaming surge. And the untamed forest maid might sing of the "*glory of its being*," while dancing along the floral landscapes that smile upon the sea! Or the native Bard, invoke his muse to grant immortal lays, while he adorned the theory of the self-made ship with his inspired song. As well might the savage, having no knowledge of the machinery, compass, pilot, or man at the wheel, speculate upon the origin, movement and destination of the proud ship, as for the Pantheist to say that orbs, revolving in the Sea of Space were not created by the Supreme Architect, and launched by skillful hands, and the law of their movement controlled by his infinite Wisdom. The salute of Columbus, as he neared the "New World," caused the Native to humble himself and worship, as he supposed, the *god of flame* and *Thunder*. Why not? Ignorant of the true character, he misjudged the cause. Or, could he have beheld the particles which, when ignited, caused the report; their composition and nature, still a mystery and beyond his comprehension, might have induced in his laboring mind the strange thought, that they were self-formed, and self-exploded. They surely possessed much ability: but needed prompting. Let those who may deem these allusions irrelevant, enter if they can, the Tabernacle of original Cause, learn the science of primitive Motion; analyze the subtle elements that form the substrata of Nature; and if their souls do not founder in the billows that roll from "the least possible atom:" let them report the Cause, means and end of Nature; and so correctly as to harmonize with known facts and sense.

He who constructs can comprehend. And

should not he who comprehends, with adequate material, be able to demonstrate? He who can in a degree comprehend the *Sun* of the *Divine Mind*, should be capable of comprehending the inferior manifestations of *Nature* in his own sphere; and also of demonstrating some laws, which the populace do not understand. If man be what "Nature's Divine Revelations" make him, and if the "Seer" is so much exalted above his fellows as he reports, why speculate so liberally and display such revealing skill, unaccompanied by potent demonstrations? The Chemist causes nature, to attest his science? The Anthropologist, Psychologist, and the imperfect Necromancer offer the demonstration of their theory. Does the Poughkeepsie Seer? In what? By the diagnosis of diseases, and the manifestation of clairvoyant ability? Does he evince his exalted condition by his assumptive and contradictory declamations and thus reveal his superior wisdom? Does gleaning historic fragments, and jumbling them together, establish him *the Oracle?* What, then, has he brought from those mystic regions, in which his intellect so freely roamed, to prove his mission? Surely the "Revelations" do not bring their own confirmation. Must we concede his pompous asseverations, unsustained by their intrinsic merit or adequate means of corroboration? What though there are truths, even important truths, embraced within the measure of his verbose speech? Does it therefore follow that his propositions, reasoning, or authoritative sayings and doctrines are founded in truth? MOSES informs us that God in the beginning created the heavens and the earth. These exist, and are above the controll of man. Nevertheless, the "Seer" denounces this statement, and declares against the character of Sacred History, as maintained by the Christian; and that Moses and the Prophets did not derive their thoughts from the source and in the manner the Biblicist supposes. Meanwhile, he affirms his superior condition, makes assertions, and then expects the tribute of our credulity. He informs us that Nature's divine ultimates, her laws and living thoughts encompassed him: that he moved amid the beaming lustre of the superior or divine spheres; that around him cluster eternal truths, wreathing his impressed spirit as with a diadem of celestial and intellectual stars, all seeking utterance, through him, to man benighted, man in clay. Thence proceeds that lofty speech, denominated "Nature's Divine Revelations," whose sayings lead the host, and proffer salvation to the Race! This causes creatures to create themselves, and particles to move as living beings, whose shuffling metamorphosing combinations ultimate in man. By this theory matter is represented more wise and capable than man, the head and perfection of Nature. Can men devise, form a globe, and bid it forth amid revolving orbs? Can all known created beings form one star, and cause it to roll along the galaxy on high? Why should they not, if the culmination of Nature?—Nature progressed? Or, to descend, can man plant the Northern mountains in the Southern sea? smother Ætna, and make vernal the eternal winter of the Poles? Can he adorn Sahara's burning sands with the floral mantle of the fertile lawn? Or hush the raging tempest? quiet the maddened deep? and buoy the laboring ship above the foundering billows? Finally, can he stay the tide of death that it shall never break over his fragile bark? or retain the spirit when the conqueror enters the chambers of his tenement of mortality?

Before these, frail man must bow, his mightitude to the contrary notwithstanding. And why? His better nature responds: "*Might is not in man.* Too frail his being to stay the wild tempest, or the tide of absolving mortality. Himself he does not know; his soul he ne'er can save. Nature counsels him not; and his days are as a span."

Whoever shall charge us with overrating and bearing the "Seer's" propositions too far, and of causing them to result contrary to the legitimate conclusions consequent upon his theses and reasonings, will, by reading "Nature's Divine Revelations," or even the extracts in this Review, discover that, although much may be said of the "Great Positive Mind," etc. still, than *Nature* he has no Divine Mind, and the Univercœlum is made to unfold into Spirit. If, therefore, the former is clearly taught by the "Seer," the latter is no less so. The reconciliation of the opposing propositions or assumptions and antipodal conclusions, we submit to the friends of this Work, merely suggesting if it might not be less difficult to *get up a new one* under the favorable auspices of a more mature magnetic condition.

This magnetic scheme of Creation concluded,
  Discloses the system of every Age,
Whose visage appears, when of verb'age denuded,
  Unworthy of Prophet, of Seer, or of Sage.

The nocturnal prism of Stoic Materialists,
  Composes the base of the Pantheist's view;
Tho' tinged by the prismatic hue of Etherealists,
  The heart of the system no power can renew.

If Orpheus, Cudworth, Aristotle and Bruno,
  Descartes and Virgil, and Spinoza, too,
Combine in the premise, it still remains pseudo,
  Tho' a magnetized "Seer," reflect it anew.

'Tis matter, and motion, self-wrought into being,
  Whose bodies form *parts* of the circle divine—
All nature resolved into thinking and seeing:
  The axiom, "Atoms to God-hood incline."

An infinite Body, the *Univercœlum*,
  A Vortex of Lava, the Positive Mind,
All Matter and Motion, all Spirit and Wisdom—
  Through Man, the immensurate *whole* is refined.

The Seer of Poughkeepsie thus uttered, ascending
  To regions supernal—the heavens on high—
While roaming in spirit, where vision unending
  Prepared him the Working of Nature to spy.

From Nature's vast Vortex, we read, he unfolded,
  The Cause and Beginning, the Mode, Means and End
Of all things in being, and how they were moulded,
  Their present condition, and whither they tend:

What atoms accomplished, when man was created,
  When the labor of Matter gave birth to the soul;
How Bible Religion by sense is berated,
  When instinctive nature approaches its goal:

The story of Nature; of Adam's creation,
  Recorded by Moses, a legend, untrue;
The Bible is not of divine Inspiration,
  As taught by the Christian and bigoted Jew:

By whom have been fostered as ethics, false notions,
  Descending through ages, oppressing the race;
From whence hath arisen Earth's dire commotions,
  Inspired by the fable of heavenly grace.

Thus reasons the "Seer" against Bible narration;
  Old Pagan arising thence heralds the morn:
The senses unite in the great proclamation,
  "The Prince of Magnetic Redemption is born."

CHAPTER V.

BIBLE THEORY OF MAN.

A DROOPING stalk invites support, and error, to be sustained needs lengthy and sophistical dissertations, and abundance of select literary embellishments. If a figure be defective, it must be clothed in a manner to conceal its deformity. If the visage be sallow, it must be rouged with artistic skill that it may appear flushed and vitalized. If emaciated, it must be inflated to render its appearance robust and vigorous. With these artificial qualifications the skeleton may survive the ordeal of showy exhibition; but not the test of analysis; nor can it endure as a means of dependence. But Truth, simple and frank in its nature, reveals without dissimulation or affectation its native qualities, its symmetrical form and harmonious movement. It displays its divine art in its works. Truth unfolds from divine Law. It moves in the eternity of its own consistency, harmonizing with existing things. Or, if born of facts, reveals the nature of its cause. Truth is unsophisticated, and needs no limner to disguise the imperfections of a malformed body, or to commend its virtue and utility to the unbiased understanding of the human soul. Truth lives as God, by means of its intrinsic worth:—like brilliant stars in night's lone abysm, reflects the perfection of its nature and the glory of its cause. Such is Truth. It is ever unassuming, therefore in simplicity expressed.

When Heaven speaks, thoughts breathe thro' purest words, and glow in the simplest language, like sacred incense in the censer of celestial form. Didactical Pantheism, on the contrary, vails its visage with the net-work of interwoven terms, fastidiously combined. And, when seeking to expound its system, bears the mind hence, by its ethereous carol whose ascending symphony blending with the ideal chorus of celestial song, trembles along the untuned chords of the human soul. First charm and then delude, is the method of error.

To maintain the Pantheistic Theory, the "Seer" roams through Nature's undefined vocabulary, and brings man out of the dumb and senseless brute—of matter, creates the human spirit. Opposed to this system and its mode of revelation, the spirit of Divine Inspiration announces to man, the will of the Supreme Being concerning him, simply declaring, what every thinking man should know, that God created the heaven and earth; and thence proceeds to narrate the order of that creation until the earth is fitted for the human race. And the object of the communication of the Spirit with man, not being to involve his sense in what his mind could never embrace, but to instruct him upon subjects immediately affecting him; and knowing full well, that human intellect could not comprehend *how* God made man; Inspiration through the chosen agent, said, "And the Lord God formed man of the dust of the ground, and breathed into his nostrils the breath of life and man became a living soul." Here is a simple statement of the creation of man. It, however, indicates volumes of exalting and inspiring thought. No dreamy mysticism entombs the truths herein conveyed. While contemplating the grandeur of the theme, the mind is not forced, for its Cause, to stagnant pools in whose viscous element filthy reptiles dwell; to loathsome dens where venomous serpents coil; the dismal jungle where ravenous beasts lurk for prey; or tropical forests of cocoa-nut and palm where chattering monkeys sport; or to the gloomy cavern where wild troglodytes herd. But the enlivening thought, that man is the purpose of infinite Wisdom, the end of design most perfect, and therefore, the object of heavenly care, quickens within his soul, and from reading he goes forth to his daily toil blessed with the earnest of joys to come.

In this brief narration, the Wisdom and Purpose of God, in man, is revealed. Saith the Word: "Let us make man in our own image and after our likeness; and let them have dominion over the fish of the sea, and over the fowl of the air, and over every creeping thing that creepeth upon the earth;" that is, Let *man be made* a being of sense and soul; the glory and perfection of terrestrial creation; who by virtue of his constitution shall be lord of the means created for his use. Having cited the mind to the creation of Adam, the Spirit proceeds in the most clear, and yet simple manner, to reveal the order of Her creation, the mysterious and complicated character of her position, who is so formed in body as to be bone of his bone, and flesh *of his* flesh, and in spirit, as to exist in the *sanctum* of his faithful soul; who was made his "angel-being" throughout his existence, and to be protected by him, and shielded from the rugged elements of earth forever, within the co[illegible]
pass of his affections; over which she sh[illegible]
rule holding the dominion of his earthly [illegible]
Hence whose influence, from her inher[illegible]
the superior qualities of her delic[illegible]
refined constitution, should pu[illegible]
refine his more external natur[illegible]
tender and affectionate natu[illegible]
bless him with the pure[illegible]

gal bliss. Moreover free from carnal desires, she should direct his thoughts to the everlasting abodes in that Holy City whose builder and maker is God; where they should dwell in one eternal union beneath the smile of their Lord.

To this end, woman, the glory of man was made; and such thoughts flow into the manly soul when in the light of the Scriptures, her creation and position is considered. For we are taught in the Word of God, that, after having created man, the Lord God said, it is not good that he should be alone; I will make him a help meet. And then from the sphere of Adam created Eve, and gave her to him. And Adam said: This is now bone of my bone and flesh of my flesh; she shall be called woman, because she was taken out of man. Then follows the divine conclusion: that a man shall leave his father and mother, and shall cleave unto his wife, and they twain shall be one flesh. How admirably this history accords with our highest sense. By it we are taught that a God of infinite Wisdom, having made the earth, and clothed it with verdure, and having enlivened it with the faunal and aerial kingdoms, created an intellectual pair, and so constituted as to form, for each other, a sphere of usefulness and enjoyment. These, as perpetual companions, were to dwell upon the earth in the perfection of peace and the fulness of that fruition which flows from unity of soul and concert of action; and also as the progenitors of the race of Man. For this purpose, they were endued with mental, moral and social abilities. Thus man was created. Need we enquire which theory, this, or that of the Poughkeepsie Seer, is the most commendable? Which most accords with the constitution of man? Or which is most likely to have originated in facts, the doctrine which teaches that God made man with capacity to enjoy the means provided for his use; to mingle in the society of more exalted beings, and to hold communion with the Divine Spirit? Or, that theory which causes his original elements to mope along dumb nature, and by means of senseless law unfold from matter into mentalized spirit?

Those who, in order to establish this system, toil to connect man with the brute and to establish the animal races as his lineal ancestry, are compelled to range creation for natural signets and exhume fossiliferous impressions to unite, by dint of imagination, ephemeral races long since perished; and from viscous pools to crawl through marshes and subterranean caverns to dry land, and to make a tour of ages, with the Monkey and Ourang-Outang; and finally construct of former assumptions added to one grand and closing assertion, a passage over the void existing between the race of man and the sphere of brutes?

Strange as it may appear, those who thus construct their bodies of self-actuated materials and tenant them with the spirit of matter, are exceedingly chagrined at the christian, because of his faith in this Mosaic account of creation and the origin of man. Moreover, because Moses wrote understandingly, with graphic precision, and therefore with brevity, they deem the history incomplete. From this conclusion, they affirm the doctrine of Inspiration a fable, and the Bible, mostly, a collection of mythical legends.

No subject that ever occupied the human mind, has elicited searching and unyielding criticism equal to this, and still it endures like the Rock of Ages lashed by the Ocean's foam, unharmed and unmoved. Upon the truth of this account depends the Bible, and the Christians hope. From it flows forth the broad current of inspired statements and the soul of religious polity. Render it frail, and the Temple of the Christians faith is razed from its foundation, it falls to rise no more forever. And he who trusted in it, is left to float, unguided and unsustained, upon the wild and turbid sea of time; and thence, with his shattered bark, to founder amid the billows of death. But it has been, for ages, tested. Upon it the true Israelite has rested his hope, and in Earth's darkest hour it has sustained him, and in death, illumined his passage through the gloomy portals of dissolving Nature.

It has also withstood the armament of the Foe, and resisted the force of Legions. It is the rampart Bible opposers strive to remove. Therefore arguments of every conceivable character have been raised against it. Every objection, or apparent objection, that could be forced from nature, or circumstances, has been magnified and brought to bear upon it. Philosophers have labored, indefatigably, to disconnect it from *facts*. In fine, every objection that wit, genius, or doubt could devise and institute, has been urged to overthrow or deface it, and therefore to weaken the Scriptures upon this vital and momentous question. But the History still remains unscathed, and, as an immutable monument of eternal Truth, looms on high, from amid the babels that an effeminate philosophy has tried to erect around it; but whose cloven tongues are ever demolishing. These crumble to dust; while this pillar of Truth, stands imbedded in eternal causes, and lifts its emblazoned dome amid the lofty pyramids of celestial thoughts. Like a Sun of unfolding glories in the midst of revolving satellites, it illumines the realm of nature and gives life to cosmical science. It sheds its light upon regions of darkness, revealing the deformity of those opaque bodies which are ever arising from unhealthy marl. Not a cosmological writer but owes the birth of his deepest and most profound thoughts to those emanating from the Scriptures; by which he is furnished, at least, with primary suggestions for his extensive schemes. Moses, in what Progressionists are pleased to denominate the dark age, the age of mystic dreaming, inscribed upon history's page, the grand and comprehensive statements of creation, which have furnished the world with material for the principles of philosophic enquiry throughout all succeeding time. His is the most ancient of all records, and enters as deep, to say no more, into original causes and procedures as any have been able since to conceive, even while inspired and conducted by his account. By this, it is proved that the Bible is the original Text Book; and that, therefore, others who attempt to record causes, beginnings and ultimates, are indebted to the Mosaic account for their leading thoughts. If philosophers and metaphysicians have been more specific in the several departments of matter and mind, they have only extended and ramified those great principles which radiate from this, as the center of all. And if science has amplified, it is but reducing to parts those great truths revealed in man's early history, and written in God's Book. This, the original account amply sustains. And the record of the creation of the Earth and the Heavens; also the order of material manifestation on the Earth, proves that the inspired writers did hold communion with that Wisdom which ordered Nature forth. Moreover, Moses by the Spirit of God conceived principles emanating from the great sanctum of original design; from the tabernacle of constructive thought; hence he wrote, not only of Nature as externally revealed, but as it existed in purpose, while as yet it had not assumed material form. To this end he saith: Gen. 2; 4–5, "These are the generations of the Heavens and of the Earth, when they were created, in the day that the Lord God made the earth and the heavens, and *every plant of the field before it grew.*" This proves that the sacred writers had conceptions of interior design; and thus is evinced their communion with the spirit of invisible truths? Who then, with the Bible before them, can deny that the Inspired Word unclosed the portals to the realms of pre-existing causes? This passage, as above stated, reveals that by some means, Moses conceived the idea of Archetypal forms as they existed in the mind of the great Architect, and which by his Will and Power were, in due time, unfolded into terrestrial order.

True, the earth and the heavens, now as ever, bespeak the infinite Wisdom of their Designer, and the Omnipotence of their invisible Creator; but how shall man determine that the race, uninstructed by the Inspired Word, would not have remained ignorant of the existence of those interior and mysterious laws which govern eternal things, and reveal the power of the great First Cause: and having no thoughts beyond gross materiality, would have been perpetual sun, moon and star worshipers? To the spirit of the scriptural statements of God, and his Works, even the Poughkeepsie Seer, as already shown, bows with reverence, after having failed to render unauthentic the Pentateuch. He, therefore admits the Bible the author of his highest and purest thoughts. And even that modern and wonder-revealing science, Geology, when correctly understood, bears irrefutable testimony to the truth of the Scriptures. By it the days or periods of creation, as recorded by Moses, are confirmed. Each degree, from the Alluvial through the Diluvial, Tertiary, Carboniferous and Old Red Sandstone formation, even to the unstratified granite, declare that Nature was formed in the divine order which the Scriptures reveal. The *fucoides* and *Radiata*, of the earliest date and all succeeding generations, of the animal kingdoms, arise in that succession which harmonizes with the Inspired account. Nor are the moving heavenly bodies opposed. If we study the Dynamic principles of nature, beyond which the "Seer" seems never to have conceived a thought, they only reveal their dependence upon a superior power, and themselves the means God has ordained to prosecute his designs. Finally, nature affords nothing to weaken, but much to strengthen the sayings of Moses, the inspired Cosmogonist. But as this review is not so much designed to illustrate and confirm the Scriptures, (that belonging to their Exposition,) as to reveal the inconsistency and untruthfulness of old Pantheism, resurrected by modern mesmerism, we shall not enlarge upon the subject. We, therefore, in conclusion, remark, that all effort to cramp the manifestations of nature into a position which shall *conflict* with the Sacred Text, or to extort from her, testimony against the word of God, upon investigation proves in vain. And until Ethnographic science shall reveal facts which will not admit of a reasonable doubt, to attest a diversity and therefore disprove the unity of man's origin, it cannot be successfully maintained that all true light man possesses of the beginning and of the First Cause did not originate in the statements claimed by Biblicists as the Word of God. Peculiar traits are, from Patriarchs, transmitted through untold generations; and *tradition*, although it assumes varied forms, may be the living Oracle of ages, to utter the leading thoughts of ancestry. Can it be shown that the heathen Philosophers and all oriental Sages were not descendants from one Patriarchal family? Or that the Indian's idea of Manitou, or the Great Spirit, did not originate in the Bible theory of God. And who can prove that Divine Inspiration, as recorded in the Scriptures of Truth, has not been the source of man's knowledge of first principles? The Bible surely leads the enquirer to the threshold of that tabernacle of immensities forever incomprehensible to man. Inspiration, however, seeking more especially man's moral good, does not dwell upon the incomprehensible, but proceeds to reveal; 1. The character of God, as affecting man. 2. His relation to his Creator and Benefactor. 3. His moral state and means of redemption from his degradation; and 4. His accountability to God, the righteous Judge. The requirements of the Inspired Word are just, the inducements to obedience laudable, and the prospects of future beatitudes in the path of righteousness, harmonize with man's highest sense and purest desires. In this system, therefore, the unbiased mind can but behold an incomparable superiority to that wandering and dreamy theory set forth in "Nature's Divine Revelations."

This closes our review of the *first principles* of the Pantheistic Creed, as reflected through A. J. Davis, and hence we proceed to consider its Ethics; a subject which more immediately affects man, being directly connected with his mode of action.

CHAPTER VI.

PANTHEISTIC THEORY OF MAN, MORALLY.

Three fundamental principles influence the lives and moral conditions of men:

I. The views entertained of the Being and Attributes of God; which embrace,—His eternity; the mode of his existence, and the relation he sustains to the Universe of mind and matter. II. The views he entertains of *his* obligations to that God; and III. Of his duty to himself and his neighbor. The *First* governs the *Second* and *Third*. The deeds of men, which are the exemplification of the Third, are also an exposition of the First and Second.

The ideas entertained of God, temper man's internal and most vital consciousness: and this inward soul or sense, gives character and cast to outward manifestations. For man socially is moved by the propension of his mental nature, and this by his moral; and his moral nature is the image of whoever or whatever he accepts as God, and is made manifest in proportion to his faith. His moral nature affects his passions or affections, and these control his conduct. (These principles are too familiar with men of thought to need illustration.) Consequently, he who conceives God to be a supreme embodiment of infinite mechanism, is stoic, mechanical, and arbitrary in his moral sense which reflects, through his deeds, his true character. Whoso beholds God as a combination of moving laws, subdued by a passional or love-nature, seeks personal gratification, obeys the impulses of his own frail being, and of his inclinations forms a self-pleasing criterion. Such virtually reject all law save that which harmonizes with their proclivity, and they therefore discard the idea of a Supreme Law-giver. Any system, thus based, removes from the human soul its reverence, and encloses the mind within the stubborn casement of arrogance; pervades the being with the spirit of self-righteousness; engenders ambition, and begets unlawful zeal, strife, and a desire for absolute supremacy. Such a system is directly opposed to the fundamental principles of the Christian religion. It meets the approbation of the carnally minded, and with perverted man readily multiplies its votaries. But the Gospel, in spirit and law the opposite, is unwelcome, because it teaches that he who exalteth *himself* shall be abased, and he who humbleth himself shall be exalted. To this end Jesus addressed his disciples, saying, "Whoever will be chief among you let him be your servant." And setting the example at the Passover, "He arose from supper, and laid aside his garments; and took a towel and girded himself. After that he poured water into a basin, and began to wash the disciples' feet, and to wipe them with the towel wherewith he was girded." John, 13: 4, 5. This is the teaching of Jesus, the spirit of Christianity, and the fruit of true Theocracy. The first requirements are, "Love the Lord thy God with all thy heart, and with all thy soul, and with all thy mind, and thy neighbor as thyself." The social polity requires man to do good unto all, and unto others as he would they should do unto him; that he should comfort the mourner, bind up the broken-hearted; relieve the needy and distressed, and turn not the poor from his door; deal justly, love mercy; visit the widow and the fatherless in their affliction, and keep himself unspotted from the world: do no evil and love the ways of Truth. This Religion, teaches man to fear God and keep his commandments; to give him his heart. "Seek first the kingdom of God, and his righteousness," and "let the wicked forsake his way and the unrighteous man his thoughts," saith the Scriptures. This system directs the mind from the carnal and perishable to the holy, spiritual and eternal; inspires reverence for God and his laws; begets meekness, forbearance and holy benevolence. Such a religion man needs. It is adapted to his condition, and therefore must be founded in eternal Truth.

A religion based upon the teachings of Nature's Divine Revelations,—recognizing in man the principles of Deity refined,—exalts his self-hood, and conveys no definite idea of a Supreme Being. Gross matter contains (is) the Pantheist's God. The Pantheist therefore considers himself a part of that intelligence, whose aggregate is infinite Sense; and whose innate promptings constitute universal Law. Hence he asserts his rights, exalts himself, and proffers wisdom to all who will heed the counsel of his lips. This system awards to finite mind capacity above its sphere, and therefore induces assumption, heedless superciliousness, and sarcastic witticism. The devotee is exceedingly wise in his own eyes, and his sayings are authoritative. He reveals that egotism which is astounded if the correctness of his assertions is questioned. The human family are his pupils, and he is ready to catechise the race, and subdue the stubborn. Though a child in years, a novice in experience, and void of true learning, he is no less eager to grapple with the sage. Certain of success, he moves with a triumphant air. He teaches that the violator of law, without redemption or palliation, shall receive to the utmost his penalty. There is, with him, no sin, and therefore no forgiveness. He laughs at pardon, and mocks repentance; denies the existence of absolute evil, and renders action the force of necessity. Such is the legitimate tendency of Pantheism. Nevertheless the author of N. D. R. although Pantheistic, is not established in any one system. He oscillates like a body having no fixed orbit or definite center. He revolves around the oracles of ancient Pantheism, and wanders at times, amid the truths of Biblicism. His theory, if he has any, is a compound of contradictory ideas, *parts* of opposing systems. In portions of his Work he besieges the Bible, and charges upon what he deems its weakest points; but the next section reveals him with his suite moving amid its everlasting columns as if Prince of the Province of Scriptural Truths. Then he is exceedingly orthodox, and preaching the fall and depravity of the Race. But ere he has established himself upon those premises, he again wanders amid the old ruins of Pagan philosophy, is contending with his former statements, and laboring with his might to raze the foundation of Bible Religion. Still, as he proceeds, having no other "land-marks," he resorts to Bible data, but seeks to take down the Temple of Truth erected by Inspiration; to bear it to the sliding sands of false ethics, and to re-erect its massive pillars about himself. Hence, in his history of Man he establishes, even in "earth's barbarous and unprogressed age," an Eden, with its innocent occupants; thence pursues the thread of Hebraic narration; employing, however, his "superior skill" to shuffle from his system the vitality of the account. By this means the unthoughtful, unestablished, unlearned, and weak believers in the Inspired Word are decoyed from Theocracy, and cajoled into the labyrinths of the Harmonial Philosophy. But without farther introductory remarks we will proceed to present the reader with the "Seer's" exposition of Man, morally.

In N. D. R., p. 124, he thus introduces this subject, which leads to his Harmonial Ethics:

"The work of the present day of creation has been more distinctly marked by unity of plan and composition, and the appearance of a general end, cause and effect, than that of any previous day. A superficial view of the whole plan of the creation of mankind, however, would lead to many erroneous and repulsive impressions. But when viewed with a scientific and reverential mind" (Ingenious method to blind) "the whole presents a connected plan and a sublime and magnificent work, inasmuch as every particle is a flowing of the interior qualities of previous existence: and each, again, as it ascends into higher forms, displays a higher degree of the same interior excellences. And so, from one order of creation to another, in which the species are only mediums of transferring qualities to higher states, there is to be seen the same united activity, the same potent energies, and the same teeming beauties; and as the confluence of all these establishes and constitutes the organization of man, man becomes the perfection and representative of them all.

"As by these harmonious breathings of Nature, the work of the present day manifestly becomes a higher example of omnipotent and divine Love and Wisdom. And this is the closing of the present era—the consummation of the creations of the whole period, and of the End contemplated; and thus Nature represents a higher beauty, a more perfect form, and a more comprehensive organization. . . . And so the vegetable creation is a substantial basis for the animal creation, even as the earth is for the vegetable. And the animal kingdom is the only basis upon which man could have been created, and therefore it is absolutely necessary to his being. And had not each of these been governed by the unchangable laws of Nature, nothing would have assumed order or refinement. But by the operation of these laws the whole creation gradually ascends, by imperceptible steps, to the perfect development of its own interior nature. Thus the germ of existence is in Nature, and the fruit thereof man. Thus the vegetable mirrors the undeveloped qualities in the earth, and represents the animal kingdom. This, again, reflects the beauties of the vegetable kingdom, and represents the formation of Man, and man exemplifies the perfect unfolding of Nature's interior qualities, and represents within himself the united and harmonious Universe. . . . From these correspondences it can be plainly seen that all things which have form and distinct existence have an interior independence, but externally they are dependent upon all things, and display a universal use. And it would be as unjust to abhor any of the lower kingdoms as it would to have a prejudice against any of the imperfect portions of the human body. For *forms* are only the temporal combinations of material substances; but the Cause (of which forms are the effects) is the invisible and therefore is eternal." If *eternal* and *unerring*, all manifestations are *just* as they should be; especially, the interior quality. This forbids perversion or depravity in any of nature's manifestations; a principle it is well to note. But to confirm his position more fully, the "Seer" adds: "And as forms, the uses of which the mind does not always comprehend, are the constant manifestations of Nature, so they are the constant and successive productions of her immutable and eternal principles." To rivet the proposition, he appeals to the highest of all his ideas of immutable perfection, saying: "And the first and most comprehensive attribute that is manifested in these forms is divine Wisdom. And their unity" (mark this) "and harmonious reciprocation prove that Wisdom is the higher attribute flowing from the fountain of divine Love." (Whatever is, is right, and without defect, according to these statements.) "Love, therefore, determines the universal relationship, and Wisdom the universal adaptation. So these attributes are the highest laws of Nature, comprehending within themselves various modifications of the same principles as all flowing from the same exhaustless Fountain" (Vortex of Lava) "wherein exists infinite Intelligence. This is the Vortex" (the Ocean of fire) "from which are unfolded successfully the receding waves of the united Universe. And one of these is an index to the expanding sublimities of another; and so their ceaseless flowings comprehend the whole Univercœlum. And as these are the flowings of the general materials in space, so the earth constitutes a similar vortex of power, which rolls forth succeeding waves from the mineral to the vegetable, to the animal, and to man: and the breathings of inherent qualities transcend Motion, Life, and Sensation, and form a pure and exalted Spirit. The wave of development is not arrested here, but it goes on throughout the unimaginable spheres in the interior world, until it approximates and is responded to by the Great Positive Mind. Thus are the concentric circles of material creation unfolded—which correspond to, and absolutely prove the concentric circles of spiritual creation, and spiritual, endless progression! Thus the great Vortex is a living, exhaustless Fountain, wherein dwell infinite Love and Wisdom, and from which flow the undefinable worlds which pervade the whole Univercœlum. And these are formed by succeeding and expanding waves, the same principle being distinctly manifest in every department of animated Nature. The Universe, therefore, is an ocean of activity, even as the Univercœlum" (original sea of lava) "is a boundless ocean of infinite Love and Wisdom. The *thoughts* of the infinite mind, therefore, constitute the laws of Nature; and the results of these thoughts are the animated forms in being, including the exalted form of man—which again form, on a corresponding principle, the interior spiritual existence. . . . It is not well, then, to doubt the existence of a use in any department of Nature; for this would be evidence that the subject is not well understood. . . . So nothing is inactive—nothing useless—nothing absolutely imperfect; but everything sustains an important position in the great architecture of the Univercœlum. These meditations are the result of the breathings of the sphere of *Causes*, in which my mind is situated, and in which all *effects* are made present. And these effects are exemplified in every minute particle constituting an inseparable chain of correspondencies ascending to the highest celestial spheres, which are illuminated only with divine Love and Wisdom."

Here is the "Seer's" *moral thesis.* It forbids retrogression or perversion of any and every quality and degree. All things, ascending to the highest celestial spheres are but thoughts of the Divine Mind. It is infinitely perfect, unerring in procedure and certain in results. All that is or can be, is necessary and in accordance with divinely perfect, undeviating and irrevocable law. Hence there can be no inefficient or abortive movements of Nature; or misdirected propensions with regard to men or spirits. Nothing could be more mechanical, or predestined to unalterable modes and fixed results. No exception is conceded, no ellipsis permitted. All is perfection. If, therefore, derangement is demonstrable from any department of nature, (perfection being claimed throughout,) the system is wanting, and from its high claims rendered useless.

Or if the "Seer," in his Work, shall admit nature perverted or defective in any degree or specific manifestation, he shall be found bearing testimony against himself. His example hitherto, however, forbids us to hope otherwise. His Physics and Metaphysics abound with contra statements, and why not his Ethics? But pursuing him in his disclosures, we are soon led to an Eden, with its innocent occupants; and that too in what he denominates man's unprogressed age. In this, also, he reveals his dependence upon Sacred History for his leading ideas, and by necessity is forced to admit what the Hebraist and Christian believe. Page 328, he remarks: "Nature, at this period of creation, presents a most beautiful reflection of all anterior creations. And it is now evident that man is created from the dust of the earth and that he is the receptacle of one of the spontaneous breathings of the Great Positive Mind. This rendered him a perfect form—a useful agent—a living soul." Why denounce the Inspired Word, and still proclaim its doctrines in stronger terms than it employs upon the same subject? The Bible says man was good; the "Seer" says he was perfect. "And thus" he continues "was male and female created. . . . And so the whole earth at this time represented the close of a distinct and pre-eminent creation, even the peopling of the garden of Eden. . . . Thus the grand Work is finished—the great End is accomplished. Nature becomes an harmonious whole—the congregation of parts. . . . And as Nature is a mirror wherein are seen all her interior excellencies, so this ultimate development of creation is a mirror wherein is reflected the truthful expression that "*the evening and the morning were the sixth day.*" Is it not remarkable that a Book so much condemned as the Bible, should afford the strong points upon which its opposers rest while striving to erect their opposing theories. Even the Poughkeepsie Seer, often cleaves to it as a means to steady him in his labors. 'Twere better by far did he not wander from it. "The germ of man," he says, "has thus been discovered in the lower forms of the animal kingdom, and traced through all its progressive stages of development, rising from the lower degrees through the great body of the animal creation, with its many and diversified branches and their modifications, up to the blooming perfection of the living tree whose fruit is the organization of man." Here man is again called perfect. Does "Inspiration" say more? As to the especial location of the Eden where he places his perfect and early inhabitants, he seems to have been absolutely controlled by the popular idea. He says, page 328; "The present" (perfect paradisiacal, or eden) "existence of man was within or near the portion of Asia which has since been termed Turkey, extending to the regions of the Euphrates and Tigris, and joining in two distinct lines to the location whereupon was built Jerusalem."

Chained by the power of opinion, and the force of education which affected his coterie and manipulator as well as himself, the "Seer" appears not to have once conceived that the Eden of which he speaks could have been on the American continent. After having located man, *perfect*, in Eden, the "Seer" seems much affected with a sudden and remarkable change in his infinite scale of progression. And strange as it may appear, that nature, which in the Beginning rolled her omnipotent tides; whose every evolution exalted by unfolding refining and immutable law her properties; from matter unfolded the fearfully and wonderfully formed human body, and animated it with an intellectual soul,—that nature in man, the perfection of her work, meets with an obstacle, by whose influence she is made to reel and fall!—to invert her course and become perverted! On page 330, the "Oracle" thus carefully and cautiously approaches the fearful *fact*. "At first and for many continuous ages they communicated their ideas by *expression of the countenance*, and *outward physical signs;* and while they remained unsophisticated by the art of clothing their ideas in verbal sounds, they were free from all cupidity and absolute deception." (Here is man's original innocence and purity maintained by this Bible opposing Revelation.) "But when they had advanced a little farther, and had partaken of a little of the fruit of the tree of Knowledge, they began to conceal their true sentiments, and to clothe them with an arbitrary vocal sound—which possessed not the power of communicating the reality of their ideas and affections to each other, but rather was liable to convey deceptive impressions." As he approaches man's fall, he seeks to provide some means for the dire effect of the violation of law; and since he must have a substitute for the Spirit of Evil, which, according to the Scriptures, *tempted* by *artifice and lies* the innocent to sin, he introduces the *human voice* as *that Seducer!* and therefore causes the vocal organs to do what the Bible charges upon an arch Fiend, even that Satanic power denominated *Devil.* Thus, by this Bible berater, Nature is represented, in creating the organs of speech, to have led the race (herself) astray. This, then,—even the human voice—is the Davisonian *Devil*, and chargable with evil equal to what the Bible institutes against Satan the old Serpent. Most fatal blunder of Nature—perfect, unerring and ever-progressive Nature! How deeply her offspring deplore it! how suffer from consequences growing out of that first Error! The christian is ridiculed because he believes that a perverted and malicious Spirit, a Liar and diabolical Deceiver, by vile artifice tempted Eve astray, and thus seduced the progenitors of the race into sin. It is considered by the unbeliever in the Inspired Word, a strange thing that God should have made man an intellectual being, and then suffer him to err! violate law! and thus involve himself in misery!! But it is infinite Wisdom for that old First Ocean of surging elements to roll its fused tide along unnumbered ages for the especial purpose of manufacturing itself into man; thence labor centuries to create organs of vocal utterance in order, orally, to express their thoughts; and by *articulation* nature became self-deceived, self-debased and self-perverted! Mark the Oracle's comments, N. D. R., p. 332. "Not long after the introduction of verbal sounds as signs of impressions, the inhabitants became disunited in social affections in consequence of the misconceptions conveyed by those sounds. They finally could not enjoy each others' society; for every expression of the mind, which was orignally pure and unadulterated, was now clothed in a false sheath; and this created disunity and confusion among all the inhabitants. Previously to this, mankind were in an innocent and pure condition; but by the constant increase of these causes, they became disunited and repulsive to each other. This has been distinguished in the original history as a state of depravity. It was in this manner that their eyes were opened; and thus they were enabled to see their own deceptions and imperfections." (But they had none—were pure and innocent—according to his previous statement, until the organs of speech were formed. How could *voice* reveal that which was not!) "And having a new power of conversing with one another, they clothed their real and imperfect thoughts by false sheathes or deceptive *aprons* of obscurity. Thus the whole race became dejected and depraved."

Why should Modern Pantheists, Harmonialists, or Harmonial Spiritualists, seek to depreciate public respect for the Bible? N. D. Revelation, their great "Text Book," boldly teaches *depravity*. Does the Bible more? But how meager the cause of all this ruin; this lamentable state of the world; a state of disunity, and wretchedness deeply deplorable, and upon which so much labor is bestowed in other portions of the Work. All the woes of man are here charged upon the human voice; as if the *thyroid*, *cricoid*, and *arytenoids*, four cartilages, situated at the superior portion of the *trachea* in the human anatomy, were capable of producing such fatal results. We are thus definite that the visage of this Harmonial monster, the original deceiver of the race, may be justly revealed. Do the disciples of Mr. Davis know, while they so significantly menace the christian religion, that their evil spirit, or the seducer of man, according to his theory, exists in the human throat! that the noble voice, which gives such delight, is a vehicle to convey words of consolation to the grieved heart, and melody to the human soul, is by him, in his philosophy, charged with this iniquity? of being the original *cause* of man's sorrows and therefore his greatest curse? His reasoning denies man's ability to deceive by look or gesture. Who does not know this to be an absolute misrepresentation? Can not the countenance shadow, and therefore conceal the real sentiment of the soul? and actions lead the observer from the feelings or intentions of the heart? But if vocal utterance was the cause of man's depravity, Nature, to redeem herself, has only to *smite the race (herself) with dumbness*, and the great work is done; the original Eden restored and man on earth shall dwell in heaven. Surely, in giving man the power of speech the Divine Mind of N. D. Revelations greatly erred, and inverted nature's progressive laws. How blessed to have remained speechless. The Bible theory of the cause of man's depravity, is said by the friends of this system to be a senseless legend. But if that be unworthy of consideration, how much more must this theory be? And especially since the Work teaches that Nature is perfect, ever progressing; and that *Man* is her crowning work, the *perfection* of her attributes and ultimates.

The human voice is capable of much evil; but the mind within prompts the utterance; and evidently, "from the abundance of the *heart* the *mouth* speaketh." It is also probable that most persons, save those who are the subjects of mesmeric influence, speak what their minds design; but the "Seer," by this rendering, reverses the order of things and makes the mind the body's agent; the body and not the mind responsible for human action. Consequently, the physical man is the superior in the scale of Nature. Having affirmed the depravity of the race he thus continues; "Not because they had violated any constitutional faculty, physical or mental, but because their faculties were wrongly and imperfectly developed." This statement involves the most vital question pertaining to man. It reaches the heart of mental and moral science. And if human happiness in any way depends upon true knowledge, and the right performance of duty, it is of the utmost importance to know the truth herein existing. Its truth or falsity, and hence the virtue of the Harmonial Theory, depends upon what constitutes the violation or imperfect development of human faculties; and in this what higher law is opposed; also what could have induced that aggression, and the consequences attending it.

There is evidently a purpose in this effort, to make a distinction between the violation of faculties and their improper development. *A nice point indeed, for a scheme so extensive.* It is, however, the pivot upon which N. D. Revelations poise man, morally; the hinge upon which the race is made to swing.

To avoid the Bible doctrine of depravity, and also the doctrine of redemption through Jesus, this form of expression is employed. As though man might be depraved; might be involved in perfect wretchedness; by reason of impurity be obliged to leave the beautiful Eden of earth; might be devoid of pure intentions; become covetous, defiled, and revengeful, and yet no faculty be violated. Moreover, if they were not, although developed into the bottomless pit, it is a matter of little moment, since Nature, although she could not keep man perfect, can easily redeem and exalt him. Thus reasons the "Seer." The fact of this depravity, however, destroys the correctness of the Harmonial Theory; for, whether or no the faculties of man were violated, by perversion unerring progression is disproved, and Nature is foiled in her purpose; at least until man shall have been redeemed.

As sure as blood follows venesection, so sure the vitality of man's purity and peace has been drained from the soul. If man was once harmonious in his nature—and this the "Seer" teaches—if his moral being was upright, and his heart pure, the censer of holy incense, the receptacle of heavenly influx, and beat in unison with the heart of heaven; if his soul once responded to the laws of celestial life, and inclined toward the home of angels, the throne of the Divine; if the *sanctum* of his nature was clothed with the garments of innocence, and shielded with the armor of righteousness; if sacred love flowed throughout the being;—then, some hand of might has opened the living fountain from which has issued the life of the spirit, the source of joy. And if these consequences are not by reason of the violation of man's faculties, some other laws or faculties of nature must have been violated. In either case, according to this theory, the effect reveals nature at fault. To imperfectly develope, pervert and misdirect the faculties; to suspend their proper action, and thwart their purpose, which was just, holy and benevolent, and render their fruits unrighteous, unhealthy and discordant, is to interrupt their intention and debase their character. Faculties thus induced or forced to prey upon themselves; or to be by any means so unfolded as to *disable* them, are most assuredly violated.

The brain weakened by disease, or deranged by over or unequal excitement so that the mind cannot perform its office, is changed, and this cannot be effected without violation. If the powers of body and mind are improperly devoted, this is a fact, and facts cannot exist without a cause. In perversion some principles are violated and misemployed; and discord is the absence of the law of harmony. Health is the product of unity and dependent upon lawful procedure. Disease follows discord, and discord is from the violation of law. To say that sickness is because of the imperfect development of the faculties is folly; but to attribute it to violation of sanitary law is legitimate, since this accords with facts and philosophy. To admit human depravity, even to the absence of purity and the introduction of absolute wretchedness, and deny the violation of the faculties, is what a true philosopher could scarcely do. Well developed organs may be so changed as to produce results contrary to their original intentions. A strong and healthy muscle becoming diseased, not only refuses to perform its office, but imparts its deleterious influence to other portions of the system.

A simple rupture, even in some unimportant part of the body, often works its destruction. Men are not always insane because of wrongly developed faculties, (that inducing idiocy or silliness,) but by reason of cerebral violation. Imperfectly developed organs cause inefficient efforts and effeminate results. But these arise from constitutional or fundamental derangement, based upon the violation of first principles, and this prevents the proper use of faculties, and therefore violates them.

Moreover, any imperfection, attending the manifestations of Nature and from whatever cause, betrays a want or weakness, in those principles upon which the manifestations depend. This reveals the violation of laws and faculties. Finally, whatever positions are assumed and principles analyzed, the results are the same; depravity reveals violation. But, perhaps the Oracle intended to have said, that no faculty was *destroyed*, otherwise the fulcrum upon which he intended to rest his lever of Magnetic-reason by whose might he hopes to raise man from the pit into which he has fallen because of sin, is a statement devoid of truth and founded in error. Upon it, however, he hinges the broad scheme of "progression out of Christ." The subject, therefore, does not close with the question as to whether the physical or mental faculties were violated:

but embraces a principle still more important, viz: the *moral nature and accountability of man*. The conditions to which he refers, the cause and maglignity of which he seems to have had no just conception, is strictly of a moral character. And here rests that Theory which denies the doctrine of Redemption through the Lord Jesus.

By analysis, it is determined that moral principle depends upon the relation one faculty sustains to another, the relation which these united sustain to the individual and social uses, and also to those heavenly or divine laws to which man is amenable.

Man is a threefold being—matter, mind and spirit. His movements are physical, mental and moral. These have, and are governed by laws originating in their several relations, the source of their being, the end of their creation; and the principles of infinite Life to which they are allied, and upon which they depend. Physical law is that of power; mental, of thought, meditation, design and execution; and moral law is that of equity, originating in the constitution and relation of things affecting man, not only in regard to his duty to his fellow, but to his God.

Physical law affects the construction, movement, harmony, and perpetuation of material bodies. Mental law has respect to the thoughts and purposes of mind; while the moral law regards the quality of human action, and reveals their nature whether good or evil.

The character of physical law is determined by its power; that of the mental by clearness of perception, comprehension, and execution; while the moral is determined by the character of inclination, ability, purpose, and results. Law is the mode, and the faculties are the means of execution. To vitiate the mode or faculties by which life, harmony and happiness are perpetuated, involves man's moral nature, since he is, by virtue of his constitution, responsible to the law of equity. Herein consists his moral obligation. If this quality of being is disturbed he is perverted. If his moral powers are vitiated they are violated, and he is fallen, the subject of violated law; debased, and the creature of circumstances. Moral ability is the capacity to do the right and resist the wrong. This depends upon the nature of the inclinations, the power of discrimination, of moral selection and choice. The will actuates men physically: decision controls the direction of the will; and choice, inclined by desire, inspires determination. What is loved most, is most sought. He whose supreme affections are fixed upon lucre chooses the miser's lot, and with undying tenacity clings to life. He whose greatest passion is the love of fame courts public applause, and spends his substance to win honor of men. While he who loves God supremely, is the faithful and devoted christian. Change a man's affections and his actions are also changed. Pervert them and he is debased; purify them and he is redeemed. "No man can serve two masters; for either he will hate the one, and love the other; or else he will hold to the one, and despise the other. Ye cannot serve God and mammon." Bible.

Again, the quality of desire, or action, is determined by its relation to right. Right and wrong are moral principles. Moral quality depends, therefore, upon good or evil. Equity is the law of justice; of harmony; and its violation is evil. Improper affections induce defective choice, and this prompts unrighteous deeds. These produce discordant results, and discord is destructive to life. Wrong affections or inclinations, then, beget evil consequences. The root of evil, therefore, is vicious desire, or improper inclinations; hence moral law is that mode which regards the affections, the end of desire, the character of which is determined by its motive, and that of the object sought, the right to secure it, and the means employed. Though an object be laudable, the means engaged to secure it may be unjust, and therefore the moral nature be evil inclined. And thus, if the powers are perverted or unjustly employed, the original principle of their being is violated; reduced from a superior to an inferior plane, and from an ascending to a descending scale. That is, the hand that gathers gold from the mine is laudably occupied; but that which pilfers from his neighbor's coffer is vilely actuated. The muscle that grasps the helm is mechanical and irresponsible; but the mind that wields it, guiding the ship to the desired haven, or to the maelstrom of destruction is tempered by the spirit of intention, and therefore amenable to the law of equity. This principle is equally applicable to all the relations of life, modified however, by the nature of causes, positions and attending circumstances.

Thus much have we remarked upon that subject which underlays every other, connected with man's moral state. It is a subject, however, too comprehensive to be fully elaborated in this review. Nevertheless, we indulge the idea that sufficient light is here reflected to reveal the unsoundness of the "Seer's" statement under consideration, and to convince the reader that his philosophy does not, by far, fathom the mystery connected with man's depravity, or approach the cause of human woe. It is remarkable though, that after having theorized so laboriously from his propositions, viz.; the perfection of nature and her works, also the certainty of her unerring procedures and faithful and divine results, he should preach depravity and its consequences as vehemently as those he denominates the undeveloped and bigoted orthodox.

Having taught the fall of man; and made an attempt to explain the cause, also the effect upon the constitution of the depraved, on p. 332, he thus continues: "Such is the origin of all deception—of all imperfection. From this moment misery and impure associations had their origin. By continued and ill-directed development of the faculties, vice and misery increased. The inhabitants acted more and more against each others' interests, and thus became disorganized and rendered entirely wretched and unhappy. At that period, when this wretchedness prevailed most extensively, they were obliged to leave the happy associations of their former days, even the beautiful Eden of the earth, and became dispersed into other lands." Then follows his statement of the worst of social evils resulting from depraved nature, viz., the sacrifice of Abel, recorded on p. 334. "And after dwelling together for the period spoken of, Cain, as a selfish tyrant, rose with all his combined forces against his brother Abel. And the latter, being so meek, gentle and submissive, yielded without retaliation, and then fell a sacrifice to a supercilious and self-exalted being—even his *brother!*"

Here, then, in the very Work, the object of

which is to establish a religion of nature, and to remove faith in the Bible, we are taught—1, Man's innocence and perfection; 2, His situation in Eden; 3, His depravity, which renders him vicious, devoid of pure desire, and wretched; 4, His expulsion from his delightful inheritance; 5, The murder of Abel, etc. Where is the consistency of the system? If man is a perfection of that nature which can never err; whose spirit of life is Love, Will, Wisdom, and whose every evolution breathes forth new and exalted forms of her divinely perfect self; whence this superciliousness, this ambition and diabolical revenge? Where is the wisdom which secures the sense and devotion of men of renowned erudition; shatters the faith, and annihilates the hope of the christian? Where the secret charm that enchants? the Reason that shall redeem the world from folly? the harmonious and truthful statements that shall battle down error? the glory of sense that shall reflect light upon the gloomy dungeons where the myriads of misguided mortals are entombed? and that shall finally consume, by its light, the christian dogma, which has for ages enthralled the race and lead those who worship at the throne of God in the name of Jesus, from their ignorance and superstition? How frail this boasted system; how disproportioned and hydra-headed, when by analysis its true character is revealed! In the former statements language failed to express the absolute perfection of nature, and the unfailing progression of her laws; certainty of her harmonious procedure and glorious results. But now no language seems capable of expressing the imperfection and wretchedness of her fallen state. Her head is bowed down, her heart sick, her love is transformed into malice and revenge, her wisdom into folly, and her harmony into discord! How great and marvelous the change. Says the "Seer," p. 336, "It has already been revealed that in the constitution of mankind there existed passions and principles which were in themselves good. But after the advance of the nations, they, by misconceiving the true elements of their nature, created unfavorable circumstances, by which the development of their passions and principles was entirely misdirected; and they became a degenerate and wretched race." Facts force this confession; but by it the very appearance of truth is forced from the scheme, and to pass away like vapor before the winds. Nature is arrested in her progression, and has thus revealed her liability to err. A good tree has brought forth evil fruit, a clear fountain muddy waters. That which from all eternity was perfect, harmonious and good, has become exceedingly imperfect, discordant and vile. The ever reliable has met with a sudden failure. Man the glory of Nature's mighty works, is fallen; his passions and principles are entirely misguided. From elysian fields he wanders upon barren deserts; from the sunny heights of innocence and joy, he is plunged into an abyss of woe, his being is shattered by the fall, and Nature has met with a strange perversion. Such is the spirit of the teachings now presented by these "Revelations" of the Nineteenth Century. And thus this grand climax of "Vortex" unfoldings confirms the doctrine of the Inspired Word, which teaches that Nature is frail, and dependent for being and perpetuation upon a Power more infinite than herself.

This theory, then, will hardly endure the test of its own statements. Most earnest has been the effort to sustain the infinite and unerring perfection of Nature, but now, in man's depravity, she is proved wanting in a marked degree, having failed to retain what she had gained by her mysterious and prolonged labors. That these conclusions are legitimate we refer the reader to N. D. R., p. 73. "The beginning and ending form one infinite circle of movement, development and progression. Representations of this great principle are seen in the movements of Nature, the whole of which is formed of concentric circles, from the smallest particle in existence to the united and perfect form of all things." And again, p. 351. "The organization of man is, of itself, perfect. In every department there is an equal adaptation—an endless amount of uses—which converge to as many ends; and these, when conjoined, display one perfect use and end, for which the whole was created. Thus man is existing. . . . He is therefore rendered a proper receptacle of the spontaneous breathings of the Great Positive Mind, through Nature, by Wisdom, to form and individualize the immortal spirit to dwell in the world within. Thus man is organized, not composed of a mutual agreement of parts, through the infinite workings of an impetuous Nature, but is rather the perfect form, the highest image, the designed organization of the Divine Mind that pervades immensity!" Also, p. 620. "The law of eternal progression also governs the constant development of all forms, both of material and spiritual nature. And from the tendencies of this law flow all the affinities, affections, relations, forms, and degrees of refinement. . . . Everything is developed in Order and Form, and all things united form one mighty external expression of Infinite Wisdom, one of the esential attributes of the Divine Mind." Thus the "Seer" labors to prove the perfection of Nature, and man the result of her eternally progressive workings. The Work abounds with corresponding statements; statements which declare that nature operates in infinite certainty; that her laws are unerring; her purposed results sure; and that she embraces all, pervades all; is from everlasting to everlasting, the beginning and end. And from his theses and reasoning, it is impossible to admit the least deviation in any of her works, for they teach that everything is the manifestation of infinite perfection; the expression of infinite wisdom; the display of infinite love; the result of infinite goodness; the demonstration of infinite harmony; and the completion of infinite design; the euphony of infinite thought ascending the divinely perfect octaves of an infinite and unbroken scale. One grand musical tone, in which combine an infinity of intonations. One voice in which are divinely expressed infinite utterances. One form in which combine the attributes of all forms. One spirit, embodiment of all spirits; and one entity embracing universal entity of inconceivable and immensurable parts. In direct opposition to this theory, we are informed, p. 337, that by reason of unfavorable circumstances the development of those passions and principles of man which were in themselves good, were *entirely* misguided; and consequently the race became degenerate and wretched. And p. 342; "thence arose envy, cruelty and misery among them. For they became jealous of each other, and lost entirely all the peaceful principles that previously united them instinctively together." This seems like absolute imperfection. To lose *entirely* the peaceful principles and to become the subjects of jealousy, envy, hatred, etc. is to fall as low as the most orthodox Biblicist would presume to claim. In addition to the above it is also written, p. 386, "Error began with man, because of his innocent and uninstructed faculties; because he did not observe those conditions which were required for his happiness;" (Why not employ the language of the Scriptures, and say, because they did not regard the Word of the Lord, "The day thou eatest thereof thou shalt surely die?" Gen. 11: 17.) "And because he cultivated a deceptive artificiality instead of interior purity and refinement." ("The serpent beguiled me and I did eat." Bible.) "and from a minute rill," (partaking of the forbidden fruit,) "human error increased to a vast ocean," ("In Adam all died." Bible.) "the many nations of the earth being tributaries." ("All have gone out of the way." Bible.) "The contaminations and sophistications of these flowed into the great stream of human iniquity. This has covered the whole face of the earth; it has washed every bosom of peacefulness, and left only the dregs of wretchedness and imbecility. It has prostrated and desolated nations; it has consumed and swallowed up the principles of morality and refinement which are man's by nature." While reading these passages, if we were not otherwise assured, we might imagine ourselves perusing a Scriptural essay from Dr. Horne, or some of the "Fathers," rather than an effort against the Bible by one of its champion opposers. Surely they remind us of the Scriptures very considerably, however much of a burlesque upon true Theology, Science and Literature, the opposers may pretend the Bible to be. The Word declares that "the whole head is sick, the whole heart is faint. From the sole of the foot even to the crown of the head, there is no soundness in it." Isa. 1: 5, 6. "The wicked are like the troubled sea, when it cannot rest, whose waters cast up mire and dirt." Isa. 57: 29.

One more illustration of the absolute contradictions upon this point must suffice. And indeed this hardly seems necessary; but lest some passing remark of his should be considered ample apology for these many antipodes, and to reveal his perfectly opposite statements upon the first transgression, etc. the following passages are introduced. Page 330. "But when they had advanced a little farther, and had partaken of a little of the fruit of the tree of Knowledge, they began to conceal their true sentiments, and clothe them with an arbitrary sound." Page 332—"Previously to this, mankind were in an innocent and pure condition. . . . Thus the whole race became dejected and depraved. . . From this time misery and impure associations had their origin." And page 334—"They became extremely depraved and wretched, such being the legitimate fruit of physical, mental and social violation." (But on p. 332 he says, "not because they had violated any constitutional faculty, physical or mental"—plain contradiction.) "They represented a being in despair, suffering as they did the full consequences of their violations: and thus Cain was represented as saying, 'My punishment is greater than I can bear.' This was humble acknowledgment—a true confession of depravity." Such are the sayings of Mr. Davis, when speaking of human depravity not having before his mind the Christian Faith. And *such sentiments as these he rejects* with withering reproach, when he opposes the doctrines of the Bible. Indeed in that opposition, he seems to be entirely in another sphere, or void of memory. From p. 482 we record the following: "Therefore the opinion is without foundation, that the race was once pure, perfect, and united, and that it afterwards degenerated, because it partook a little of the fruit of the tree of Knowledge." Could there be greater and more glaring contradiction? Even the same phraseology is employed in the opposing statements. But again, p. ib. he continues, "The *third* opinion is exceedingly derogatory to the character of the Divine Mind, and absolutely charges him with a want of foreknowledge, and predetermination, when his living energies were engaged in creating and organizing the Univercœlum. For the supposition that he ever instituted laws (*which are the very elements of his Will*, and which are as unchangable as his Divine Essence,) and afterwards found himself incompetent to carry them out, and to perfect the system he had erected—is a supposition exceedingly unrighteous, and altogether opposed to his celestial dignity, and therefore it should be discarded and never more promulgated to the children of men." Can language introduce greater contradictions than these? Having taught the depravity of the race, the suspension of nature's progressive movement, and the fall of man from harmony with the laws of being, to mental and physical violation; from a pure and happy state to one exceedingly vicious and wretched; from innocence to guilt, from love to hatred, and from peace to war and bloodshed: having himself established such as the state of man, and consequently the interruption of nature in her purposed course, he proceeds to condemn the doctrine, saying that even the supposition is exceedingly unrighteous! If it should be urged that the charge is not against the doctrine of human depravity, but that which teaches a want of ability on the part of the Divine Mind to carry out his purposes, we reply; that to such charges no one need plead guilty but himself and his disciples. For he reduces all power and being to the capacity of Nature. And as heretofore shown from his declarations, whatever he may say of the Great First Cause, Divine Mind, etc. he has taught that it originally consisted of Matter and Motion, and that too in a molten state or vortex of lava; and that man is a perfection of the Divine Mind. Consequently when man became perverted these principles were responsible. That is, the laws and attributes of his own being constitute his dependence, and when he is degraded, nature in him is vitiated. And if man fell from his dignity, being the head and glory of Nature's works, a perfection of the Divine Mind, who shall aid him from his degradation? Or, if the principles of nature not only enter into the composition of man, but encompass him, and he be the casket exalted and supported by universal law as a perfect vessel for the spirit, and if then by any means he descend from a superior to an inferior plane, from harmony to discord; and from progression becomes retrogressive, his condition is equally as helpless, and nature also equally involved with him, and therefore "the Divine Mind" is impeached. And what hope can nature have in herself, if, after having contended successfully during the lone and laborious night of her unfoldings until the morning; and until the flower of her being kissed the sun of opening day and disclosed its divine stamens arising into the realms of celestial sublimation; if she then could not sustain the blossom of her being upon its divine peduncle, but overcome by retrogressive agencies, drooping, hung her opening bud in the muddy waters of infamy, and drank that poison which neutralized her virtue, how after this can nature restore herself? If, when healthy and vigorous, she fainted and sank by the way, how, when sick and palsied, unaided, arise and pursue her pilgrimage? Verily, here is a difficulty; one out of which there seems no way of escape, save by the gracious interposition of some superior Power. This remedy Heaven proffers in the Person of the Lord our Redeemer. Thus the "Seer," inadvertantly however we suppose, preaches the necessity of "the Savior." How strangely, bewildered man revolves, unconscious, around that Divine Center while laboring to construct a way of his own to the heaven of peace; and to avoid the humiliation of a full confession of his guilt and dependence upon the grace of God for salvation. But however much he toils, he does not remove the frailty of his being or the dependence of his soul upon Divine Favor for spiritual health and heavenly joy.

The christian believes that man, when innocent and pure, partook of the fruit of the tree of Knowledge of good and evil, and in so doing became depraved. So unfolds the "Seer." For, as already noticed, he thus teaches: "But when they had advanced a little farther, and had partaken of a little of the fruit of tree of Knowledge, they began to conceal their true sentiments. . . . Previously to this, mankind were in an innocent and pure condition. Thus the whole race became dejected and depraved. . . . They represented a being in despair, suffering as they did the full consequences of their violations. . . . And consequently they became a degenerate and wretched race." The christian charges this defect upon created beings: but he upon the Divine, through nature, in man, since man is a perfection of the Divine Mind. To whom, then, or to what theory, does his anathema apply? Not to the christian nor his faith. For he regards man a creature formed by the Infinite Creator upon whom he is dependent for all things; who possesses all Power and Goodness;

and who if his children err is merciful to forgive. If through violation they become depraved his graciousness provides means of redemption. He stretcheth out his hand to save the rebel, and guards his people with a shepherd's care. This is the christian's faith. But the so-called philosophy of nature combines the principles of cause, existence and perpetuation in man, who, according to its teachings, is depraved. *This*, then, is the opinion which "is exceedingly derogatory to the character of the Divine Mind, and absolutely charges him with a want of foreknowledge and predetermination—is a supposition exceedingly unrighteous and altogether opposed to his (the Divine Mind's) celestial dignity; and therefore should be discarded and never more promulgated to the children of men." Page 483. Such is Mr. Davis' own verdict—his own decree.

The next proposition in these "Revelations" worthy of notice is found in the following language: p. 482: "I am impressed that nothing has been forfeited as pertaining to the spiritual nature of man, so as in the least degree to require a supernatural restoration to the position which man once occupied."

The *cause* of depravity is charged, in this Work, upon the human voice. In this passage direct reference is had to the extent of the *effect*.

The two propositions, when jointly considered, serve to convey the idea that the *cause* and *effect* were merely superficial; that the outer and not the inner being, is implicated; and, that, therefore the spirit will naturally renovate the man. Hence, with proper time he will, of himself, arise above the ills of misdirected life. The former of these propositions (the cause of depravity) has been considered; the latter (the *effect*) being *one* of the *principle* propositions and *most important*, invites criticism. Connected with this, and in relation to the entire scheme are two substantial considerations.

First, Mr. Davis, notwithstanding his former theses, so states his metaphysical theory of the human constitution, as to render the spirit the seat of, and therefore the principle engaged in man's depravity; hence responsible for the ills of life. The *Second* consideration is this: If the spirit is depraved, the constitution and position of man in matter of fact and agreeable to this Theory, also, are such that his depravity will endure, unless aided (redeemed) by Life uncontaminated, and Omnipotent to save.

In illustration of the *First* of these, the following passages from pp. 608, etc., are introduced: "The all-important truth to be established in the mind is, that the interior essence is the soul and creator of all external forms, which forms determine and demonstrate the mode of such soul's existence. The form which every particle of matter assumes, is that created and determined by the peculiar essence which is latent in the particle itself. . . . So *Sensation* is the soul, essence, and creator, of the Animal World; and in, by, and through this, all the qualities and essential attributes of its *interior* are made manifest to the *outer* world. . . . Thus all things are unfolded to the outer world by the incessant activity of the qualities, attributes, and unchangable tendencies of the internal essence or soul, which is the interior or life of all external and material existences." Page 610. "Keeping in mind then, the uniform developments from the inner to the outer world, a knowledge is received concerning the corresponding development of the animal world. For as by understanding one particle of matter, with all its properties, tendencies, and capabilities, a corresponding knowledge is obtained concerning the structure of the whole Universe—so by understanding the mode of the existence of Life, an understanding is at once established concerning the higher degrees and similar modes of existence, as determined by *their* Soul or essence. And as by knowing the measurement of *one inch*, a rule is obtained by which may be measured the length and breadth of all material existence—so it is equally plain, that if the existence of Life and Sensation is understood, the same laws and principles which govern these will introduce the mind into higher degrees or planes of corresponding exterior development."

Guided by this rule, if this earth and its depraved inhabitants may occupy the magnitude of *one inch*, in the scale of universal measurement, then the vast Univercœlum must be in a deplorable condition. The system, however, affords no other conclusion. For by it we learn that man is the crowning glory of Nature. If so, according to the state of Man given by Mr. Davis, little order, harmony or proper development exists in the immensurate realm. "The mode," he continues, "by which Motion, Life, and Sensation, exists as one united essence and Soul in its relation to the material world, consists only in the perfect structure of the *human organization*. Then it is not the *body*, the *form*, the *material*, that develops and organizes the *spiritual* principle: for if this were true, then indeed the human mind could not sustain its identity as disconnected from the instrument by which it was developed." By this reasoning, it is seen, that the *mind* or *spirit* develops, fashions and controls the *body* or outer manifestation. To confirm this theory, on p. 611, he remarks: "And it is in the human world that Motion, Life, and sensation, become united and perfected as one living organized essence—an *individualized Soul*, by and from which every human form is created. Each *individualized* human structure also possesses an organized soul, composed of the subordinate attributes existing in the lower planes of material forms. Therefore this essence unfolds and displays its interior qualities in the human form, which is Man. Thus the exterior form of man is the perfect representative of the peculiar constitution and qualities of his spiritual essence or soul. In other words, it is an exact correspondent of all the tendencies, attributes, qualities, and possessions of his interior soul, essence, and creator. . . . The *interior* or inner essence, in every instance, and without variation, is the soul, substance, creator, and cause, of all *effects*, which are the forms visible in the outward world. The external evidence of this consists in the appearances of all external forms; in the relation which they sustain to one another; in their invariable manifestation and developments, and in that general relation which they all sustain to the great structure of the Universe."

By these declarations we are taught; I, That man externally, is but the outward expression of his inward spirit; hence improper manifestations are not of the external man, but are from the spirit; moreover, are an exact representation of the interior or spiritual being. Depravity, then, cannot depend upon the material form or its deeds, but is the work and exact representation of the living essence or soul. It is, therefore, the spirit which is depraved, and engaged in the work of vice. Hence, whatever loss or depravity man suffers, the spirit sustains. And to restore that loss the *heart* or *soul* must be renovated.

II. This teaching makes the spirit or soul-essence, not only the designer, but the cause and creator of the external. All outward display is, therefore, according to the pattern of the inward principle. "The *interior* or inner essence," he continues, "in every instance, and without exception, is the soul, substance, creator and cause of all effects, which are the forms visible in the outer world." The inner principle, according to this, is absolute monarch of the outer manifestation. Again, p. 612: "Here, then, is the *sensuous* evidence that the human form is a form determined by a corresponding essence, which is man's organized and immortal soul. Not only in viewing the whole Human World as one Form is Intelligence discovered as an interior quality and essence, but in every *individual* structure are all the required qualities to demonstrate an absolute individualization of the interior creative essence. . . . Moreover, a single human form is a perfect organization, representative, and reflection, of all the other lower compounds in Nature. And thus man is a perfect *flower*, being progressively developed from all the lower parts of the same great Tree of ceaseless causation." No one can mistake the meaning of these passages. We have been constantly instructed that the body is a mere vehicle for the use of the spirit; and if so man is only revealed through these external agencies. Hence the human form is but the development, or assumed form, and its deeds but the procedure of the spirit. The following passage from p. 74, fully confirms this view: "And in the process of natural development, each particle, substance and form, enters into the composition of vegetable, animal and all else existing, by which process the substance or essential principle becomes *individualized*, but not until *Man* is made the instrument. And by such individualization, it becomes the future and corresponding principle, *Spirit*—representing, in a second condition, the instrument of its individualization. And as Matter contains the essence and properties to produce *Man*, as a progressive ultimate, so Motion contains the properties to produce Life and Sensation. These together and perfectly organized, develop the principle of *Spirit*. This is not a production consequent on organization, but it is a result of a combination of all the elements and properties of which the organization is composed; and organization serves merely as an instrument to *develop* the principle of Spirit. But such principles must have existed eternally—as emanating from the Great Source and Fountain of Intelligence; but it could not be individualized and made manifest without a vessel like unto man." The movements or deeds of the body, then, are only the demonstrations of the spirit. The body being intended for the individualization and use of the essences or spirit of nature, acts only as its agent, through which it is revealed. And therefore as the body is a representation of the principles of material nature, so its deeds are an exact representation of the spirit. Agreeably, on p. 614, it is written: "Thus the body is merely a coating, a garment, a sheathing of the spiritual principles, whereby the latter is enabled to communicate with all material things within its plane of existence." Again, p. 615: "But the *body* is subordinate to the spirit, and is dependent for its motion, life, energies, animation, and even for its existence, upon the immortal spirit within, whose continuous identity is determined by eternal law, according to which, matter in all cases stands only as its representative and external development." And p. 618:

"Thus it is that *form* is the express image of its interior or first principles of life and being. And the use of everything is determined by the specificness of its own interior possessions. . . It is on the same principle that the *human* form is an express likeness of the qualities of the interior soul." The body, therefore, is a mere machine; a model or representative of the spirit within. It depends upon the spirit for life, energies, motion, etc. If so, the voice, when it articulated, proceeded in obedience to the spirit actuating the organs of speech. And as it is a perfect representative of the soul, it moved strictly in accordance with the impulse given it.

"The forms of thought," says the Seer, p. 619, "are words—these always bring the express likeness of the thought evolved." The utterance, which he formerly declared "possessed not the power of communicating the real reality of their ideas and affections to each other, but rather was liable to convey deceptive impressions;" (p. 330.) and by which means, "every expression of the mind, which was originally pure and unadulterated, was now" (by the voice) "clothed in a false sheath," (p. 332) —even that utterance, he now declares, always brings the express likeness of the thought evolved: and is, (was) therefore, precisely what the spirit designed. Such is the letter and spirit of these statements. And however adverse his former theorizing may have been, the tendency and ultimate of this lengthy metaphysical dissertation declare that if the voice cursed the brother, or the hand was raised to slay him, both proceeded by the will of the interior prompter—even the spirit that was in man. The reasoning renders it equally so with every human action. The spirit or inward being is, therefore, the cause of all external manifestations, and hence responsible for the deeds of the body. How else can it be? If, then, Man is depraved, it is his spirit; and if he has suffered loss, it is the spirit that sustains that loss. If the loss is restored, it is restored *in, and to the spirit.* In the following, this sentiment is still more emphatically urged. Page 622: "Love is the first or rudimental element of the human soul. It is that liquid, mingling, delicate, inexpressible element which is felt in the depths of every human spirit, because it is its germinal essence." In this statement love is made the deepest and most vital principle of the being. Again: "Love perceives and conceives that which is congenial to its affections. The end to be obtained is the *cause* of Love's prompting the Will to act upon the body in order to accomplish it. In other words, *Will* is employed as a *means* by Love to attain the end for which it has an affection. Will in all cases is subject to the promptings of the element of Love, and its acts therefore originate in the suggestion thence derived. Will is the faculty employed to move the body in the performance of any external work, for the accomplishment of which the Love has conceived an affection." Such is the "Seer's" exposition of Love, which he denominates the essence of the soul; the prompter of the Will and thence the body, in pursuit of any object of the affections. Love, then, is the prime mover, and indicates the character of mankind. Therefore, according to the nature of love is that of the deeds and lives of men. Upon the character of this principle of the human soul, he remarks, p. 623, "Love being the first element or the essence of the soul, is accordingly imperfect, unguided, and, like the lower forms in Nature, is developed *angularly*." Here is the seat of depravity, according to Mr. Davis' own theorizing. Let it be remembered that it is Love, the Will and body prompter: love, the "liquid, mingling, delicate and inexpressible element," he renders thus defective and "the parent of eccentricity, impulse, fantasy, imagination, and inflated conception of all things invisible, intangible, and unreal." The cause, then, of human woe is deep in the soul. For if, as he affirms, love prevails with man, it must infuse its spirit throughout, and determine the external manifestations of the being. From this faculty, therefore, must issue those fountains which reveal themselves in man's misguided life. Hence, whatever may have been the original cause, it is this element within the soul which is depraved. However, lest the friends of the Work should decline from this conclusion, in connection with the above extracts, we again introduce the following passage from p. 328: "And it is now evident that man is created from the dust of the earth, and that he is the receptacle of one of the spontaneous breathings of the Great Positive Mind. This renders him a perfect form — a useful agent — a living soul." At the period when man was a perfect form and the receptacle of *one of the breathings of the Great Positive Mind*, which breathing constituted him a living, intellectual soul; at that period, being perfect, he was not imperfect, the creature of fantasy, and of inflated conceptions of all things unreal. If so, the term "perfection," has no meaning, and the manifestation was a sad comment upon the character of the Great Positive Mind, and more especially, since man was, according to Mr. Davis, a perfection thereof. Either man was created imperfect, and vitiated, (and that annihilates this system of perfect nature's perfect unfolding,) or the most vital principle of his soul has *suffered loss* by perversion. The latter the Work fully maintains: also, that the love element partakes primarily, of that defect. The human spirit in this case, is the direct subject of depravity—is implicated in, and responsible for man's viciousness. Hence it is again proved that human misdirection did not originate in, and by reason of physiological development, (viz., the voice,) or by outward deeds; but by reason of some counteracting influence, directly affecting the heart: and outward manifestations are only reflections of inward character. And this, also, reveals the vital conflict ever existing between the fundamental principles of this scheme. In the following language, p. 625, the "Seer's" thesis that Love controls man is clearly and unmistakably expressed: "From the faculty of Love as a basis of the soul, flows the faculty of Will, . . . Love prompts the Will to act upon the body; . . Will is employed as a *means* by Love to attain the end for which it has an affection; . . Will in all cases is subject to the promptings of Love." Upon love then, rests the responsibility of moral agency. Thence its nature determines the moral quality and state of man.

This sentiment of these statements, and that of others in the Work upon the condition and tendencies of the soul, are directly opposed to its original premise and intention; condemn the leading principles and first reasoning, thence the Harmonial philosophy; and also confirm the Scriptures. They make man a depraved and wretched being, subject to sin, and the consequences of violated law; enthrall his spirit and reduce him to moral degradation of a most malignant character: and the cause, according to the reasoning, exists in the love-nature of the soul. What orthodox urges more? And why should Mr. Davis, and the friends of his Harmonialism, oppose as they do the teachings of the Inspired Word upon this subject?

At length, after having taught depravity, an effort is made to avoid the doctrine of Redemption through the Savior, by simply stating that "Wisdom is the perfection of Love, and the faculty that analyzes, calculates and imperatively commands obedience from all the subordinate passions of Will and Love." Page 622.

When we speak of perfection, we embrace in our mind the extension of first principles to their highest attainment. And it is a law of nature that what is begotten derives its leading character from that which gave it birth. From the acorn arises the oak, and not the palm: nor is the citron a fig-bearing tree. The trigress would scarcely give birth to a lamb, or man beget an ape. If Love is imperfect and the parent of eccentricity, impulse. fantasy, imagination and inflated conceptions of *all* things invisible, intangible and unreal, the ultimate perfection of its imperfect nature and paternal qualities might militate against the theory. Perfect eccentricity, impulse, fantasy and inflated conceptions of things unreal, etc. would savor very much of perfect *Folly*, rather than perfect Wisdom. Excresences may be removed from a body, but when elements are eradicated or transformed into opposite natures, the body is also changed from the original to another type. If love is the first element of the soul, it must forever endure as such; and if its germinal nature is likely to beget the full catalogue of unrealities, and these are the fruit of its innocent state, will not such inherent tendencies accompany that faculty throughout every mode of existence? And as the soul shall enlarge its capacity will not that element "grow with its growth and strengthen with its strength?" The soul is the essence, the intelligence of the being, and love being the first element is a constituent thereof; and as unreal, or erroneous consequences flow from it, do they not prove its nature? Can the Ethiopian change his skin, or the Leopard his spots? How then can Wisdom, which is called the perfection of love, fail to partake of this element, and be liable to unwise decisions? the pursuit of objects of fancy? hence inherit foolishness? Even more than this is charged upon love, the imperfect element of the soul; for it is said to have embraced objects so much the opposite of the real and good, as to render the heart void of pure and tender sympathy, and to beget the spirit of vice, tyranny, revenge, and murder. Love, innocent, and pure, gave place to hate, and those who had dwelt together in harmony, peace and happiness, began to contend, and finally became disorganized and entirely wretched. Page 332. This principle is represented as having so far gained the ascendency as to have usurped the throne of reason, and by vile dictation ruled man as with a rod of iron. Fantasy bade, and he wildly pursued every imaginable false light; chased the phantom, engaged in manifold vices, and went forth multiplying human sorrow, and stained the earth with the blood of his brother, and thus made the land desolate by reason of carnage and death. Hence he became reckless, unmerciful and cruel. To these conclusions, man's history and present state bear mournful testimony.

In accounting for this condition the "Seer" most fatally involves the soul by rendering man, whom he denominates a perfection of the Divine Mind, constitutionally imperfect. Even his love-nature, which was formed under the advantages of the attributes, progression and ultimate attainments of the Great First Cause, or principles of the original Vortex, he declares the author of fantasy, etc. If so, and man is the crown and glory of Nature and her works, how can he ever eradicate the imperfect element from his soul, and still retain his entity? Nay verily, if the imperfect element has prevailed over the being and impelled him into the vortex of vice and folly, and if the christian's theory of God and nature is unfounded, no hope exists for man. If man must depend for salvation upon his inherent principles, and if wisdom and goodness bowed to the baser propensions in its incipiency, now that it is monarch of the soul, (for thus it is rendered, p. 332, etc.) the destiny of the spirit is sealed forever; and the Race may despair of heaven and happiness. This is the inevitable, the only conclusion; for the premises and reasoning afford no other, when the strong points are justly arranged and compared.

Conditions may be varied when they are not the legitimate consequences of elementary principles. But until nature shall change her laws, and the order of her manifestations; and reconstruct her stupendous Temple, elements must retain their constitutional properties, and also their mode of being while the organisms they compose mantain their original type. And if love is the first element of the soul, and it begets vagaries, which leading to every imaginable evil, commit the being and overcome it, the soul shall be liable to like results so long as the principle dwells therein. And until man shall cease to be, the components of his constitution shall endure. The properties composing the hippopotamus and controlled by the same laws could not assume the human form; neither could man become that pachydermatus mammal. And since nature has revealed her weakness in her most vital part, and lost her equilibrium, and dominion in the most important realm of her kingdom; and since man is the especial display of her shortcomings, he has no hope unless a God of more might than that of this Pantheistic Theory appears to save.

Lest some superficial reader should confound this system with the doctrine of depravity taught in the Inspired Word, it may be well to observe, that the Scriptures charge the perversion of Man's inclinations upon the violation of law. They deny that an original evil-inclined element existed in his nature when from the hands of his Creator which finally subdued the nobler qualities of the soul; but they do declare that by reason of transgression the soul lost its innocence and thence its power to control the being in the way of life; and that the weakness thus induced rendered man the subject of evil—of death. The Scriptures also teach that in order to reinstate the spirit's pure and heavenly inclinations, it requires Divine Aid; and that the Grace of God alone can change the heart, convert and save the soul from death. The Harmonial or Pantheistic Theory, on the contrary as already shown, allows an original and imperfect element to prevail—hence teaches that depravity arises from constitutional inclination, and that man's redemption depends upon inherent ability.

Again, on p. 623, we find the following contrary statement relative to the constitution of the soul: "Love is the element that conceives of all loveliness, of gentleness, of sweetness, of fragrance, and of beauty, in all their various modes of exterior manifestation." These qualities are the direct antipodes of the former named abilities and tendencies of Love. We are not, however, now inclined to contend with the "Seer" for having awarded to the soul these opposite elements and this complexity; and will only observe, that perfect Nature in her most perfect work has presented us with a peculiar compound in demonstration of the *infinity of her Divine Harmony!*

Allowing these two elements to constitute the Love of the soul, it then follows as an unfailing sequence, that their perfection in what he denominates Wisdom would render that of like nature, since it must harmonize with the embodiment whence it arose. Therefore Wisdom *must* favor both extremes. And if it controls Love and Will, it is as likely to command their obedience to a fantasy as to a reality. Nothing is gained therefore, by this especial effort to introduce Wisdom as the savior of perverted man; but the difficulty is evidently increased.

Should the "Seer" maintain that the better qualities shall overcome the imperfect and evil inclinations, and prevailing exalt him supremely above all ill, we reply that this may do (?) for theory, but that to demonstrate by the cultivation of human propensions has ever baffled the skill and powers of his class of philosophers. Earth is wanting in a single instance where their theory has been verified by such flattering results. This, however, is the soul-thesis of the system. But the very many statements and arguments in favor of man's vileness and absolute misery by reason of perversion, completely deprives it of life, and mutilates the form. As silently, however, as this clause ("Wisdom commands obedience from Will and Love,") may have been introduced with the other passages, it is evidently intended as a key to Harmonial redemption. It may bear the test and withstand the severest criticism; and it may, in other respects than that just considered, be found wanting in its capacity to meet the demands of the system. Love is a living fountain. It flows spontaneously from the soul, and is capable of sudden development. From a genial and heavenly grace, it may be unfolded almost *instanter* into might sufficient to move the being whither it will. But Wisdom never. The Soul possesses those principles which from germs may be cultivated into the dignity of Sages. This however, invariably requires time and a faithful application of extrinsic means. However it is rarely that wisdom is chief with man. Who does not know that love is the strongest passion of the soul? In life it manifests its superiority, and in death it is the last to relinquish its hold upon the objects of its affections. Wisdom adjusts the affairs of life, counsels the friend and gently retires: while love contends with the destroyer to the latest moment, moves the convulsing hand in token of the last farewell; compresses the cold and dying lips at the touch of those of its dearest friends; and struggles to say adieu; and finally looks out from the glassy eye-ball until the mortal vision fails and closes from its view the loved ones lingering around the dying couch. This is the power of love.

The savage spurns the counsels of wisdom

and hastens his steps in the ways of cruelty and revenge. But by the power of love he is subdued, and becomes as docile as the lamb. Love is a living liking of the soul: an outflowing of desire. It animates, quickens, and moves the being in the pursuit of its object. It is not mechanical or artistic. It gushes forth like a fountain issuing from some compressed siphon. But Wisdom is cold sense. It is mechanical. It is not life, but the vehicle thereof, by which the living principle seeks expression: the mere agent of inward desire. The man of superior erudition is subject to the passions of his soul. Illustrations of this fact are abundant. How frequently men of brightest intellect and highest attainments fall victims to their passional natures. Go to the Halls of Nations, where Statesmen congregate. See that manly form, that high and commanding brow. Read the depth of that intellect which beams forth through that eye from the soul within. Fathom it, you can never. Listen while the lips move, to the profound thoughts expressed. Observe how the chest expands with the increasing volume of the inspiring theme; and how the countenance glows. You are awed with the sense, and fired with the zeal. The blood courses rapidly through your veins. He tells you—for he is the Nation's Counselor —he tells you of the perils that o'erhang his country. With masterly skill he pictures before your excited imagination the glory of former conquests; the honor and dominion of your National Polity. He unfurls the streaming banner,—signet of the Nation's renown, saying: "This Ensign of Liberty is periled. The Foe nears our coasts; his fleets cruise our seas. His legions already congregate upon our shores. And to rescue the Nation, *you must arise,* and go forth to battle. You *must force* the enemy into the maelstrom of death, else the country will fall dishonored at the feet of the proud usurper." While listening to his appeal, before you the nation's blood appears already running like rivers, and standing in pools o'er the plains. Fathers are agonizing in their gore, or lying dead upon the battle fields, while the aggressors ravish their defenceless homes. You are ready, yea, eager to go forth. A momentary pause ensues, and in breathless suspense you wait the conclusion of his speech His eye is upon you. His countenance flushes with the excitement of his soul. At length, from the depth of his being, inspired by the awful grandeur of his subject, and in tones that move the elements, and make the nerves quiver through your system, he thunders forth. "*To arms!*" and lo, at his bidding a Nation arises, marches to the field of battle, and engages in the dread conflict. Her belching cannon echo along the Continent their booming thunders; and earth trembles at the din of war.

This is the display of human wisdom. Its power, how great. But mark that mighty man, as he retires from the magnificent Hall, having closed that speech which moved a Nation to the field of death. And lo, in yonder banquet behold him. He sips the ruby wine, and whirls in the giddy dance, until his brain is fired and his being bows before old Bacchus. At length he leaves this scene of mirth for one of lowest infamy, there to render base homage to perverted love. Wretched man! Where now thy wisdom? Hath it not failed to "command and secure the obedience of all the subordinate passions of thy will and love?" Thou canst control a Parliament or Congress, and thence nations with thy sense, and by thy eloquence wield them as thou wilt; but a stronger passion has thee in its fatal grasp. Thy love, imperfect, fantastic and unreal, holds thee as its slave.

This, reader, is a true comment upon the theory of the soul, as maintained in N. D. R. Truth, facts and man's forlorn condition unite to condemn this Harmonial System.

Again, according to the "Seer's" own reasonings, love, the imperfect element of the soul, overcame wisdom, or the race would not have been perverted and unwisely employed. Is wisdom depraved? or is it influenced by those faculties which are?

Finally, we proceed to consider more directly that question which of all others is the most important, viz.: *Does man's depravity so disqualify him as to render supernatural aid necessary to his restoration?* Mr. Davis says he is impressed that it does not. We are impressed that it does. And indeed, as we have already and repeatedly shown, his declarations, as also much of his philosophy, sustain our impressions. Nor does it, in view of such considerations, seem proper to again introduce the subject. But the following statements touching the question at issue require analysis. "Many theologians," says Mr. Davis, p. 481, "have conceived, from observing superficially other isolated passages in the Bible, that Jesus was a being expressly destined and created for the purpose of redeeming the race from a fallen and degenerate condition. Others have supposed that he came merely to establish a connection between the spiritual nature of man and the Divine Mind, and thus to serve as a medium through which spirits from the rudimental sphere might approach the presence of Him who made from internal Essence the Universe. Others have supposed that he was a material organization capable of receiving the Divine Mind itself, and that as such he came to reconcile and elevate the spiritual nature of man to a degree whereby perpetual communion with holiness and righteousness might be established. The first opinion is in a measure true; he *was* a destined medium and agent to unfold a higher degree of perfection than had been before possessed by man; but, for this purpose, he was created, as all the human family are created, by the workings of the laws and elements of Nature. But the supposition that he came to redeem the world of mankind from a fallen condition is exceedingly contrary, both to the laws of Nature and the teachings of the Primitive History, and is derogatory to the unspeakable perfection of that Essence which has breathed life and animation throughout space. "By the word *redemption*, the mind is instantly led to the idea of something *lost* or *forfeited.* I am impressed that nothing has been forfeited as pertaining to the spiritual nature of man, so as in the least degree to require a supernatural restoration to a position which man once occupied."

It will be noticed that Mr. Davis in approaching the denial of any necessity for the Savior, proceeds to class the Lord Jesus with other members of the human race, and places him upon the scale of natural creation. That is, he makes him *the product of the elements of this earth*, saying: "He was created as all the human family are created, by the workings of the laws and elements of Nature." He furthermore states that, "the supposition that he came to redeem the world of mankind from a fallen condition is contrary both to the laws of Nature and the teachings of the Primitive history." Thus he 1, denies that Christ was Divine above men, and 2, declares that the idea of his supernatural Divinity is not derived from the Primitive history. The latter is unworthy of a reply, and a consideration of the former is hardly called for in the review of a Work so replete with error as to consume itself; a Work made of tangles, and as multi-faced as the notions of men.

We shall bestow a few, and but a few, thoughts upon the last sentence in the passage quoted, because upon its truth and bearing depends his opposition to the Savior. And this depends, in like manner with his principal thesis, upon that all important phrase—"*I am impressed.*" Aside from this, however, there seems a weakness in the principle involved. It suggests the following important questions: What is lost or forfeited? What constitutes supernatural restoration? and lastly, Does man's state indicate such beneficent aid? When a limb is amputated it is lost to the body. Severing the ligaments, tendons, bone, etc. breaks that sympathy which once existed between them and the body; thus the means of support are destroyed, and the mutual uses are sacrificed. The heart is the fountain of life. When innocence, purity and perfection reign in the perfect soul, the fruit, or consequences are harmony, love, peace, joy, and righteousness. But when these principles are removed, hate and revenge, etc. take possession of the heart, they result in vice and wretchedness; and the being is deprived of what it once possessed. When the "true faculties, true passions and pure associations of men, were *turned into unholy and polluted paths,*" (p. 335.) they were not in those of the holy and pure. And as purity and holiness are the opposites of impurity and unholiness, this change must have been a complete transformation. No man can serve two opposing masters, or proceed in opposite directions at the same time. A sick man has lost his health, and the insane his sanity. If the vessel containing life's elixir be emptied of its contents and *filled* with deadly poison, there is more than a loss of the life-giving principle sustained; for it is not only deprived of that boon, but is burdened with, polluted and endangered by the baneful drug. He who receives into his system sufficient of the element of death to destroy his life, has thereby *forfeited* it.

Whoso keeps the law is just, but whoever violates, removes from himself his innocence. Law protects the righteous, it is his shield and strong defence, his tower and hope in trouble; but he who violates its precepts, or infringes upon its claims, forfeits that protection which the law affords. Yea more, brings himself into contact with its power, and suffers the tortures of its iron grasp. "Sin revived and I died," said the Apostle. "And the commandment, which was ordained unto life, I found to be ur to death. For sin, taking occasion by the commandment deceived me, and by it slew me. Wherefore, the law is holy, and the commandment is holy and just, and good." Rom., 7, 9-12. If the body or mind be weakened or maimed by excess or the violation of laws and faculties, it may recover, apparently, its original tone, but according to the theory of progression, it has lost, if no more, the advantages of time and space misimproved, nor can that loss be restored to all eternity. Hence the disabled or depraved has fallen rearward of his fellow of equal capacity, a degree proportionate to his aberration, and without unequal benefits that disparity will everlastingly exist. The fallen brother again progressing, may sigh for reunion with the advance group, but when endless ages have fled the distance still remains. Here is loss and forfeiture.

and this is upon the supposition that having deviated, by self ability, the equilibrium can be regained: but if this cannot be, the *loss* who can compute?

The offender may be pardoned, but not fully restored to his primitive state. He may be made free, but his condition is not equal to those who never erred. He is not justified by virtue of his loyalty, but through mercy. If man, once innocent and pure, by transgression became impure, he first became unjust, since moral purity has reference to equity. This his deeds establish. He then is amenable to that law whose principles he contravened in himself, and thence whose cause he opposed. In a literal sense he became a rebel to the Divine government, and therein forfeited his harmonious inheritance—his original condition. When Cain slew Abel, the meek, he forfeited his primitive relation to law; and also his fraternity with his brother whom he had sacrificed upon the altar of revenge. He who steals from his neighbor, or commits murder, is not, nor ever can be what he was previously. If he shall be restored to a justified state, he is not literally reinstated. That is, his righteousness is not by reason of original purity and unerring obedience, but because of compassion and forgiveness on the part of the offended;

and repentance and a return to the way of righteousness on the part of the offender.

Unrighteous deeds violate law, or no law exists. To charge the perversion, iniquity and unhappiness of man simply upon the imperfect development of the faculties, and to claim that innocence and justification is not forfeited, is an invasion upon good sense. The man who by excess induces opthalmia, and who is thereby made blind, by the breach of physical condition forfeits his external vision. And to restore the lost eye, would require supernatural means, or rather, means more capable than the infringed organism possesses. If by violation man's moral nature becomes so benumbed that he does not sense the right and therefore pursue it; (and it is so if he is really depraved) or if his spiritual vision be so lost that he does not discern the truth, but spiritual things are to him as trees walking; to restore that moral nature will require means in character superior to those native powers which fell a victim to the aggressor. A power that could thus restore, is what christianity regards as *supernatural.* That is, a power not inherent and available by virtue of constitutional abilities; but that which is bestowed from the absolutely superior and independent upon the inferior and dependent. Christianity maintains that man is so disqualified by reason of transgression that he cannot be restored to personal harmony and concord with Heaven without divine Favor. This is denominated supernatural: 1, Because it is from Life and Ability, unperverted, unfallen and infinite. 2, Because it is Divine Beneficence from the Supreme Spirit. When, therefore, Mr. Davis combats the christian, whose religious philosophy he seeks to rebut, by saying: "I am impressed that nothing has been forfeited, as pertaining to the spiritual nature of man so as in the least degree to require supernatural restoration,"—when he thus seeks to overcome the christian, he should be conversant with what the believer in Divine Inspiration considers supernatural, and also remember that the Biblicist is not bound down to *his* Pantheistic notions of God and Nature, but looks far above material manifestations for the throne of the Divine Being. However, viewing as he does, man to be a congregation of the refined elements of the First Ocean of Fire, he may well say, as recorded p. 508: "It is perfectly clear that nothing *is*, and nothing *can* be, but the Divine Mind, which is the *Cause*, and the *Universe*, which is the *Effect*." (The Vortex of original and co-eternally existent Matter and Motion.) "Cause and Effect thus *uniting* and *harmonizing* in one sole System, it follows that whatever occurs in any of the innumerable departments of the Universe *must* occur because it is caused by a natural instigation." It was natural then, for man to proceed in a manner calculated to make him entirely wretched—Nature, even Divine Nature, instigated—the Divine Mind prompted, and Man obeyed. But he continues: "Nothing, therefore, can occur in the vast empire of universal creation opposed to, or transcending the principles of nature." Go on, then, O man, in thy evil way. Thou assassin, sink the glittering poignard deep in the fallen victim's bleeding heart. Nature, whose ways are equal and just, *instigates* thee. The Divine breathings inspire thee. Urge the war-horse to battle and strew the field with your mangled brothers, ye mounted cavalry! the Great First Cause prompts you according to this Work. Horrible! Heaven forgive the blasphemy! But again: "All things, then, whether organized or unorganized, developed or undeveloped, must be strictly and unequivocally NATURAL." It may be *wisdom* for the author to display his marvelous powers in condemning, yea denouncing the honest Bible-believer for his faith. But which savors most of sense, a belief that the Supreme Spirit pities his erring children and offers to save them; or for this Revelator to charge all the wickedness, all the crying sins of man, upon the Divine Mind? His propositions and reasonings will allow no other conclusion. The dreadful thought disturbs the soul. And who that reads understandingly, does not feel like assuming sackcloth and bowing low in the dust; and weeping tears of blood, in view of this God-dishonoring charge. It is even mocking Mr. Davis' Nature-God; that which consists in the eternal *Motion* of Liquid Fire.

And was there sufficient consequence in the matter of these revelations to arouse her, Nature herself would murmur, because of these irreverent accusations. Yet the land moves with advocates of this pretended philosophy, those who are making much ado about the foolishness of the Christian Faith. And the youth are taught to scorn the Bible and follow this worse than false light.

In pursuing his theme he continues: "If anything, therefore, *transcends* Nature, or the natural movements of the Universe, it must be an effect of absolute nothing. The term *supernatural*, then, indicating something above Nature, is a solecism; and nothing is more distinct than the untruth of the theological proposition, that Miracles were accomplished by *supernatural* power: for that is clearly teaching that they originated from *nothing*, and consequently never existed." This is a tedious method of avoiding the Divinity of Jesus Christ, and the acknowledgement of his Mission to the World. To accomplish this, although he evidently does not intend it, and notwithstanding he and his friends may affirm to the contrary, he denies the existence of the Supreme Being. In the paragraph above quoted, we have the following statement: "It is perfectly clear that nothing *is*, and nothing *can be*, but the Divine Mind, which is the *Cause*, and the Universe which is the *Effect*." In this sentence there is a distinction made between *Cause* and *Effect;* and the only idea conveyed is, that the Cause first existed and then the Effect; that the Cause having had Being before the Effect, was not connected with it in its mode of existence; and that the Effect came by, and is, therefore, dependent upon the *Cause* for perpetuation. (In this sense they may unite and harmonize.) Such is the true meaning of the passage, or language is useless. The Cause, then, in its relation to the Effect, is the superior. In this the "Seer" is evidently correct, for, as the *Cause* must have existed prior to the *Effect*, it *must*, also, excel it. Therefore, the Divine Mind which he declares to be the Cause of the Universe, did pre-occupy a superior Realm, and had character above that of the Universe, which it caused—created. In the same paragraph he also remarks, as already noticed: "If anything, therefore, *transcends* the natural movements of the Universe it must be an effect of absolute nothing. The term *supernatural*, then, indicating something *above* Nature, is a solecism." Matter, Form, Motion, and Life, constitute *Nature*, Nature is the Universe, and the Universe is the Effect of the Cause, and the Cause is the Divine Mind. The Cause or Divine Mind, therefore, must be supernatural—that is, above nature. And hence the Universe, according to his own propositions and reasoning, must be the *Effect* of an "absolute nothing." "It is indeed remarkable," he still observes, "that any system of religion could have been so effectually established by manifestations in evidence of its truth, caused by an Omnipotent NOTHING." It *is indeed remarkable, we observe*, that one so illumined as Mr. Davis, in opposing the Christian Religion, should become so zealous as to forget the interest of his own system—a system to establish which he traveled over nearly a thousand pages; and above all, to disprove another theory should absolutely prove his "Divine Mind"—"Great First Cause," an "Omnipotent Nothing!" To this opinion we *have been much inclined*, as the reader will have already observed; and now to strengthen our belief, we are favored with the "Seer's" own words, yea *his* argument. Who awoke thee, thou "Seer," from thy dream? Or hast thou entered a still more giddy realm? Thy former contradictory statements seem sufficiently unnatural to be a miracle; (contrary to nature) but this, if possible excels them all. However, in the Work, all positions appear to be assumed: Nature is reasoned up and down. Supernaturalism, human depravity, natural perfection, etc. are proved and disproved. Nor can sophistry answer for these defects. All, therefore, he may say of Legends, Ancient Mythology, spurious prophets, magi, false creeds, and vague and dreamy records, is not worthy of analysis. And although he may weave into his sayings many, very many substantial truths, that cannot make right a wrong, or give soul and life to a dead system. He acknowledges a condition so depraved, that redemption from it would require a Savior endued with almightiness, but rejects the doctrines of the Gospel and denies the Lord of Life and Glory.

Finally, we conclude with the following, by which the author intends to overthrow the doctrine of Redemption. "The first of these," p. 501, "is the opinion concerning the use and intention of the birth and teachings of CHRIST. It has been supposed that he was a designed instrument, possessing in spirit the Divine qualities of the Creator, to redeem the race from a low degree of physical wretchedness and spiritual death, so that they might thus be restored to a position they once occupied, and become subjects of the favor and goodness of the Divine Mind." Christians believe that men were the subjects of Divine Favor, if not, that favor could not have been bestowed; and by reason of merciful interposition the humble recipient is restored to a state of justification. In this, therefore, he so misrepresents as to present the doctrine in an opposite aspect to its true nature. He would represent the christian as believing man not the subject of heavenly favor and goodness until after the Incarnation. But the Savior said: "God so loved the world, that he gave his only begotten Son, that whosoever believeth in him, should not perish but have everlasting life." John, 3: 16. And in Rom. 5, 8-10, it is also written: "But God commendeth his love toward us, in that, while we were yet sinners, Christ died for us." These passages disprove the above statement, and reveal God's love for man, while an alien.

"This speculation," he continues, "is founded upon the assumption that man at one time was pure and unsophisticated, and far more advanced in physical and intellectual attainment, than at the present period. It is plain that *this* is founded upon a very equivocal and unwarrantable basis, because it is strictly mythological—an opinion that arose from the early conceptions of original evil. It is entirely imaginary, and was handed down through each succeeding generation, undergoing successive modifications, until it was historically introduced into the Old Testament, from which it has been extensively disseminated by theologians." Having himself enforced the doctrine of depravity, does he not in this confess *his* dependence upon the Bible and theologians for his knowledge? Or does he, free from that influence, claim to have discovered *that truth* in the condition of things. Either his theory is mythological, or the doctrine of depravity is a truth. However, although his statements may be thus dependent, Bible teachings do not depend upon his assertion or visionary reasoning. In continuation, he says: "Moreover, the belief in such a defect in the human race—in such an absolute retrogression—is a virtual denial of the superior harmony of Creation, and of the perfection and universal knowledge of the Divine Cause; and the Deity is thereby charged with a want of Wisdom—with an incompetency to produce an *Effect* (which is the Universe) corresponding to himself who is the Cause." How such a system or catalogue of sayings can adhere, and above all, secure multitudes to worship before it, would be a *mystery* but for the fact that *man is depraved*. But he thus concludes: "From this, it is made unequivocally evident that this speculation concerning the design of Christ's advent is only attributable to the fertile imaginations of those who confined their spiritual and natural observations to the superficial inconsistencies consequent on human existence." When the *heart* is the seat of envy, pride, and malice, it is not exceedingly superficial; and when Cain murdered Abel it could not have bordered upon the superficial. When the vicious, tyrannical and blood-thirsty nation subdued and dispersed the meek and innocent, it must have been more than superficial. "Thus," p. 334, "the two nations warred together. Devastation was the result: but soon the terrific combat was ended; and Cain, the overpowering nation, usurped the wide dominion of the whole earth!" Was this *superficiality?* If so, what would constitute *reality?* "Again," says the "Seer," p. 502, "it is supposed that Jesus came to inform the race of principles never before taught, by and from which mankind might be restored to primitive innocence and spiritual perfection." Here is another defect in his statements, for although Jesus appeared the very embodiment of heavenly Wisdom, it is not claimed that educating the mind alone will save the soul, but it *is taught* that his Mission was to influence man's cold, perverted and dormant heart with divine love; to quicken the soul into life, and beget within it desires for the holy and good, thereby removing the spirit of wickedness, even that which Mr. Davis affirms possesses the heart or internal man. Said Jesus to Nicodemus, John 3: 7–8: "Marvel not that I said unto thee ye must be born again." (Born from above.) "The Wind bloweth where it listeth, and thou hearest the sound thereof, but canst not tell whence it cometh, and whither it goeth: so is every one that is born of the Spirit." And Rom. 10: 10, it is written: "With the heart man believeth unto righteousness." This is the language of the Scriptures upon this subject. Shall the Bible speak for itself, or shall we accept the "Seer's" misstatement as the true faith of the Christian? The doctrine of salvation through Jesus does not therefore depend upon simple intellectual culture, as *the* means of redemption—as *the soul's Savior*, but its Wisdom counsels, and Divine Life by renovating the heart or inclinations, secures the devotion of love, and the obedience of will. "Again," says Mr. Davis, p. 502, "it is supposed that he came to act as a mediator between the Divine Mind and his children. That is, to be a creator of a mutual affinity, such as might join together the universal creations and their Creator!" (This the Bible never indicated, its teachings having reference only to the human family, a very minute part of the universal creations. Does the "Seer" intend to misrepresent?) "to form a connection between Cause and Effect so that a relation might exist between them which never existed." (This is too glaring to merit a reply.) "If he was designed as a mediator, then he was entirely incapable of performing the office for which he was set apart. For how is it possible for a medium to be added to any *already-united* system, the relations of which are the relations of Cause and effect? This proposition is also superficially founded; and its tendency is to destroy in the mind the order and uniformity of the vast creations of the Universe, ALL of which sprang spontaneously from an inconceivable VORTEX by the impulse of one ETERNAL CAUSE."

These statements deny the possibility of the separation of parts or bodies once united; also the existence of a mediumship, or of a mediatorial office. The refutation of the first is demonstrated in common with physical and spiritual action. Two bodies which are held together by attraction, affinity or whatever law may unite them, are frequently separated and their magnetic attraction or centripetal power is either destroyed or so deranged as to be inoperative. This, even the magnet fully proves; also, that when two bodies or substances become through any means so severed as to lose their united action, by extrinsic agents, they may be placed in proximate relation and again become united. This needs no illustration.

The "Seer" will not pretend to deny that minds once affiliated, and bound by the strongest ties may become alienated. If two minds may be sundered, may not more, and if embodied spirits may sustain antagonistic relations to each other, may they not also occupy opposite relations to the sphere of the disembodied? Surely, if there is any law. If these derangements may exist between effects in the earthly sphere, and also between the external or mortal, and the interior or spiritual state, may not a disunited condition, by reason of man's deflection exist between him and his Creator? Or, in other words: if by the violation of law disunity may be effected between man and man, may not the harmony existing between him and superior laws be also affected? And if man violates that law which controls his spiritual and moral harmony, will not that violation affect his relation to the Divine and cause the separation of his soul from the principle and enjoyment of heavenly peace? To these interrogations there is but one truthful answer. Discord is rife with man, and he evinces a want of concord with heavenly or divine spheres. The *great proposition*, therefore, which the "Seer" states, without proof, and by which he tests the Main Doctrine of Christianity, is unfounded. The supposition that a medium or mediator according to the nature of things could not exist, is equally untrue. For in social life the law of mediation is prominent, and every mind is more or less a mediator. Individual and national discord is not unfrequently adjusted by mediatorial aid: and the mediator, to prevail, must be in sympathy and possess the confidence of the dissevered parties. Moreover, his capacity must accord with the nature of the undertaking, and be adequate to the office he is to fill. By such means prodigals are restored to the bliss of home and the full possession of parental love and favor. Rebel provinces are also redeemed from hostility and consequent ruin, and blessed with the protection of those governmental laws, which by their violation had been a terror. And may not the sinner be brought back to God by means of a suitable Mediator? And by the union of the Divine, or Spirit of Life with perfect humanity in the person of Jesus, the doctrine of Redemption renders him a suitable Mediator between God and man; between perverted souls and the Supreme and Infinitely perfect Spirit. And the object of this Office of Reconciliation is not to *create* a union which *never existed* between the race and Heaven; but to restore that harmony lost by reason of perversion. This is a simple and unadorned statement of the doctrines of the Inspired Word, upon that inconceivably important question. And how unlike the Seer's expose.

It is indeed strange that a Work so lofty in its pretensions, should wander so far from truth. But, although its profession is to reveal Nature, it evidently is an intended effort against the Scriptures; and having that object ever most prominent, it does not seem to regard so much the truth in what it assays to reveal, as the destruction of what it has undertaken to overthrow. Thus, and thus only, can we account for its many unphilosophic declarations; especially those pertaining to metaphysical and moral sciences. Truly the entire display reminds us of one who, although ignorant of the laws of health, and also those of remedial agents, proffers his diagnosis and prescriptions to the sick, not knowing whether the treatment will destroy or save life. To assume the discussion of all the abstruse questions pertaining to physical, spiritual and moral philosophy, and display so little knowledge of their principles, is but to quack in Science and Religion.

Immediately preceding the paragraph last quoted, the following bitter denunciation of the Christian Faith is recorded: "The belief that Christ was to be a medium, by and through which man might ultimately ascend to higher spheres, is a belief which is most unrighteous, and has a tendency to create hostility, exclusive sectarianism, and presumptive arrogance. It elevates one above another, and tends to establish exclusive privileges." Had the author of these epithets been a heathen and never heard the name of Jesus Christ the "Anointed" as "Savior," we might not wonder so much at his charge. Or, had he been dealing with christian imperfections, with the manifestations of spurious professors of the religion of Jesus, there might be some apology for him. But when expounding the *Christian Faith* there is not; for he either should have understood the Principles of that Faith or not made the attempted expose. If he had understood the name "Emmanuel," "God with us," or been familiar with the great social Criterion given by Jesus to his disciples: "Love one another as I have loved you: greater love hath no man than this, that a man lay down his life for his friends." "Whosoever would be chief among you, let him be your servant." "Blessed are the meek, for they shall inherit the earth," etc. Had he been familiar with these Christian principles he never could have introduced this catalogue of unjust epithets against the Faith of the Gospel. But rather, would have reproved the professional world for want of perfect faith and obedient lives. But he continues: "It breathes envy, bigotry, and superstition, into the heart of man, into the bosom of society, and almost causes the human judgment to sanction the same. It is a belief that depreciates the constitution of Nature, of man, and of spiritual principles, together with that CAUSE who breathed them all into being. It is indeed a belief unworthy the human affections; it is too unholy to be entertained even by the uncivilized of earth; it should be banished from the world forever, because it is destructive to a proper knowledge of the cause of human existence, of the characteristics of man, of his spiritual possessions and of his immortal destination."

We have finally arrived at the true character and intent of these remarkable Revelations. And here the Christian can see what the Harmonial Philosophy and Harmonial Spiritualism *are*, and to what they tend. This, christian, is the light in which the doctrines of the Cross are viewed by those who are promulgating the sentiments of those "isms." They may declare their high regard for true christianity, but the spirit of these passages from their "Great Book," is the spirit of their fundamental principles. They detest the Bible and its religion. Their Prophet, A. J. Davis, affirms that the doctrine of Salvation through Jesus—the Gospel—"is too unholy to be entertained by the uncivilized of the earth, and should be banished from the world forever." This is the head and heart of the system. It is directly at war with the christian Faith, and fain would banish it from the world. And if it would banish the cause, why not the believer and advocate? Did the Pope say more against the heretic? And having power did he not put to the torture whoever dared protest against his creed? Is the spirit of this denunciation better? If so, in what does it consist? Banishment is absolute removal, by whatever means. Might not circumstances strengthen this, and rather than didactically *urge* the banishment of the Christian Faith, *decree* that it *shall* be banished forever from the world. Moreover, if it became necessary, would not circumstances also introduce the Inquisition, Dungeon, Rack and Faggot, for this object? These are grave questions to propound in this day; and especially with regard to an "ism" that externally presents a visage so bland. But does its mildness, its complacency, change the spirit that prompted those epithets—epithets that appear to emerge from the very heart of the system? The canine creature when young may be as harmless as a babe, but in later years, become most savage. The lion's whelp may sport like a lamb, but in maturity he ranges the forest in ferocious majesty, and at his roar the beasts thereof tremble. Apply this to man, and how verified. He knoweth not himself. He may be republican until the people give him power, then his spirit may unfold into the proud Emperor. Mahomet, when he retired to the cavern in Mount Hara, may not have intended the results that followed. But having first converted his wife, Rhadijah, and his most intimate friends, he proceeded until he drew the sword and forced allegiance. A religion of the perverted heart unsheaths the sword; and the elements of this system are such as to render coercion more than probable. In its present form it originated in, and by the law of magnetism, Mesmerism or Psychology—wears a smile externally most captivating, but its main power is *will.* It holds the victim with a hand of iron, and when once in possession moves at will the subject. It is superficially a law of affinity, but fundamentally that of irrevocable decree. The history informs us that Dr. Lyon mesmerized the author of these Revelations; and while under that influence he delivered his lectures, and Rev. Mr. Fishbough recorded them. The primary law, then, was magnetism. That is, Mr. Lyon, by certain laws of mind induced the young man into a condition not natural to himself. Was not that state one of necessity? Mr. Davis, therefore delivered his lectures under the most stern necessity.

Thence he declared, as above, the christian's faith unworthy of the world. Reduce one half of mankind to a like condition, and then let the inspiring cause determine the banishment of the christian religion with its subjects from the world, and would they not arise to execute the decree? Those familiar with this Science can readily determine in their minds the consequences. The nature and tendency of this power is such as to inspire dread in those of exceedingly nervous sensibility who understand it.

It is also understood that having been moulded by this law, the magnetizee subsequently became the subject of the element and current idea, and often without the aid of a magnetizer passes into what is termed a self-induced state. Such is long since said to have been the case with Mr. Davis. In this, the probabilities of ultimate force are enhanced, for then the prevailing idea will control the passions of the affinitized mass, who thence will move like the headless and unconquerable tide. Obedient, then, to the law which begat N. D. R., if that anti-christian spirit shall obtain to a sufficient degree, no mercy will be shown, but the object of its intention must abide whatever consequences it inspires.

Let not the unobserving call these reflections "dreamy," and lulled by the friends of the cause, deem us wild in our conclusions, for as sure as seed sown in fertile soil ripens into a luxuriant harvest of its kind, even so the spirit which inspired that bold denunciation, and the law that ultimated it, unless checked in its growth, will thus culminate. Should it he claimed that wisdom controlled this law, we reply that the same is also claimed for the dictations under consideration. And this renders the consequences still more sure and fatal. But as the subject will be discussed at length in our "Review of Spiritualism," we will not further pursue it in this relation.

Let those who are disinclined to favor this conclusion, read and carefully observe the spirit of the following, with which we shall close this review; and then enquire if when reason failed, the prompting genius might not deem it important to the good of man for the exercise of force to relieve the world of the dreadful bane? "Again," (p. 504.) "it is supposed that Christ was designed as a medium by and through whom man might escape eternal condemnation. This is indeed an opinion not transcending the theology of the early inhabitants. It originated in darkness—it developed darkness—and is itself so exceedingly dark, that it cannot approach the serene and brilliant light that surrounds the throne of an enlightened reason. Men have been led to believe in the existence of an ocean of unceasing flame, where one wave of fire succeeds another, sustained by the fuel of discarded and damned human spirits, whose sufferings would add to the glory and majesty of the Divine Mind, who, with all complacency, receives the perfume thereof as the fragrance from an open flower! By him this burning abyss is thought to have been created; and that from him also proceeded the fiery darts aimed by the omnipotent vengeance, of dark and *terrible* damnation. Indeed it is supposed that he is the great *Fire Kindler*, and that he fans the flames by his own breath, and consumes innumerable spirits of his own creation in the bosom of that terrible gulf, that he so *divinely* and so *properly* originated." According to poetic license the bard may sometimes build without foundation, make airy flights without wings, and ride along the etherial regions without conveyance, and hence we suppose the "Seer's" song is admissible, especially since he indulges so freely in his eloquence; and more particularly since he began with a song of Fire, of flaming Vortices, of Lava Oceans; and in One of immense heat and magnitude discovered his great Positive Mind, and the soul of the races of intellectual beings: and finally, since he develops in one grand ultimatum all men whence they originated—the great Beginning, a burning abyss, a molten Vortex, by whose ceaseless evolutions one wave succeeds to another to all eternity. We repeat; this being his favorite theme we must tolerate his eloquent strain. And now we will leave him in the midst of his fire-song—back again, where he first began.

REFLECTIONS.

From the peculiar character of this Work, it will be natural to enquire, what the real state was that Mr. Davis occupied, what caused that condition; and also, what principles were engaged in the inspiration of his lectures. As an introduction to our suggestions, the reader is referred to the prefatory remarks on pp. 43–4, A. P. In addition, we observe, that according to the laws governing the mesmeric state, the subject is not the author, and therefore not responsible for what he may say or do. He must, however possess an organism adapted to the development or reflection of whatever is produced. Farther than this, his being has no part in the phenomena, he is only a passive agent for the work. Dr. Lyon, Rev. Mr. Fishbough, and others immediately associated with the magnetizee, were the authors of N. D. R., rather than Mr. Davis. It is hardly necessary to appeal to the science or its demonstrations to confirm this position. Every Magnetizer, and Psychologist, by each trial or exhibition supports this idea. Indeed, otherwise, there would be no such science. By the laws of mesmerism or psychology realities may be rendered as fictitious or as substantial. A phantom may be made to appear as most divine. All is the same to the subject. He speaks and does what the circumstances inspire or the position mentally controlling him prompts. While in the magnificent and illumined Hall he may be made to believe himself in some subterraneous vault tormented by fiery demons. He may seem to gather ripe clusters of fruit from trees of Paradise, which he imagines stand in luxuriant growth around him. He can ride Pegasus to the remotest star, or paddle his canoe in the raging sea. The dunce may be made to suppose himself Demosthenes, or Galileo; Cæsar, Bonaparte, Washington or a blooming sylph. The man of sense can be made to imitate the booby, or believe himself a monarch and issuing his murderous edict; an humble peasant or a doomed inhabitant of lost worlds; or even in the presence of the great I AM. And all this can be produced by one controlling mind. The subject then, is, by the nature of his condition, compelled to speak what the circumstances inspire, hence what he cannot avoid. All being a work of necessity induces in him a sense of right, and especially so since he cannot conceive of power to move in an opposite direction. To him the influence of his sphere is Omnipotent. It encompasses and pervades his being, and therefore he feels its immensity. The force of mind operating with him overcomes him, and the influx upon his sensitive soul is so overwhelming that he supposes himself the recipient of divine breathings. His spirit is quickened, his perceptions become exceedingly active, and he fancies himself sipping at the fountain of Wisdom. Such was evidently the case with Mr. Davis when in his superior condition. The united minds about him encompassed him, and he existed beneath it as beneath a divine pavilion. Its compass transcended the capacity of his intellect, hence he deemed himself in an exalted sphere of intellectual immensity, whose movement appeared as the ceaseless breath of infinite thought. He roamed beneath a magnificent dome of inconceivable magnitude. The currents of mentalized nerv-aura converging upon him caused him to believe himself in the immediate sphere of the Divine, the presence of the Unknown. The magnetizer and his group, ignorant of the real state of the subject, and awed by the novelty of the scene, imagined the sleeper in the presence of new and more exalted modes of existence, and become impatient for the revelations. This desire changed the form of Mr. Davis' sphere, and he became *impressed* that he must bestow upon man *some* of his divine conceptions. Obedient, therefore he began. His novel condition, induced a somewhat novel mode of expression. Thus interested, his circle, of necessity, began to anticipate superior disclosures, the exposition of nature and the character of causes. By this mutual operation upon each other, extreme transcendentalism was induced, hence the Revelations. Nor did the subject for a moment conceive his sphere composed of the elements immediately connected with his mundane nature. In other words, that he rested upon the mental apex of his magnetizer, which was sublimated by marvelous and imaginary excitement, and his magnetizer upon that of the friends around him. And that from this position he was gathering the fruit of that mind sphere. Neither did the circle for one moment imagine themselves recording their own thoughts, somewhat transformed by the circumstances, and uttered by the instrument of their united minds.

Such are the consequences of mental illumination by means of animal magnetism. And Mr. Davis' Works prove such to have been his condition, and the major causes of his inspiration. Upon these principles alone can the vague complexity and contradictory nature of the lectures be accounted for. True, he claims sympathy, yea, direct converse with super-mundane spheres; but however much man's nature renders him capable of such sympathy, N. D. Revelations evince *very little, if any,* of that attainment. The entire philosophy, seems only a repetition of the knowledge or the notions of men; and that, upon which so much is expended, viz.: the ignorance of the young man, Mr. Davis, is merely a play upon the marvelous. Time was when this extraordinary claim might pass, but modern developments are revealing the mystery, as the result of the most common laws of human existence.

Mr. Lyon was a disbeliever in revealed religion, and the Rev. Mr. Fishbough was a man of superior literary and scientific attainments, as his writings abundantly reveal. Add to these,other men of noted ability who were in almost constant attendance, and the marvel is accounted for, and upon principles connected with the mind and magnetic nature of man, and without calling to aid the higher spheres. The Book has awed into profound reverence its thousands, but the day cometh when its marvel-mask will be removed by the familiarity of the phenomena of mental sympathy, then men will wonder why well informed minds became so easily led by it.

We only add, that although the Work admonishes the world to discard the marvelous, and seek for truth in Nature, simple and undisguised, still the very marvel of its production by an unlearned youth is foremost in its commendations, and by this means has most obtained.

APPENDIX.

DAVIS ON SPIRITUALISM.

As Mr. Davis is now figuring quite largely in the spiritual ranks, and as his sayings are by many considered unfailing truths, we propose in this connection to consider briefly some of his reasonings upon that subject. And we shall select that portion which reflects most directly upon the moral philosophy of N. D. R.

It is unimportant that we inquire into his mode of conversion to modern spirit manifestations, any farther than to say, that when the "Rappings" were first emerging from Hydesdale, N. Y., he declined endorsing them as real. However, as he has since written much in favor of "Spirit Manifestations," we accept him as a convert to the truthfulness of the phenomena.

That which we propose to consider is his philosophy of good and evil spirits. Upon this subject the reader is referred to p. 206, of a work written by him and published in 1853, entitled: "The Present Age and Inner Life of Man; A Sequel to Spiritual Intercourse." "Although I have impartially examined all so-called demonstrations of evil spirits, and have been careful to be led in willingness of mind to any legitimate conclusion, nevertheless I have been utterly unable, from the evidences, to arrive at any results antagonistic to those expressed in the foregoing chapter. But the doctrine of evil spirits will be reconsidered in succeeding pages. . . . I am persuaded that the reader who has accompanied me through the 'Table of Explanations,' will not be terrified by the demonological disclosures to which the present chapter is devoted. These are a class of nocturnal, mysterious, and exceptional phenomena quite worthy the consideration of thinking men. Swedenborg and his followers—'The Receivers of the Doctrines of the New Church'—unreservedly advocate the theory, that corrupt and evil spirits, of both sexes, utterly dissolute and abandoned, enter in at the open door of every correspondingly-inclined mind, and tempt it to the commission of crime,—deeds dark and destructive to all the divine interests of the soul. And a doctrine no less hideous, though not so manifestly involved amid psychological complications, imagination, and pandemoniacal windings, is indefatigably taught by nearly every catholic and protestant clergyman. These doctrines, I think, are not wholly imaginary. There is, unquestionably, some hidden psychological source whence they spring. And as the media through whom these revelations are professedly made are usually firmly convinced, as already shown, that the communicators are malignant spirits—real demons from a veritable pandemonium—therefore kind reader, it becomes us, as candid examiners of all facts in the wide field of spiritual intercourse, now thrown open, to let no prominent demoniac cases pass without a careful and impartial inquiry. With this motive prompting us, we will hesitate no longer, but proceed directly to cite and examine several strange revelations. In the 'New Era,' dated Boston, March 9, 1853, I observed an article containing graphic descriptions of several 'Astounding Facts,' arranged for publication by J. A. Gridley, M. D., which should not remain unnoticed. The circle in which the facts are reported to have occurred, was composed of strong nerved men, with their families, who could not be induced to continue in the circle while several of the astounding facts were in process of development. It seems the proceedings were terrific. 'We have seen the medium evidently possessed by Irishmen and Dutchmen of the lowest grade.' The medium was seen to 'snap and grate his teeth most furiously, strike and swear, while his eyes flashed like the fires of an orthodox perdition.' These are strange freaks of Nature! Few facts come to us so freighted with discord and indications of pandemonium. 'We have heard him (this medium) hiss, and seen him writhe his body like the serpent when crawling, and dart out his tongue, and play it exactly like that reptile. These exhibitions were mingled with the worst wrangling and horrible convulsions.'

"The preceding and subsequent facts are related with particularity, and the writer is manifestly a full believer. 'If we have ever been skeptical before,' he remarks, 'after what we have witnessed, we shall never doubt again the Bible statement, that an obsessed man in olden time, who was well acquainted with Christ and Paul, but who possessed but little respect for the seven sons of Sceva, a Jew, so he leaped upon them, and before they could make their escape from the house, he overcame the whole of them, stripped them of their entire clothing, and tore their flesh, so that they left the house naked and wounded. We have heard these evil spirits lie a score of times, as fast as they could speak.' One of the spiritual friends of the writer, Briant, 'has told us that if he and his associates in goodness should deliver N. over to his tormentors, during his worst seasons of obsession, these demons would, in all probability, permanently possess him, like the man 'who dwelt among the tombs.'' Such facts are truly startling, especially to persons who cannot penetrate the thin gauze which separates effects from causes. . . . What shall the reasonable mind conclude from the 'astounding facts' above related? . . . The narrator is unhesitatingly and peculiarly emphatic, in the employment of the epithets and unbrotherly terms of description. . . . Not to question the assumptions of the relator," continues Mr. Davis, "let us enquire on the supposition that the spirits were low and undeveloped in character and motive, 'did the writer feel kindly toward them?' Did he feel commiseration for them in their low and degraded state? Did he experience combativeness, and throw out from his individuality a positive sphere of repugnance and hatred toward the opposing powers? . . . Nay? He unqualifiedly termed them 'demons,' 'devils,' 'Legion.' etc.—thus developing sentiments of opposition in the spirits present; a result, under the circumstances, scarcely avoidable, even on the hypothesis that the contending powers were intrinsically righteous."

It will be noticed that in his comments, he discards the idea of evil spirits. And indicates, at least, that no unpleasant manifestation would have occurred had not the spirits been provoked, leaving us to infer that his opinion is, no discord, absolutely as such, exists beyond the pales of mortality. He also admonishes against employing unkind epithets; that is, he would teach us to employ terms not indicated in the nature of the case, least by giving discordant and malicious manifestations their appropriate appellations, or even indulging unkind feeling, we should offend the spirit, and cause him to reveal a demoniacal disposition. As if a sleeping lamb, if awoke in a way not pleasing, would arise a ferocious lion. Thus he makes the nature of the spirit, or manifestation, dependent upon the mode of extrinsic inspiration and not an inherent or absolutely incorporated principle. It doubtless is wisdom not to disturb dormant evil, but how a dove can, by annoyance, be transformed into the vulture, is, as yet, unexplained. It is quite probable with all his sophistry he cannot induce the christian to believe that opposition can change the heart of a holy angel into that of a mad fiend. Or that by antagonistic manifestations, Jesus of Nazareth could have been made angry and inspired with the spirit of a madman. The "Seer's reasoning would reduce all heaven to a condition liable, at any moment to be transformed into a perfect pandemonium; or, by opposition, change the character of the Almighty, and thus reverse the order of universal movement. No! such reasoning is fallacious; it proves too much; it can never be verified. And what is most strange, is, that while seeking to avoid one condition, he has removed his own "platform." But, if discord and manifestations of a most grievous character are mere effects, it is quite evident that there can be no effect without a cause, neither can cause, unless it be absolute creator, which this philosophy denies, proceed to effect without adequate principles to operate with. Explosion would create no sound if there was no atmosphere, nor could oral speech affect the sense without the organ of hearing, or the mind conceive of color without the eye. And there must be the existing element, else such a discordant and demoniacal manifestation could not have so suddenly developed. Therefore, the manifestation was either entirely dependent upon the external, or the spirit was primarily evil inclined. If entirely external, it goes far to disprove his theory of spirit manifestations. If evil inclined in a primary sense, the foundation of his magnificent scheme is removed and all his efforts vain. Again of this clause: "We have heard these evil spirits lie a score of times," Mr. Davis remarks: "This is assumed. He may have heard the *medium* utter a great many contradictory things. But how does he know that spirits provoked the utterance?" This is indeed, strange language for a spiritualist. How does Mr. D. know that a *spirit ever* provoked utterance? It is proof equally as strong against one character of manifestation as another. The inference from his criticism is that the spirits are no way connected with discordant manifestations; that they do not originate in the interior. This cannot especially favor his theory, for it must be equally so with harmonious communications, since men have no means of demonstrating that discordance *does not exist* in the spirit world, and may not be revealed to the external by spiritual intercourse as well as harmony. Therefore the principle of his effort is false, or "spiritualism" is not a reality but a fiction. Hence his labors, from the first page of N. D. R., through the Great Harmonial, etc., are founded in imagination.

Again he quotes: "The devils stung to madness," and replies: "How does he know this? The medium may have been *frenzied* by a contention between the cerebrum and cerebellum—a severe struggle between the vital magnetism and vital electricity in the nervous system—implying the imperfection of his psychological state—implying, moreover, that spirits, or the terrestrial circle, had *partially* got him under magnetic influence." This is as much to his own disadvantage, also, as against the cause he is opposing, for relative to his spiritual "Congress," p. 82, etc., it may be with equal propriety propounded: "How does he know? Perhaps he was under the influence of unbalanced excitement. Not that of contention; but, the one portion of the brain may have been entirely dormant while the marvelous and imaginary may have been actuated, hence he may have supposed he saw harmonious spirits." Such reasoning is plainly one-sided, and entirely sectarian. He has *assumed* against the doctrine of evil spirits, and distorts even his own manifestation into uncomeliness, if he does not entirely annihilate it in order to carry his point.

Mark his reasoning on p. 212: "Permanently established in numerous minds is the oriental philosophy of good angels and evil demons. . . . It is a thoughtless, unintellectual, barbaric method to explain *the discords* of humankind—the good and evil apparent—the human and the bestial characterization of our species." If this idea, false or true, be "permanently established in numerous minds," according to his own theory, man may bear his permanent impressions with him beyond the grave. And there are many who have "permanently established in their minds," if they die while unholy and discordant, they will exist in an evil state, yea, will be evil hereafter, Such in the spirit world, admitting they are not really so, will, in their own estimation, be evil. And being discordant, should they possess a medium, would produce all the effects that an evil spirit could, hence the manifestation of such spirits would be virtually evil, and betray, really, what a mortal could properly denominate demoniacal. In this, also, his own reasonings provide for all the "writer" of the article he is criticising claims. But in the following he strengthens this application of his reasonings, by saying: "The ideas of the brain, 'uttered or unexpressed,' descend into every department of the dependent organism. From hence a sphere issues, which tinges and affects favorably or unfavorably as the ideas are, every thing as well as every person with which the individual comes in contact. . . And, so if his ideas be false in their relation to each other, all beneath, according to the established principle, must also be characterized in a similar manner. The subtle essences of the thinking principle in man, with all their inconceivably minute attenuations, flow beneath and ascend above every thing pertaining to the Individual and to the orbit in which he moves. As this is true of every person, so it is that minds assimilate to each others' structure and inclinations."

From his own reasoning it has been shown that spirits may be evil in their own belief, (and as a man thinketh, so he is liable to be) hence he may be evil in his deeds. Now he states that one mind may influence another. And as there are really inharmonious and evil minds as well as harmonious and good, it follows that evil minds may influence each other. If so, bands of evil-inclined spirits may exist in the spirit world. This borders very much upon that orthodoxy he dislikes so exceedingly. And if spirits can approach and affect the medium in the external, it also follows, according to Mr. D., that they will impress them with their own likeness. Therefore, while laboring to expose the error of the "writer" upon the manifestation of evil spirits, he has most certainly established the possibility of its truth, and disproved his own theory. His philosophy, also, proves that good and holy spirits affiliate and strengthen their sphere by association; and if they communicate with man their influence will be decidedly good. And as the imperfect sphere is negative to the perfect, it is not probable that a word uttered by a mere mortal, and by reason of an honest misunderstanding, will be liable to set a band of good spirits into the manifestation of diabolism. If, then, spirits do commune with men, in this age, and connected with the phenomena are evil, or discordant manifestations, they are as liable to be from discord, existing with the communicating spirits, as are the good and harmonious to be from pure spirits. And especially so, if his "perception," recorded p. 216, "Present Age and Inner Life of Man," is correct. "It is," he remarks, "most beautifully clear to my perception, that the indwelling forces of the mind are pure, and, in germ, as perfect as THE FOUNTAIN from which myriad streams of spirit-life flow."

When media are *en rapport*, with spirits, it must be the indwelling forces of the mind which are thus sympathetically affected. Those forces being proximate to the spirit sphere nearest earth must first sympathize. And the Author's perception is that they are as "pure and perfect as the fountain from which streams of spirit-life flow." If the spiritual element of man is pure and perfect, it cannot transform the character of the manifestation from good to evil and thus prove an imperfect conductor; but is a faithful reflector of the Cause within, which is seeking through such means, manifestation without. Neither can the defect be attributed to the physical medium, for it is a mere instrument for the spirit, and is, moreover, according to N. D. R., a perfect representation of the spirit. The character of the manifestation, then, as to good and evil, must depend upon the spirit communicating. One of these positions must be true; either the spirit is evil, which at once destroys the system; or the spirit of the medium is exceedingly imperfect; and this also renders void the scheme. Or the body is a horrible jargon of principles and parts, a pandemonial epitome. And such would also prove fatal to his cause, for he informs us that the body is a perfect representation of the spirit, and therefore in that light the body would reflect back upon the spirit again, yea, even upon the Divine Mind! Test, then, the Author, by whatever law existing in nature, or mode of her manifestations, and the result is the same. To avoid a confession of the most natural cause, he does away his own philosophy. But notice his conclusion, p. 213: "Hence theologically or mythologically to separate the world of mind, in this sphere or in any other, into opposite parties and factions, or even to have *the mental* tendency to do a thing so prejudicial to human happiness and universal Brotherhood, is simply adding fresh fuel to an old altar-fire, whereon *Reason* has from the first been sacrificed; it is bowing the knee to an Egyptian Myth; paying reverential homage at the shrine of sheep and goats. I must lose all power to penetrate the nature of man—I must die to the sublime and unchangable philosophy of the Universe, replete with endless concatenations of cause and effect—and become confirmed in error or sectarianism—before I can consent to poison my affections and stupify my judgment with the doctrine that the earth, or any lower or higher plane of the divine creation, contains positive antagonisms, in any intrinsic sense whatever." We have quoted this paragraph at length that the reader may see how self-blinded a man may become by a sectional notion. The author expatiates upon his position "that no positive antagonism in any intrinsic sense exists." It will be remembered that he is equally as eloquent in disclaiming the existence of *effect* without adequate cause. Antagonism does exist, and to a very great extent, with man. Indeed, it is most prominent, by far, in human history. It must have a cause, for no such effect can exist without a cause, and that cause must be positive, and in an intrinsic sense, being essential to the production and existence of the effect. The "Seer" is going to "lose all power to penetrate the nature of man—die to sublime and unchangable philosophy, and become confirmed in sectarianism!" *before he will* poison his affections and stupify his judgment, by consenting to the existence of that which exists wherever he can turn his eyes; which *severs families*, communities and nations; and which has hung its dark pall over the whole earth; made desolate homes and covered battle-fields with the dead. If the causes of such results are not positive in some intrinsic sense, positiveness does not intrinsically exist, and vast and mighty effects may be produced without cause. But such are the labors called into action in order to avoid the doctrine of evil spirits. A doctrine that is demonstrable in its consequences perpetually with human kind.

A physician wishing to induce convalesence in his patient, seeks the real *cause* and *malignity* of the disease, rather than to *smother prominent symptoms.* He does not tap the nerves to draw blood from the system, nor amputate a limb for the tooth ache. If the patient is laboring under an affection of the heart, he does not strive to locate the disease in the head in order thereby to treat the brain. Hydrocephalus is not the dropsy of the chest, but of the head. Nor is bronchitis an affection of the dorsal vertebræ, but an inflamed state of the membranous ramifications of the trachea. Winter is not because the first month of the year is denominated January rather than May, but because of the absence of what constitutes the vernal season. Discordance is not because men believe in its existence and thence announce it, but because of the absence of elements necessary to harmonize; and also the presence of principles which create disunity. Evil is not, because unnamed good, but the want of purity; and because of the existence of opposite principles. To say that the sea is *terra firma*, and the idea of its liquid state a myth, or the result of diseased nerves, might do for song, but he who attempts to cross it on horse back might pay dearly for his folly. Even so with the questions relative to evil. Name it whatsoever you may, it is nevertheless evil.

After having quoted extensively from the narrative of evil communications given by J. A. Gridley, M. D., the Author, in the following manner introduces another instance selected for his purpose, and by his comments evidently expects to *close up* this foolish dogma (as he deems it) of evil spirits. "A *most thrilling* narrative," he says, p. 222, "has recently come into my possession, and as the witness or writer has experienced many wonderful things, bearing on the question of evil spirits, we proceed to place him with his 'astounding facts' (?) before the bar of judgement."

Succeeding this statement is a narrative occupying many pages. But as our limits will not admit of the history in detail, we introduce the following abstract: "For many days," says the writer, "I had not been in my usual health. . . . My attention was aroused by hearing my name distinctly pronounced. . . The thing was repeated so often, without my being able to find any clue to its meaning, that I became seriously annoyed. . . . I distinctly heard a considerable company of persons talking with each other. . . . I looked to the right hand and left, but no one was near me. . . .

And yet this talk continued to go on, and was heard by me as distinctly as I ever heard any thing in my life. And now, if I could credit those ghostly whisperings, a group of demons had long been hovering about me, prompt to seize the occasion of my peculiar physical state, to urge me to that which, they trusted, would be my destruction. . . . No sooner had I addressed them, than they evidently became greatly excited, and one of them was sent to summon their superiors. He soon arrived, as I could judge from several sounds, and brought an additional throng of demons with him. . . All this while, I may mention, this diabolical troop had cursed and blasphemed more wickedly even than men are wont to do. . . 'We must have him,' they exclaimed, 'or he will do us infinite mischief; he will betray us to the world, and we shall lose all our power over men.' . . . Every moment new spirits arrived, and as before, their torrid atmosphere enhanced the violence of the fever-flames that preyed upon me. . . . But I suffered in mind too, as well as body. . . . The horrible thought came over me that the Divine Being had forsaken me!" Speaking of one whom he seemed to have recognised as one he knew while on earth, he continues, p. 228: "There seemed no bound to his fury at my detection of his identity and present condition. It seemed to me as if forgetting his want of a material frame, he had tried to dash himself against me and rend me. Certainly he hissed serpent-like in my ear, and put in action a new engine of diabolism. He made a sound, as if spitting at me; and he no sooner did so, than I heard the others exclaim, 'That is right—that will weaken him.' . . . How dreadful was the complication of my sufferings. I could feel the deadly simoon go through and through my brain, burning and stinging, while before my eyes was a wavering and shimmering, as of heated air-currents. At last from my inability to sit up longer I went up to my bed-room, with how much awful forebodings you may possibly conjecture."

In his bed chamber he reports they assembled and continued the torture until he was overcome. "On—on—monotonously, sonorously on—went those fiery respirations, till without and within, from the head to the feet, my whole frame felt as if, like that of Kehama in Pandalon, it were transmuted into one living coal! . . . A strange accompaniment of all this was, that outside my window their seemed to be a vast world, which was not this our material world, or at all analagous to it, but in which, as in their famed whispering gallery of old, the faintest sound, uttered in one extremity, ran reverberating round a vast concave, till it passed off like thunder tones at the opposite. In that world, I heard the noise of a countless multitude of demons and men. . . It was hell in very truth, the home of all jarrings and clashes and blasphemies, and mad mirth, all having a pungency such as naught can create but the sharp ministries of pain alone. I never listened elsewhere to such wit and fun; I never heard before such peals of laughter, now rising into screams, now exploding into stunning uproar. Voltaire never mocked with such razor-edged keenness at religion, its office or its historic claims; nor Paine uttered ribaldry so brutally coarse. . . . Thus they went on a long while, vaunting themselves the hidden springs of numberless crimes and disasters in all quarters of the globe; and ever and anon, as they completed some relation of wretchedness and ruin wrought by them, a peal of blood-curdling laughter ran roaring and shrieking around the echoing concave that overhung them. . . . There was the keen pungent jest, whose keenness could come only from a mind whose faculties were edged by habitual suffering; there was the sarcasm cast upon religion and its requirements, and upon virtue and all its manifestations, evidently prompted by despairing remorse at having proved recreant to religion and virtue; there was occasionally a snatch of singing, and once a song of several stanzas chanted by several accordant voices. And, oh, what a song was that! The voice was exceeding fine, and it seemed as if, for a moment, the very soul of early innocent days had come back to breathe through them, and mingling with the sadness of the hopeless present, gave pathos to the tones as they swelled and sank, that made the chant inexpressibly touching. I could not restrain my tears, even on that couch of fire. . . . It was now approaching morning, when feeling an unusual intensity of heat over one vital organ, I heard one of the party exclaim, 'Now you are going to hell—now I'll pay you for charging me with low dissipation. . . . I'll repay you, for you shall burn in hell before morning.' . . From this, strangely enough, I got to questioning my agreeable companions about the place of their abode, its appearance, usages and conditions. Two or three of them made some few replies, though it seemed, (I knew not why,) difficult for them to speak on the subject of my inquiries, so that I could understand them. I asked them if hell resembled earth in outward appearance. They said yes; that there were lands, waters, trees, grass, &c., there as here. I asked if they dwelt in houses. They replied in the affirmative, but did not give a clear idea of the architecture used among them. They said, too, that they had certain species of grains, on which they subsisted, but they had no horses or other locomotive animals. They told me they all dressed in garments made of a yellowish-brown material, and shaped in the mode prevailing among our oriental people. They bore, they said, much the shape and appearance as when living on the earth. . . . They had among them some thing like the marriage relation, but it was dissoluble at the will of the parties." (How much like the sentiment of some modern philosophers.) "I put sundry other questions, some of them relating to their beliefs on various topics, but the information I obtained was not very satisfactory. . . . I began to strongly hope that the ordeal was over; that by some merciful intervention I was plucked from the grip of the demon host. How then was I startled, when suddenly I heard a stunning outburst of noises without, which showed plainly the whole fiendish throng to be awake and waiting! At the same moment a loud commanding voice called out, 'Have you finished him? Is the work done?' One of the party within the room replied, 'Finished him! no, he's unhurt and sound as ever; and they are asleep. The voice outside, with a blasphemous execration, then exclaimed, 'I must kill him myself, then, and have done with it, for we must and will have him!' In an instant after, some being flew or bounded into my window. . . . I could not see him, but I could clearly discern something like a stick or branch, held, as I supposed in his hand; this he kept waving to and fro over my head. It made a sort of crackling electric noise as it moved, and I either grew or imagined I grew, faint under the process. . . . Fancies began to crowd thick and fast of some new and strange anguish, suddenly to sieze upon the very springs of life, as a consequence of the work which this malignant being was performing in ominous silence. The thought, too, fell blightingly upon me, that I must have been absolutely surrendered by Heaven to the power of the demons to wreak their whole will upon me, else I could not have been left helpless so long in their ruthless grip. . . . I then relapsed into a silence, in which I still had my will, braced as firmly as I could against any consenting surrender to his efforts. . . . At length, as I was on the point of yielding to despair at the thought of my present state, and the recollection of what I had gone through for the last few hours, the 'benediction of the covering heavens,' the merciful deliverance I had so many times implored in vain, descended upon me in the form of a dewy, profound, dreamless sleep, from which, after several hours, I awoke, completely free from the recent disturbance and affected solely with a slight unpaining languor. But the impression of the last night's .events remained; and I thought then, as now, after the lapse of years, I think, that there was more in those events than can be explained by, or than is 'dreamed of in our philosophy,' shallow, skeptical and material as it is. I leave the reader to draw his own exposition. Many will, perhaps, be able to define the nature of my condition; at any rate to their own satisfaction."

Relative to the above narrative, Mr. Davis remarks: "We surely cannot reasonably expect to obtain stronger testimony than the foregoing. And now kind reader, what do you think? Verily, no one can desire *more thrilling revelations from pandemonium.* Now, the explanation of all this is necessarily metaphysical; but I will proceed to give it. . . . In the first place let it be lodged in the mind, as an universal principle, that every man *is a duality*—a double being—a *One*-ness, growing out of the interpenetration of *two* natures. Every man has two different spheres of consciousness—an external, material or sensuous sphere, and an interior, spiritual, or super-sensuous sphere. The external sphere, in man, is the medium of communication with the objects, sensations, and phenomena of the external world, in which we now reside; and the internal sphere, is the medium of communication with the objects, sensations and phenomena of the spirit world."

This dual nature of man, is the hypothesis, upon which he accounts for the discrepancies of his system, manifest in phenomena like that just quoted. Accordingly, p. 240, he thus remarks: "Fifth, It will be found that all the 'devils' of the universe are living in the symbols of the mind—on the *middle ground* between our material and spiritual organizations. What are called 'evil spirits,' originate in the conflicts of the nervous system, when one state of mentality is indulged to the expense of the blessings which the other may contribute or confer. . . . Eleventh: Experience prompts me to affirm, that *good* communications depend upon *good* states of mind. . . . A fever is one state of the body, a chill is the opposite; both are wrong, being out of harmony with nature; and both, therefore, develope 'devils,' in the shape of internal disorders, and 'evil spirits,' also in the familiar shape of pains, aches and mental disturbances. But this is a merely physical illustration! Let us apply this thought to the mind. Now the mind, be it remembered, is the greatest and most fertile source of perplexities. . . . But enough! This explains all; that mental discord, and the symbols of such discord, develop all the conceptions of hells and of demons that ever obtained a footing in this rudimental existence."

Thus, the Author in his comments upon the evil communications under consideration, and all manifestations of an evil nature, claimed to be from spirits, charges the sole origin to the unhealthy state of the medium, or seer, and the result of a deranged and discordant imagination. Hence, whatever manifestation, however great the probabilities of its spiritual origin, that savors of demonology, is not at all the work of evil spirits, but the fruit of medium discordance. For, "What are termed 'evil spirits,' originate in the conflict of the nervous system." Spirits, then, never originate such impressions, because they are from nervous conflict. The author therefore settles one class of so-called spirit manifestations, as having no claim to spiritual origin. And that class amounts to quite considerable of modern spiritualism. So much, therefore, of the phenomena, is, by the "Seer" accounted for upon principles no way involving the spirit world. Perhaps the same kind of reasoning may reduce the other class of manifestations to a like condition, and thence the entire phenomena is proved by him a delusion—himself not excepted. For if all manifestations purporting to be from evil spirits are the manifestations of false conception, and belong entirely to the consequences of a nervous state, why are not all, purporting to be from good spirits, attributable to like origin, viz., the state of the nerves? Who can tell? The narrator of the above scene, truly appears actuated with honest motives, and his vision of, and communication with, the spirits, seems much after the ordinary communications of the day. As to whether the narrative recorded by Mr. Davis was entirely fictitious or real, we have no occasion to offer our opinion, especially in this connection; but we do say that its style and general character, as regards the record of what transpired before the victim's mind, classes it with modern spirit manifestations. And if that was a gross delusion, and all such appearances belong to the human nerve, and thence the false conceptions of the mind, it renders the whole manifestation exceedingly precarious. And who can rely upon either class? The "Poughkeepsie Seer" himself may be, though as truly honest, yet as truly deceived, and his heavenly spheres may be the different octaves of his harmonious nervous system! By this effort, and especially if his philosophy be correct, he has exposed himself and his Oracle-ship to the severest criticism, and rendered his own delusion more than probable. Not willing to *rest* our reasoning and conclusions upon *our im-*

pressions, the following references are had to his works.

In Nature's Divine Revelations, p. 660, while describing what appeared to him as passing before his mind, and when he supposed himself in the heavenly spheres, he thus remarks: "I can read from memory of the spirit; either in the human form or in this Spiritual Sphere, with as much ease as one can read from a book." (How does he know that? Perhaps his nerves deceive him.) "I can converse with spirits distinctly, and learn from them the peculiar impressions and affections of their souls; and this I can communicate to any person in the human form."

The narrator of the "evil manifestations," P. A. and I. L., of M.," p. 234, said also: "From this, strange enough, I got into questioning my agreeable companions about the place of their abode," etc. This Mr. Davis, in substance, says is a conversation the deluded seer held with his own nerves, or the phantom spirits that dwelt in the tabernacle of his own discordant system. Perhaps his (Mr. Davis') communication was also dependent upon what 'symbols' and phantom ghosts his nervous system might be capable of producing. And as mesmeric influence is usually soothing in its effects, Dr. Lyon may have so quieted his nerves as to cause him to have fancied himself transformed into some beautiful and heavenly sphere, honored with the presence of celestial beings, whereas his divine sphere and ecstatic state consisted in the pacific condition of his being, thus induced. By what means can we determine he saw spirits at all?

Page 663, N. D. R., he thus continues: "They are guardian angels to those below them, to whom they are constantly descending, with no other end in view than to gratify their thirstings for purity, and their desires that are holy and celestial." The "evil communications" say that spirits had congregated to torment their victims. Is there more evidence for the truth of one than the other? Mr. Davis only proves himself in the most desirable state. But he continues: "I perceive, also, those plains that are undulating as the gentle waves of the ocean. I behold also those valleys and placid rivers." How does he know but those undulations are the gentle flowings of his quieted nervaura? and the plains the dominion of the nervous system, where softly glide the peaceful currents of his spirit? But again. p. 665, ibid: "Every spirit has an exhalation or bodily atmosphere, which is an exact indication of the quality and purity of its interiors, and thereby are all distinguished."

The victim of the diabolical manifestation, which Mr. Davis judges to have been the effects of delirious fancy, speaks also of the encompassing sphere that attended each spirit. "I felt," he remarks, "the influence of his burning sphere. . . . Every moment new spirits arrived, and as before, their torrid atmosphere enhanced the violence of the fever-flames that preyed upon me." This seems to chime very much with the philosophy of the "Poughkeepsie Seer," differing only in the quality of the sphere. And if this is only the consequences of self-emanations, what evidence is there, that his, is not also? Hence the entire system labored as the Harmonial Philosophy, is likely to be a self-wrought world of thought and imagination? And therefore man is no better for those wonderful Revelations. They were only evolved from the nerve-sphere of the "Seer" and his group.

The next instance recorded by Mr. D. which we will bring into account, is that of the dying child recorded in a pamphlet written by himself, and entitled, "THE PHILOSOPHY OF SPIRITUAL INTERCOURSE." "The hour came at last, and the weeping neighbors assembled to see the little child die. The dew of death was already on the flower, as its life-sun was going down. The little chest heaved faintly—spasmodically. 'Do you know me, darling?' sobbed close to her ear the voice that was dearest; but it woke no answer. All at once a brightness, as if from the upper world, burst over the child's colorless countenance. The eyelids flashed open; and the lips parted; the wan, curdling hands flew up, in the little one's last effort, as she looked piercingly into the far above. 'Mother!' she cried, with surprise and transport in her tone—and passed with that breath into her mother's bosom. Said a distinguished divine, who stood by that bed of death: 'If I had never believed in the ministration of departed ones before, I could not doubt it now.'" p. 53.

This Mr. D. quotes as "a truthful and beautiful instance of spirit seeing;" but how does he know it is truthful? Sure: *because it suits his ideas.* Nevertheless, his reasoning upon the philosophy of 'evil spirits,' greatly clouds this "truthful instance." For the child was sick—her body was dying. It was impulsive, therefore the nerve system could not have been in a good condition, but as it approached its repose in death, the child's foremost idea arose. She had *lost her mother:* THAT was her *great thought.* She was sinking to rest, her pain of body died away, her mind became freed from physical suffering, and then her *mother-thought* assumed form—hence the vision. Such is the truthful interpretation according to Mr. D.'s theory.

Again, p. 73, ibid., Mr. D. remarks of himself: "By direct influx or impression from the highly accomplished spirit of Benjamin Franklin, I learned that we owe principally to him the discovery of this electric method of telegraphing from the second sphere to the earth's inhabitants. The substance of my communication with him on the 6th day of January, 1851, was as follows. I give his own words, faithfully rendered." How do we know that? And how can we know it is a truth? That he saw the celebrated Dr. F. at all? The great idea, forsooth, wrought itself into that notable personage. "In searching out," says that great mind (Dr. Franklin) the numerous manifestations of spiritual presence among the multitudinous sects and nations of the earth, I percieved that the great *general* principle of aromal intercourse had been observed, but never particularly understood, by spirits (the so-called inhabitants of this sphere) whence they have from time to time communicated. In compliance with the great, inextinguishable love I feel for scientific research and exploration, I have steadily—with calm and fervent joy, progressed from point to point in this attainment, by following the principles of *panthea*, or of electricity, into their innumerable windings and diversified modifications. I have contemplated this element's mighty workings in nature's great nervous system," etc. Tried by Mr. D.'s own rule, what evidence have we that he saw or heard any thing at all? Indeed, no address could partake more of the purely external sphere in its style or spirit. It supposes that because Dr. F. discovered the properties of that subtle element, electricity, more fully than had any other in his day, therefore and of course, Dr. F. must have been the great inventor of "Spirit Rappings." If any communication ever bore greater evidence of human nerve-sphere origin than this, it has not come to our knowledge. And it is rendered still more dubious as a spirit communication because given by the "Seer" who claims for himself very rare accomplishments in his Seer-ship; and for whom exceeding much is claimed by his friends. "I then listened," says Dr. F., "to the serene observations of FENELON and WILLIAM ELLERY CHANNING, who declared that from their co-equal researches into the moral and spiritual necessities of mankind, it was their knowledge that, in case such aromal communication could be established, the people on some portions of the earth would listen, and be thereby advanced toward enlightened wisdom, unity and truth. Thus I was assured and positively encouraged that the time had arrived when our *terrestrial* friends had reached that point or *apex* of intelligence which would cause them to investigate whence could proceed those 'sounds'—to search whence came the 'manifestations.' . . . We passed over Western New

York. And particularly at Auburn and Rochester—perceiving there the required pre-requisites—we opened the first communications which have, to any extent, engaged the world's attention and interested the skeptical intellect."

This communication has some peculiar features, and suggests some thoughts of enquiry. While copying from it, we cannot refrain the impression, that the author whished to lead in the exposition of a phenomena to which he was not converted until some time had elapsed from its first appearance at Hydesdale. And also, that if Mr. D. had been as familiar with the spirits as his works profess, why he did not obtain this information, before multitudes were admitting the phenomena, and report it to the world? He should have known that Dr. F. and his associates were experimenting. Why did not the rappings at Hydesdale, when they first reported their spiritual origin, rather than say they were by the spirit of a man murdered in the house, whose body was laid beneath it, simply state that Dr. Franklin, Fenelon and Channing had succeeded in the discovery of a method of communication between the two worlds? It would seem quite as easy to tell the truth as to misrepresent in the outset of their philanthropic mission. But why prolong the analysis? Wherever we read we find the "Seer" involving himself, his writings, and the cause he advocates in endless contradictions. Nor can a distant apology reconcile him with himself or with the divine harmony he professes to unfold.

THE ANTI-PANTHEIST.

AN ORIGINAL WORK,

BY JAMES LEANDER SCOTT.

TO BE PUBLISHED IN NUMBERS.

THIS work will be devoted to the discussion and elucidation of Theories, Principles, Facts, Legends and Traditions — Historical, Social, Scriptural, Ethical, Metaphysical and Cosmical — connected with Man, with his Genesis, Depravity, and prospective and anticipated Exodus from mental, moral and spiritual Darkness.

It will expose errors of False metaphysics, give a full history, reveal the character and falsity of modern "PANTHEISTIC SPIRITUALISM," and prove the incapacity of the "HARMONIAL PHILOSOPHY" to meet the wants of the human soul. w

Being devoted to no party or sect, the ANTI-PANTHEIST will labor to conduct the reader beyond the pale of false religions, and the vagaries and conflicting inconsistencies now flooding the world through Clairvoyant and Necromantic sayings, to the doctrines of the Bible.

TERMS.— 12 numbers, of 32 pages each for $1,00, strictly in advance. Specimen numbers sent to any address

ANTI-PANTHEIST, VOL. I.

PANTHEISM — A. J. DAVIS REVIEWED — ANALYSIS OF NATURE'S DIVINE REVELATIONS, ETC.

This vol. of 288 pages, bound in embossed muslin. Price $1,00.

ANTI-PANTHEIST, VOL. II.

SPIRITUALISM REVIEWED — Reveals two opposing currents from man's earliest history. One Divine, the other Satanic. This work proves the Mesmeric Spiritualism of the present day but the revival of ancient diabolism. m

Printed on good paper, contains 320 pages, bound in embossed muslin. Price $1,25. These Vols. (1 & 2 — 603pp.) bound together, price $1,75.

ANTI-PANTHEIST, VOL. III., For 1857.

THE NIGHT SPECTRE — SPIRITUALISM UNMASKED.

THIS vol. will reveal the hidden mysteries of Spiritualism, disclose the secret workings of the system, together with its deleterious effects upon individuals and community, and will give some instances of the most horrible and tragical character connected with the phenomena.

Those subscribing for 1857 can receive the Jan. and Feb. Nos., now ready. Twelves Nos. $1,00.

A THRILLING NARRATIVE.

THE exciting story of Marietta Davis, related after a nine days' trance. Fifth edition. Bound in embossed muslin. 226 pp.

Address J. L. Scott, or Stephen Deuel, Dayton, Ohio.

DAYTON, O., Aug., 1856. STEPHEN DEUEL, Publisher.

Agents wanted. Agts. & the Trade furnished on liberal terms.

THE REVIEW

OF

ANCIENT AND MODERN

SPIRITUALISM.

L. SOLENTIA.

VOL II.

PHENOMENA ATTENDING

ANCIENT AND MODERN

SPIRITUALISM.

NEW YORK:
O. W. SCOTT & A. G. MARTIN, PUBLISHERS
1862.

CONTENTS OF VOL. II.

CONTENTS.

PREFACE.

THE design of this volume is to analyze Spiritualism as reflected from the earliest history of man, and along succeeding ages to the present era. And by the review of ancient spiritualism is revealed the absolute distinction between two currents, their opposite natures, and antagonistic procedures; the Omnipotence, when tested, of one, and the effeminacy of the other. The Bible is sustained as the Book of divine Inspiration; and the opposite current, by revealing its own character, proves itself evil-inclined, and at perpetual variance with the Spirit of Life. The following is the order of the Work.

I. As a competent counterbalance to the modern visions and so-called spirit productions of anti-Christ, and as an introduction to the analysis of Spiritualism, past, present and to come, an Anti-Pantheistic vision, given at Louisville, Ky., June, 1855, is introduced, and without comment respecting its genuineness, further than its absolute utterance by one in a trance state. Its sentiment being strictly Biblical, maintaining the doctrine of a "Satanic" influence affecting man, the doctrine of "the fall," of "depravity,' and of "salvation through Jesus," render it unobjectionable as to its teachings, and therefore admissible as a religious argument against spiritual infidelity.

II. The Scriptures are also introduced, and their record of divine Interposition contrasted with the modern Manifestations, by which the developments of the present age are discovered most inferior, and unworthy, while the Bible is honored and decidedly proved the Word of Inspiration—the manifestation of divine Dispensations; hence unworthy of equal comparison with the spiritualism of the Nineteenth Century.

III. The phenomena of mesmerism, clairvoyance, somnambulism, psychometry, spirit-seeing, etc., of former times are proven of like nature to the present, and by virtue of their proximity to these times, absolutely as delirious and also linked to modern spiritualism; therefore, the phenomena of this day are found not to be a new development, hence afford no evidence of man's having greatly progressed, thus establishing a false claim on the face of the manifestations.

IV. In the conclusion it is shown that the mesmerism of the Nineteenth Century, and the phenomena connected with A. J. Davis, who, by his friends, is called the "Poughkeepsie Seer," are the sub-principles in, and were the foreshadowing of Magnetic Spiritualism, since developed. It is also stated and amplified, that the Lectures of A. J. Davis, given while under the magnetic force of Dr. Lyon, comprehend, if they do not beget, what has been exhibited by the media of spiritualism; that "Nature's Divine Revelations" reviewed in Vol. I. of this discussion, contains the philosophy and theology of that Spiritualism now so active and which is, from its nature, mode of manifestations and results, properly donominated "Magnetic Spiritualism."

V. That those who composed Mr. Davis' circle while in his incipiency, are now with the foremost advocates of that Spiritualism.

This volume leads to the direct review of modern Spiritualism, which is the work of Vol. III.

Finally, the Work is offered as a defence of vital Christianity. Not of an improved Christianity, but of the Gospel as primitively taught, believed and lived by the early christians; and also to furnish those who have not thoroughly studied the subject discussed, with means ample to defeat the influence of that Spiritual Infidelity, which is now flooding the land, and deluding thousands.

PROEM.

SPIRITUALISM: term how full of meaning; and how little understood! Of how much said, and yet how unrevealed. Man's life and sphere, his substance; all—himself! His joys are from its harmonies combined: his sorrows from its wrong. Ever present, yet to him most strange. Sense of his being! Spirit of intelligence. Its nature man doth little know. No moment absent, still he seeks it as of foreign clime. *Its good is thence*, but when disclosed man's grosser sense beclouds its heavenly form. Nor deigns in humble vales to seek it; but pursues imaginative schemes its dwelling place to find. His efforts to secure it outwardly incline, while deep, deep within his sense it has its altar; or deeper still within the Sanctum of the Cause it holds its throne. Man is not *the Spirit*, but the spiritual.

ETERNITY: word of awful majesty! Kingdom unlimited. Infinity in its bosom nestleth as doth the nurseling on its mother's breast. And man the infinitesimal germ trembles round some wandering beam as meteors in the sun-realm of terrestrial spheres. Duration is a faint resemblance of its nameless self.

JEHOVAH: August appellative! is but the retiring echo of a truer name:—Majestic utterance, yet the expiring cadence of the CAUSE thus orally expressed.

THOU most HOLY—BEING eternally unknown, THOU art our FATHER, and heaven the Pavilion of thy Thought thou givest as *our home.*

MOST BENEFICENT. THEE we adore, whom as the Word we know; and best we know thee when in our heart thy Love we feel. All Perfection thou! Our weakness brings us to the dust: thy hand of Mercy lifteth up. In Thee we live; from Thee our sense derive.

POWER OMNIPOTENT! Thou movest immensities. Universe Terrestrial, Spiritual, Celestial, Seraphimal, God-like, Divine; are as inferior stars in unimportant constellations encircling Thee.

LIFE: define it? Never! It *is*, and that is all frail man may know.

SPIRIT: Who hath known thee? Who of thy element conceived? Thou art eternal, and thy shadows dwell in man. Mortality seeth thee not; nor doth gross nature sense thee. Neither materiality confine thee. What thou art, who knoweth? Of what thou doest, peradventure, dependent beings know somewhat! Can read thee in thy works; thy goings forth; and comprehend the degrees of thy movement the retiring wake causeth in thy immensurable Procedure: or in thy receding presence bask as on the bosom of infinity beneath the glory of the eternal Sun. All Spirit-forms are as minutest dew drops trembling on the open flower of time terrestrial, or of duration in the realms above.

THY MANIFESTATION: is whate'er thou doest, and in whatever form.

HATH MAN A SPIRIT FORM that shall survive the ordeal of Mortality? and when the body is dissolved shall it still exist?

QUESTION of immortal worth: how answered? Man endure forever? But why? And where? The Holy Word informs us. BUT DO THE DEAD remember whence they were and those still groping in the dismal realms of shadowy time? And ever to the earth return? Ah! this, *this is the question* of the age! Men seek to know? God of the just do they presume? Have any right, or cause, or means to touch the vail that mortality hath woven?

SPIRITS OF THE DEAD! are ye arousing mortals from their dull lethargy? the pall and sepulchre removing hence forever? inviting men amid the tombs where millions sleep, from whence to pierce the death-night air, that clouds the vision of thy home? Is what we hear the work of your own hands? Are ye "Rapping," "Tipping," "Chaunting," "Unfolding mortal seeing," and "unmasking heaven?" O, ye dead! is this your work? Wisdom from on high, wilt thou the answer give!

TO THE READER.

This volume is devoted to the history of spiritual phenomena, commencing with the race in Eden and concluding with the introduction of modern spiritualism.

As somewhat lengthy passages are introduced from the Scriptures, it may be well to notice that many remarkable events recorded in the Bible, and many prophecies pertaining to all time, and which bear directly upon the subject under discussion, are quoted in full in order to show that the Bible's claims to divinity are infinitely above any and all of the phenomena of modern spiritualism.

There are facts presented in this volume which must establish, in unprejudiced minds, the truth of the scriptures beyond criticism. For the revelation of Divine Power, as shown by the record quoted, reveals the contrast between Divinity and "Spiritualism" in such a manner as to disclose the Divine Nature of one, and the human frailty of the other. And it is moreover established that a like spirit to that revealed in this age, entered Eden, and also induced sun, moon and star worship, possessed and inspired the false prophets, aud opposed Jesus and his apostles. To defend the Christian Religion, to remove the doubts of some, establish the faith of others, and sustain the Truth, has been the author's object in this volume.

THE VISION.

INTRODUCTION.

As the reader has been engaged with the visions of Mr. Davis, all of which are directed against the Christian Religion, the following visionary narrative is introduced as a suitable antidote. We do not represent this as an authoritative revelation, but claim that it possesses evidences equally as favorable, and has as much to secure the world's credulity as the visions of Mr. Davis, or the productious of the various "spiritual media" of these times. If their statements may be admitted as worthy of confidence, this should be. If this is imaginative, and the scenes represented unreal, others of similar origin are quite as likely to be, which may be suggested as the most rational conclusion with regard to the subject.

We employ this peculiar production, and it is in truth peculiar, as before noticed, to prove that the minds of this age, as in all other ages, which incline to visions, are as contradictory as in former times, and also, that modern visions and transe disclosures are not all anti-biblical; and because it is equally as novel, and in style as poetical, and sublime as any modern anti-Scriptural effusion of this strangely visionary age.

INTRODUCTION.

This vision bears date Louisville, K. Y., June 14, 1855, and is reported to be the substance of what was uttered at the time by a person while in an abnormal state.

In view of the above considerations, and to place in opposition with Mr. Davis' visions, this is here introduced and offered to the reader, who will by comparing the two perceive at once their antagonistic natures, and by this determine that a production originating under somewhat strange and marvelous circumstances, does not necessarily endow it with especial merit.

ANTI-PANTHEISTIC VISION.

CHAPTER I.

FIRST IMPRESSIONS OF THE ENTRANCED.

'T WAS mid day in the month of June, while meditating upon the state of man on earth, how little peace, how much of care composed his lot: together with his hope of future bliss, that suddenly the world grew dark, my eyelids closed, and I thought the hand of death upon me. Strong seemed the efforts of the outer man to resist the power now rapidly subduing the energies of my being: but failing I seemed to sink away. I knew no more until apparently awakening in another realm. I thought the struggle over and my soul had found its long sought home of peace. A new and exalted world began to reveal its glories. Immortal groves stood before me fanned by the gentle zephyrs of that holy land. Floral lawns lay smiling in the beau ty of divine perfection. Music, infinitely excel ling all human thought moved along the heav enly atmosphere. Myriads of immortal beings, whose excellency was above a name, appeared before the vision of my enraptured spirit. It seemed some silken veil had been removed, and eternity with its blest inhabitants had appeared in view.

"Is this death?" I enquired as one drew near me.

"Nay! this is life out of death," was the kind reply. The music of the speech overcame me, and again I sank into unconsciousness.

VIEW OF EARTH.

As I slumbered, I seemed dreaming, and in my dream I stood upon a high tower from which I beheld the earth I had just left. Its continents, islands, oceans, seas and lakes, lay beneath me, as one vast plain of loveliness. Large and expanded forests adorned the main land, while verdant islands dotting the seas, gave variety to that which would otherwise have appeared one broad waste. Ships too, were traversing the waters in every direction, like living creatures moving on their different errands. Rivers I also saw. These rising in the mountains, where gurgling fountains emerged from their earthy beds, rippled down the forest hills, until they formed the little brooks, thence dashing along in leaping cascades, gathered with the converging streams, formed majestic rivers. These rivers widened into friths, thence sweeping with their currents the rock-bound base of high promontories they poured their torrents into the broad seas.

"Fit emblem of man, in birth, in life, and in death," said a voice from some one I had not noticed in my dream.

CHAPTER II.

THE VISION: ORIGIN OF EVIL.

Again I awake as from profound slumber, and in a world unknown to me. Strange are my sensations. I am prompted with unusual desires to know and comprehend. The light encompassing me is as the light of wisdom, the illumination of super-spiritual existence—the reflection of living thought. It pervades my being; by its influence I arise, and its inspiration enlarges my soul. Its glory is my pavilion. Former scenes, and their remembrance are receding. Earth appears as an opaque body, far in the distance, and enveloped in a cloud of night. Shall I no more return? And have I passed the river of death? Fain would I still my thoughts, lest their discord disturb the harmony of this sphere.

My destination is toward a sun-like orb whose light infolds me, and as I approach, it reveals a landscape transcendently beautiful: a country most glorious to behold. No abrupt and frozen mountains, ribbed with broken rock-belts, mar the beauty, or break the harmony of its lovely features. But the broad and beautiful plains are relieved by gentle undulations; and the surface appears as if overlaid with a luxuriant carpet of moss, green and velvet-like. The wood presents an appearance of unequaled majesty. No fluctuating climate disrobes the vegetation which thence is clad in perpetual and unfading verdure. The order of the floral lawns bespeaks the perfection of Art, and the trees are arranged in rows, circles, coils; and also direct and wind ing avenues.

There are pools of clear, transparent waters, and jetting fountains interspersed throughout the land. From many of these the sparkling waters are emitted to a very great height, thence terminating in spray are diffused through the heavens, whence purifying the atmosphere fall again in dews upon the luxuriant vegetation. The high jetting fountains are upon the eminences, and jet their waters periodically, that is, once in what man would call sixty hours; while the smaller, located in the lawns and upon the sloping grounds, send forth perpetual streams of the liquid element. From this cause, I perceive the land adorned with an almost infinite variety of rainbow reflections. These combining every imaginable shade and hue, and blending over each other in every conceivable form, render the scene one of surpassing loveliness. No limner can approach the artistic beauty and picturesque grandeur these blending colors reveal. Nor is there in the atmosphere thus softened by the dewy element, that damp chilliness consequent upon like aqueous disseminations in the earth, but it is so pure and graduated, that no excess exposes the climate to change, or any living thing to inconvenience. Here is perfection in very deed: here nature undeviatingly obeys divine law; and here the infinite wisdom and harmony of the Maker is truly reflected. Here is an exhibition of the law of proper development —of progression. No surcharged cloud sends forth its whirling tempest, destructive tornado, and dreaded thunder-bolt; but perfect unity reigns throughout material manifestation. This is harmony, loveliness and divine order.

There is time and measurement here, for I perceive that sixty hours according to Earth's calendar, are equal to one minute, and sixty of these one hour, and sixty hours one day. There is no night, but varying periods: the morning, meridian and eventide. The evening is cool and refreshing, well calculated for repose, and with its balmy calmness merges into morning; and the morning arises into exhilerating noon. Each exerts its benign influence upon all existing things.

I also behold palaces, most magnificent, composed of materials pure and transparent. One of these not unfrequently occupies an area of many acres, and has many compartments of various dimensions. The most capacious are round, but the inferior are octagonal. All are encircled with magnificent corridors, arising many stories high, and are capped by a dome formed of most precious and transparent stone. The center of each discloses an arena graduated according to the general dimensions of the edifice. Within this arena are scales so constructed as to ascend by the application of weight. Each tier has its separate scale. The architecture throughout displays very superior wisdom and skill.

Animals of every imagined species are gamboling over the lawns, or reposing beneath the groves upon the rolling grounds. But there are no beasts of burden.

This is evidently an Orb, but I am not able to determine its true character. It is encircled, tropically, by a channel of limpid water, and at what may be properly denominated the poles are two vast seas. They are animated with living creatures that sport in the bright element, while above, the aquatic bird soars in the aerial realm. Along the shores of these waters are floating at ease vast numbers of pleasure barges of the most beautiful and perfect construction. Bordering upon and encompassing these seas are many inviting cottages and stately mansions, in the midst of beautiful lawns.

Into these seas many rivers empty their bright waters, and thither broad avenues converge.

The woodlands seem animated with birds of brilliant plumage and melodious with their song.

There are eight vast cathedrals, two of which face each other opposite the equatorial channel, and are connected by an arched suspension passage. These situated equidistant from each other around the orb, divide it into four great sections. Midway between these temples are other channels leading from the main one to the polar seas, and bordered with the vegetable and floral productions of the land.

The banks which gently descend from the upper plains to the water, thus adorned, present a landscape of unsurpassed beauty. These rolling grounds are divided into lawns, in each of which are mansions for the homes of the blessed inhabitants of this happy world.

In the inlands are vast pavilions formed of thrifty, properly proportioned, and interwoven trees of a peculiar kind, which are productive of most delicious fruit. The fruit hanging in clusters within the dome apparently forms the inner wall. There are also natural corridors constructed by the interwoven branches. I have no means at present, of describing the interior of this natural structure. Within are females and youths who appear to be partaking of the fruit Persons, however, of different ages and appearance do not indulge in the same quality, but select that which seems adapted to specific conditions. In form and general expression the occupants are perfect. No improvement could be made in their figure or physiognomy. Their complexion is exceedingly fair. Their cheeks are of a rosy tint. Their eyes are lively and the very expression of loveliness. Their hair is of a golden auburn, varying from this to a pure and lovely silver hue. They proceed without effort; and their thoughts are known to each other without utterance. Their motives and actions, are pure and harmless. They think and know no evil. There is music in their speech and harmony in all their movements. I perceive the males of maturity gathered in and about the great Temples for purposes of wisdom and counsel. The light here is entirely unlike that of earth. It is of a gold and silver cast — a happy blending of innumerable shades and colors. The regions seem illuminated with the light of pure and harmonious life, that being void of particles, has no connection with materiality. It is the light of truth, spiritual illumination, and material reflection.

"Truth, primarily," says one standing near, and who now appears as guide and counselor, is the procedure of divine life. The mind encumbered with materiality, or which expects no other light but material, cannot conceive of the nature or existence of this illumination. But as in the physical universe light is reflected from orb to orb, and travels in the vehicle of substance, and is only adapted to material things: so spiritual illumination moves in the chariot of Divine life; and reflects from orb to orb throughout the spiritual realms. God is Life and Truth. In him there is no darkness. From him proceeds, as from the fountain of life, truth and goodness, The radiance of truth, blending with the infinity of moral goodness illumines every intellectual realm which rests upon the durable foundation of moral purity. Light, therefore, is the essence or life of truth. Truth is the eternity of God; and forms the home and mansions of the pure.

"Every plant, flower or tree is pervaded with, and partakes of that light. The very orb itself appears like one transparent body, and being permeated by this principle reflects back its image. The waters, too,—the fountains, brooks, and rivers, the channels and the pacific seas—are of like nature pure and illuminated. Every living thing, seems an embodiment thereof. But the intellectual inhabitants are as lesser *orbs*, from whom radiates the life of light, and proceeds the living energies of truth divine. All are united by this great law, in purest, most vital, and most sacred sympathy; and hence are in harmony with superior realms.

Each individual is a spiritual reflector. They partake of food immortal, drink of living waters, are indestructible, and therefore not liable to physical decomposition. They are immortal!

Their social relations have no just comparison on earth. Each is an epitome of all, and the whole but the enlargement of the characteristics of one. In feelings and concert of action, they are as one heart and voice; the harmonious sense of one great soul—of holy affections.

Far above is an orb in appearance like a sun, whose descending glory illumines this. Volumes of light therefrom, in cloud-like forms move gently in the serene atmosphere, and the effulgence dissipates whatever is of less degree, or purifying, exalts it to superior planes.

"How perfect are the ways of God! How just and right! Whoe'er rebels, ne'er knoweth what is lost, or seeth in God's works the Maker as he is."

CHAPTER III.

THE INFERIOR ORB.

THUS spake my guide, and lo, the scene changes, and we descend to an orb of inferior cast, one somewhat resembling; but more refined than Earth.

Upon the purified orb, there was no evidence of important changes save that of increasing perfections. Upon this, are fallen timbers, broken soil, gathering harvests and beasts of burden. The streams and fountains do not manifest that order which marked the former. The water-courses are more irregular, and abrupt. The beauty of the plains is broken by marshes, and the hills and mountains, (for there are mountains,) by rocky fragments and bold projections. Here the animal races are not as harmonious, and there is less melody in the notes of the feathered songsters. The architecture is less perfect by far than that upon the purified orb. The inhabitants, though comparing in some degree, are inferior to those in the transparent realms. There is not that music in their speech, unity in their movements, nor openness of thought and action; yet compared to our race they are almost infinitely superior. They are industrious, yet their labor is not forced; but is the result of intuition. The exercise does not seem prompted so much by necessity, as the inspiration of delight. If theirs may be denominated labor, it is only the use of their faculties in the sphere of their greatest pleasure. Nature appears spontaneous in her productions, unaided by the hand of art; and their delightful employment seems equally natural and prolific of good. Hence the movements of nature and the habits and inclinations of the inhabitants blend harmoniously, and without interruption result in unitary productions.

There are no signs of death either with ani mals or men, but undisturbed they progress. There are not only the youthful, but also many that evince a life of ages.

Within enclosures of a very peculiar character, there is a fruit-bearing *tree*, having no likeness in the land; and the fruit differs as much from that of the land, as the tree from other fruit-bearing trees.

There are officers appointed to admit those only whose age qualifies them, and, also, to superintend the selection of fruit, which in maturity must harmonize with that of the participant. The fruit resembles the Banana. Its pulp is very white and pure, and the seeds correspond somewhat to those of the Muskmelon. These the partakers preserve, and at stated periods dissolve them with the juices of a fruit common to the plains, and drink the compound. None returns short of seven years from the time they first entered the enclosure, and this they continue until seven such septennial periods shall have passed, when they return no more whence they came; but leaving the natural enclosure, pass into an arched passage, or corridor, on the opposite side from which they entered. This pass is formed of arching trees and interwoven flowering vines, which complete the enclosed archway. The fragrance within is exceedingly exhilerating; and when inhaled infuses itself throughout the system. The construction of this passage is such that no eye from without can witness what passes within.

There is also a kind of air-curtain formed of more condensed atmosphere, which separates the passage into many apartments. Hence, though many are passing, each appears alone. Within each of these, is an attendant, who furnishes the pilgrim with a change of garments. On the right, and also enclosed, are pools of water, in which they purify themselves; and leaving their old apparel, pass to the next apartment, clad in raiment adapted to their advanced state. Thus they pass seven times seven of these purifying processes. Each seventh division is supplied with fruit which grows upon the enclosing vines, and of this they partake. Its effects are not only refreshing, but chemically transform the system. From the forty-ninth, and closing purification, they enter a vast pavilion, around whose walls are magnificent galleries arising tier above tier to an immense height. The occupants are much like those upon the purified orb.

The crown of the cupola has an extensive aperture, over which rests a bright cloud. From this descends the water of life, whose principle pervades the arena and permeates all within.

He who attends me remarks: "Such was the globe on which the inhabitants of the transparent orb once existed. The tree bearing fruit, of which they partook in the enclosure, was, what was known, on that globe, as the *tree of life*. To the possession of which the inhabitants aspired; and were careful to observe all things preparatory to a fitness for the enjoyment of its inestimable benefits."

CHAPTER IV.

CELESTIAL MIRROR: THE UNIVERSAL REFLECTOR.

THE vision has departed, and in a vehicle of light still more perfect I am borne far above, and to an exceedingly high tower in superior realms. Above this tower rests an overspanning canopy, so constructed as to reflect the likeness and reveal the character and movements of all things either animate or inanimate, pertaining to the vast sphere of which it is the center.

From this position I behold the orbs, systems, and their spiritual inheritances throughout what appears immensity of space. The vastness of the magnificent scene is entirely above the comprehension of man while existing in his state of moral depression, spiritual darkness, and mental derangement. No means are afforded to reduce to human capacity a proper miniature of those expanded heavens. Earth's abilities combined cannot furnish the one hieroglyph from which may be read the outlined characteristics of one of those unbounded plains.

While reclining upon the breast of my guide I behold what is transpiring in the light of the dome above me, where figure passes figure, and scene succeeds scene, as imaged from the moving heavens through this Celestial reflector. There I behold the members of every system and the transit of every orb. Yea more, from another and more perfect mirror, which is within the former, I perceive even the inhabitants of different realms, in the vast assemblages that move in the spiritual heavens within the compass of this divine speculum.

"Here," remarks my guide, "thou shalt at the appointed time, sit and read the history of that portion of the vast universe to which thy race doth belong. But for a season, that which is more immediately important shall engage thee. Learn however, that all these orbs, all these moving bodies, which enliven the space embraced within the scope of thy conceptions, are, or have been in like condition to those orbs thou hast just beheld. That is, the same laws affect them, and their inhabitants, when in like condition.

"The vision of thy earth, (when viewed as an example of the works of God,) in its deranged, inharmonious, and perverted state, reflects unfavorably upon the order of divine perfection. To its inhabitants God has revealed the solemn truth of its derangement; that it is not in harmony with universal nature, and that man is a violator of law. And also, in order to redeem and unite him with unperverted beings, God the Life, Creator and Preserver, must interpose, hence it is revealed that he is the Savior of sinners. But man, intent upon finding cause in nature, of all his ills, and also means for his exaltation to the plains of harmony, has rejected the Revelation of God in which is epitomized the cause and effects of transgression, also the means and end of salvation. It therefore behooveth Wisdom to disclose that which hath heretofore been a SEALED MYSTERY to the race."

CHAPTER V.

THE INTERPRETATION OF THE TREE OF LIFE.

"HEAR the interpretation of the TREE OF LIFE of which the inhabitants of the unperfected orb partook.

"The liberty, indulgence and exercise of the youth of that orb were restricted, and they were required to live obedient to laws adapted to that period of their existence; and to partake of appropriate nourishment, until after they had eaten of the *Tree* standing in the enclosure. Thence they were required to live in obedience to the laws adapted to the first seven years; which laws and conditions varied as they advanced. The fruit of which they partook possessed a quality calculated, when taken into the system, to neutralize, and expel therefrom the grosser properties of their being, and to serve as spirit of life, to purify and exalt them to a more refined condition. As the refining process removes from the pure metal the dross, so this served to refine the system. And thus the spiritual being was sustained in its efforts to rise above the more material, and to attract to itself from physical nature, that which was in sympathy with the spirit, and inclined to the spiritual realm.

"The virtue of the seeds, uniting with the juice of the pure grape of that orb, served to perpetuate the action of the transforming element, taken with the fruit, and to inspire and support the more refined properties as they arose with a spiritual being above the material plains.

"The arched passage to the great dome was enclosed by that growth which repelled the influence of the external atmosphere, and shed a fragrance within like spiritual aroma, which uniting with the essence of the fruit partaken, prompted an increased purifying and spiritualizing action.

"As the garments received the material properties expelled, they were frequently exchanged for those new and more refined. The pools served as cleansing and healing fountains.

"Within the great Temple they were baptized with the principles of immaterial Life from the divine effulgence which in a cloud-like form rested above. Beneath that effulgence they remained until the properties of their beings capable of sublimation, were translated from the material to the spiritual; hence, until their bodies became immortal. Thence, existing in a sphere of life superior to the natural plane, they were qualified to repel the gross and perishable influences, and receive as breath of life, supplies from spiritual realms. Thus the immortalized inhabitants became fully prepared to proceed, unaffected by the perishable elements, upon the orb of their genesis, and to be, in due time, translated according to the will of their Creator, to a more spiritual world.

"This is the process by which the transformation of all unfallen beings is effected. But the pre-requisite state, together with the immortalizing fruit has been forfeited by man on the fallen orb. And without especial and divine aid, man, there, cannot arise into harmony with the heavens, or obtain an immortal body. The cause and mode of this loss will hereafter be considered."

CHAPTER VI.

CONSTITUTION OF MIND.

"UNNUMBERED ages elapsed, and the happy beings upon the orb whose immortalizing process has been revealed, had obtained to immortality; and genesis was no more. The vital elements were already controlled by the law of spirit life; the vail was removed that concealed the worlds of superior light. Freely did holy Angels visit the orb, and mingle with the happy multitudes. The song of final transmission from that to a higher plane already moved along the octaves of harmony, and arising mingled with more hallowed notes. Joy and gladness pervaded the peaceful throng, and a deeper life seemed waking from within,—quickened by the inspiration from above. Nature herself, awoke from her sluggish repose, as if newly animated. The animal kingdoms also, felt the animating spirit. The fowls of the air rose higher in the heavens. When lo! as if shocked by some sudden and awful collision, the orb reeled and oscillated in its movements. The mighty dome gave way, fruit dropped from the trees, the beasts ran wildly across the plains and through the forests; and the fowls of heaven, frightened, fled as if hurried by some wild and furious tempest. A sombre cloud encompassed the orb and night set in The angels from heaven departed; mourning and consternation reigned, and the voice of lamentation arose from myriads of prostrate beings.

"Wouldst thou know the mysterious cause? Verily, it is a mystery to fallen man; how, in the universe of mind, those consequences should exist which have succeeded the cause of this deplorable change. And how sin originated is a greater mystery still."

THE EXPOSITION.

"Deep and unfathomable are the laws of mind, and strange that mental and spiritual combination that constitutes an intellectual being. There is a power, by reason of the united attributes, which confirms and individualizes created intellect and forms the soul capable of selecting for itself. Otherwise, men and angels have but brute instinct. There is a combination of spirit-principles whose union ultimates immortality. These are dependent for origin and adaptation upon the creative energy of the Lord; and without him could not have been, could not be. Nevertheless, mind in the abstract, forms its character by its ruling choice. It possesses ability to enjoy—to accumulate means of pleasure. It can not only add to its useful facilities, but can, by appropriation, enlarge its capacity. That which can accumulate means for useful ends, can also neglect that which would redound to its benefits, yea, even withhold the soul's supplies. These abilities so prominent in the human mind, now depraved, are by the unfaithful philosophy of the race rejected. Hence, by improperly combining principles, his complement is self-destructive. He toils to win a way to the lands productive of gold unalloyed; to a kingdom of mind eternally pacific, and beneath a cloudless sky; but ne'er attains. And why? Because he denieth this simple principle—*the power to pervert the intention of the soul.*"

THE CAPACITY OF BEING.

"ALL, whether men or angels, possess powers of research by which they investigate; of discrimination, by which they compare and judge. They have the powers of computation, by which they define, and comprehend; powers of analysis, by which they separate and distinguish; powers also of repulsion and attraction, by which they accept or reject; and powers of incorporation, by which they appropriate to their own use, according to their own determination.

"The soul, or heart, has the faculty of inclination or affection. By this it loves and admires. Also the principle of aspiration which prompts desire of superior attainments and inheritance. And finally, the principle of reverence by which superior respect is bestowed upon objects deemed worthy.

"These faculties properly cultivated and harmoniously employed, unfold to degrees of refined and exalted being. Such perpetually glorify their Creator and benefit the created; and such, throughout the realms of the vast universe, where they exist united, compose one living octave, the utterance of whose pure emotions and ascending praises, unite in alleluiahs before the throne of God.

"The aspirations of such beings, when self-devoted, become transformed into ambition. Ambition prompts reverse tendencies, thence perverts the powers to individual aggrandizement, which should be devoted to universal uses, and the glory of God. Hence refraction, opposition to law, and therefore *rebellion.* Rebellion confuses and deranges the organism; hence *discordance.* Discordance causes one principle to prey upon another, thus enfeebling and preventing the appropriation of sustaining and unfolding means. This is succeeded by imbecility. Weakness and discord engender disease; and disease induces decomposition. Hence death."

CHAPTER VII.

THE REBELLION.

"In the process of time, one of those who had passed from the great dome, having attained to immortality, in his self-complacency, especially considered his own merit, and while contemplating, neglected to honor his Creator as the Author of his existence—the cause by which he had immortal character. And thus becoming careless to his instructions, strictly applied his meditations to himself, therefore became self-devoted. This prompted a desire of display, and consequently of ambition. And arising in the pride of self-sufficiency he proceeded to display his own dignity; and thus perverted the law of harmony praise and ascension! *And infolding the faculties of his internal being, he became selfish.* By this he failed to realize his dependence upon God; and assumed self-ability—arrogance. Thus he disturbed his sympathy with divine life; severed the golden link that united him to the heavens, AND FELL! Breaking the bond of union between one soul and the spirit of harmony, affected the kingdom of peace and life afar, and was felt throughout the heavens; shocke the orb and removed it from its orbit. The a -

gels left, and the veil of darkness encompassed that distracted sphere. *This was the first violation of law*—THE REBELLION! Hence the origin of *evil*—of SIN.

"When he felt the consequences of the fall his soul became envious and he blasphemed his God, for the affliction he had brought upon himself: and HEAVEN PRONOUNCED HIM UNJUST.

"Moreover, since he was immortal, death as a consequence could not be alloted. He was therefore, by the laws of his condition, self-doomed to banishment, and regions of perpetual night.

"Becoming malicious, he sought and induced others into evil who with him declared their opposition to heaven. Hence *fallen and rebellious spirits*—opposition to God and his government.

"Having secured his followers, he declared himself Prince and sought to subdue those who could not by artifice be led from the Law of the Lord.

"Thus is revealed the *origin* of EVIL."

THE SUPPLICATION.

"Those who did not sin bowed before Heaven and implored protection. This was the *first* prayer of affliction, and such were its causes. Their importunities ascended as breath of sorrow and in mournful accents arose on high. Silence prevailed. And the unnumbered myriads of angels and seraphs felt the burden, and united in the solemn prayer. GOD HEARD! The finger of his Almightiness touched the orb: and lo! the suppliants arose. The law of disintegration decomposed the orb. Thence obedient to his Word, the refined particles were transformed and spiritualized, and arose into the intermediate heavens. The Lord reigned thereon, and made of it a home of many mansions; and blessed it, and gave it as the inheritance of those who would not sin, but kept their first estate. And this is the *transparent orb;* even PARADISE: and these the *blissful inhabitants* first beheld in the *vision.*"

THE WORLD OF WOE.

"But the gross, imperfect and igneous elements of the decomposed orb, being collected, became a thirsty, barren, and unfruitful sphere, encompassed with a heated and discordant atmosphere. Void of power to attract light, and destitute of all means of reflection, it wanders in perpetual gloom.

"Over its surface hangs a self-generated, ghastly, pale sulphuric cloud. It is the inheritance of those rebellious and fallen spirits.

"Being immortal, they increase in energy and violence of movement. Their thoughts are the reverse of integrity, purity and frankness. They are subtle and serpent-like; have no desire of heaven, and, if possible, would blot out the SUN OF PEACE. They can at will encompass themselves with artificial splendor like a garment, and wear the smile of artifice. But their heart is black and full of deadly poison."

MAN SPIRITUALLY INSPIRED.

DURING this address my position was such as to behold the images reflected within the dome. As my instructor spoke of earth I saw its image; and its contrast with those harmonious orbs cannot be described. Dark shadows hung over the entire surface. These, however, were penetrated by rays of light. Far above stood a mighty angel, holding in his hand a trumpet. As he spoke bright beings without number, descended into the gloomy atmosphere that encompassed the earth. As the ministering angels endeavored to influence the forlorn and bewildered inhabitants, to impress them with the image of the cross and its attending truths, dark spirits, inhabitants of realms of night, sought to imitate their appearance and mode of procedure, and by reason of perversion, the inhabitants of earth could scarcely distinguish the bright beings. From these causes also, they were inclined to the dark spirits, and more readily perceived them; and as their teachings harmonized with their vain hearts, they believed them true. Many were influenced, and blinded by the illusive reflections from fantastic spheres; and receiving the false philosophy, as agents of these perverted beings, became the heralds of untruths. I was solemnly impressed with the correctness of the vision.

During the interpretation of the laws of life on the rudimental orb, I beheld its image and movements, until decomposed. Thence the orb of night appeared as if eternally fixed. It was a dark spot upon the broad features of the universe.

RETURN TO THE TRANSPARENT ORB.

As my conductor closed his dissertation upon the origin and consequences of sin, whose truths appeared self-evident, we immediately descended to the sphere of the Orb-Paradise.

Upon approaching, I beheld the male inhabitants gathered in and about the principle Temple. I enquired the cause, and learned that intelligence had just reached them of the creation of man upon Earth. How? at this period? I enquired, since many ages are already passed in the history of man. "Nevertheless," answered my guide, "every scene, with each minute part or act is reflected, as upon a spiritual mirror. Nothing is lost, or the trace of its existence permitted to pass into oblivion. All nature daguerreotypes itself, indelibly, upon eternal duration. Not one thought perishes or fails to infix its character upon the pages of eternal records. This principle is sealed to the actors until they pass certain fixed degrees in the scale of existence. Thou art impressed with the realities of scenes long since closed in their active manifestations; but whose image still lives. Duration in its unfoldings, unrolls itself, a scroll whereon is inscribed whatever is. It is a book of records, a transcription of events. Each fluttering leaf, crawling insect, thought or deed of man or angel, is written in that Book of everlasting ages. Whoever reads nature from this Book, arrives at truth. Dost thou understand?

"This is a page revealing the past; the memorable scene when the existence of Adam and Eve, the innocent and pure possessors of Earth's Eden, was announced to this world. What thou hast previously beheld of this realm, is connected with that event; hence this assemblage explains why at thy former visit here the inhabitants were not in their usual occupation upon the land or seas. He who is now represented as addressing those assembled is an Angelic Messenger from superior heavens. The anxious expression of his countenance, and which was also revealed by his audience, was because of a vile deceiver, who was seeking the ruin of the blissful pair on earth, who though then innocent and unsuspecting, by reason of a constitution heretofore explained, were capable of neglecting the counsels of Heaven, and of becoming the prey of carnal desires. * * * Let us depart."

CHAPTER VIII.

ORIGINAL EDEN OF EARTH.

THUS saying, we descended from that Paradisiacal world to the earth, and paused above ancient Eden. Before us appeared Adam and Eve in their native loveliness. But how little they compared with man as he now is! And nature, too, how superior to what earth now presents. Alas! for the consequences of sin. Eden was a model of perfection. The ærial and faunal kingdoms, manifested divine order, and vegetation unfolded earth's unalloyed virtues. The foliage upon the trees gently moved under the influence of the balmy zephyrs. Fruit rich and golden, hung upon the pendant boughs, and Earth's surface was clothed in Flora's choicest garb. Above, the heavens smiled and reflected their glory from a cloudless sky.

"Behold," said my counselor, "Eden as it was! But in the distance observe that orb of night, dark and dreary. It is the habitation of rebellious souls. They seek to tempt this lovely and innocent pair, and pollute them with the spirit of their unhallowed natures. The law of being has been revealed. Each soul must choose the right and reject the wrong. Upon this ability depends intelligence. Without it there could not be man or angel. Between the laws of mind and matter there is no analogy."

A dark cloud now drew near, which disclosed a clan of fallen spirits most malicious. Dreadful was that sight. Their purpose was obvious, and although Adam and Eve had been formally instructed in the philosophy of their natures, the chemistry of matter, the vegetation suited to their present condition, and that which would prove exceedingly deleterious if indulged prematurely; and the exercise of their own functions, also relative to the existence and character of the rebel beings; still *they* must accept or reject, obey or disobey. And the fate of earth seemed to rest upon their decision. Thus was their primitive state revealed. To seduce them the arch fiend resorted to unnumbered machinations. He sought sympathy with them by secret influence, breathed upon them his vile magnetic life, but as he approached was careful to infold himself in a kind of deceptive light; hence they did not perceive him. Finally, after many futile efforts to possess them, he resorted to the animal races for one suited to his purposes.

In the rear of the garden, and under the shadow of a grove, he approached a creature in appearance much like man, but whose head was serpent-form. This creature, having a heavy base or sub-brain, was readily possessed, and thence inspired at will.

THE TREE OF THE KNOWLEDGE OF GOOD AND EVIL.

"In the midst of the garden," said my instructor, "behold a tree whose fruit is immature. This 'is the tree of the knowledge of good and evil.' Herein consists a mystery never revealed to fallen man. When mature, if eaten, it was calculated to unfold and confirm the faculties of generation. If eaten before ripe would unavoidably induce premature development, and engender disease. Of this fruit the Lord forbade Adam and Eve to partake until the fullness of time. This constituted the principle requirement. Now, it came to pass, that he who first rebelled, having possessed the creature, as already shown, sought to effect his purpose by enticing them to pluck and eat of that fruit before the time. By so doing, he was assured the baser propensions would prevail, and they inevitably be perverted, hence become sympathizers with evil. Man denies this, because of its apparent (as they affirm) reflection upon the knowledge and power of God. But the law of mental ability awards a power of choice. That renders the being a moral agent, and moral agency gives ability to determine the mode of actions. This has been discovered in the exposition of the first violation."

At this period the creature, now possessed by the Satanic Power, was manœuvering in the garden. But the peculiar manifestations of Adam now absorbed my thoughts.

CONSTITUTION OF ADAM.

It appeared that he was by various movements responding to every quality of his nature. There was true dignity in his demeanor, his physical and mental constitution, in reality, appeared to qualify him for the government of earth, as the under shepherd of the Lord. He evinced a soul capable of enjoyment. I perceived that his brain was composed of *three* grand divisions. The base or cerebelum, united him with physical and material nature. By this he sympathized with the lower orders of beings, and was capable of enjoying harmony of physical sensation. Its union with superior qualities rendered it the sensational crown or seat of animal life, conjoined with mental and spiritual sense. Hence by this union originate human propensions.

The second division was that which forms the blending sphere, or the intermediate region between the material and spiritual being. This is composed of the superior essences of the inferior realm, and the inferior declination of the world of mind. This union constitutes man in human form a spiritual being, and identifies the spirit of life with a created organism, hence a spirit entity. By this, man physically is exalted, and becomes upright. He is therefore above the animal. He is the ultimate of the physical and a member of the spiritual universe. This intermediate degree is the link which unites the material and spiritual. Its life is from the spiritual and not the physical. The material man, therefore, is dependent upon the principle of spiritual life, by which it has form and exaltation.

The result of his union constitutes human ability in the external sphere. *The third and superior division* is pure mentality. This actuates and engages man in his earthly procedure. It is that by which he conceives, analyzes, determines and executes. It promotes the inferior man, when the soul and body harmonize with each other and the laws of their existence.

Thus Adam revealed a combination of capacities, superior, beyond comparison to other manifestations around him; and attributes which united him with two universes—the material and the spiritual—the earthly and the heavenly. Moreover, by his nature, thus innocent, he was decidedly inclined to the divine. Therefore, in unfallen man, matter and mind are so united as to harmonize in every function, and by every movement to increase in degrees of refinement, until, by Heaven's appointed means, the changeable shall obtain to the unchangable—the immortal state. But, to strictly analyze, definitely reveal and clearly define the intricate blending, and silent procedures, together with the modes of inspiration, reception, incorporation, and progression of unfallen man, is not within the capacity of perverted mind.

If the body be by any means rendered defective, or the mind become depraved, the purposes of the union are suspended. Physical deformity however, alone, cannot prevent the final development of the spirit, since such deficiency only affects the external manifestation and immediate growth. The body is the agent by which the soul reveals its character to the outer world, the casket for the unfolding spirit: therefore in the earth sphere the free and healthy movement of the mind is accelerated or suppressed by the functions of the external being. Still though the body be perfect it cannot correct the errors of the mind. Nor can spiritual depravity, even by a perfect medium, manifest health and harmony. Hence righteousness is not by means of physical health, but because of spiritual, mental, and moral rectitude, neither doth unrighteousness pertain to material nature. The physical man cannot, therefore, transform the spirit, or disparage its moral worth. Nevertheless, proper development of body or mind in the rudimental state depends upon their unitary health and harmony. If, then, either is depreciated or becomes unduly excited, wrong will be inflicted upon the system. If the body suffers, the spirit will sympathize; and if the mind is diseased, the body shares in the consequences of its ills. And as the health, development, and longevity of man depend upon his state of mind and condition of body, it follows that overaction in any attribute or faculty will infringe upon the rights and uses of his constitution. And thus improper tendencies by any excess may be induced in man. Therefore to pervert any attribute or faculty of mind or body is to interrupt its harmonious development, suspend its progression, and retard or prevent its healthy ultimation. A law of force is a law of necessity, and that is mechanical. Adam revealed inclination and decision, therefore the power of choice. Hence, although he may be advised, urged or tempted, he alone must decide the character of his actions. This renders him intellectual—constitutes his manhood. He is therefore responsible for his deeds. Thus man is made but a little below the angels.

Eve manifested greater refinement and susceptibility, by far, than Adam. She was to him an angel-being, existing in a material body. Her gentle spirit qualified her for his companion, to comfort and bless him evermore. She was God's great gift to him. How blest that happy pair. Hand in hand they moved amid the trees of Eden. Smile answered to smile, and heart beat to heart in holy sympathy and perfect confidence. Thus might they have lived while eternity endures.

CHAPTER IX.

THE TEMPTATION.

A peculiar musical sound now arrested my attention, and I beheld hovering above the tree bearing the forbidden fruit a large and beautiful bird, which was also under the charm of the evil spirits and influenced to attract the attention of Eve. The tree shone brilliantly, but its lustre was a fantastic halo which concealed the many demons within its boughs. Beneath stood the beast-agent of the prince of fiends, and the encompassing atmosphere was transformed into a base magnetic element. "Malicious yet most perfect design," remarked my guide. "If Eve shall hear and be enticed into that magnetic sphere, *farewell to her purity and peace.* The cloud of death shall encompass her, and unborn generations shall be the victims of the enemy of innocence and heaven! Father of mercies spare! Yet why should I pray? They know their duty; they *can not*, surely they *will not* heed the Tempter. Behold!" he ejaculated, and lo, Eve had heard and silently withdrew from Adam in the direction of the demons. As she approached, dissolving views most captivating played around the tree. Their influence reached her sense! She lost her self-government—was charmed!

"Eve, thou favored of God," exclaimed the angel, "why dost thou wander? False beings allure: pause, or in a moment thy doom shall be sealed!" She heard him not. Her ear listened to the charmer's song, and her eye gazed upon the fantastic and bewildering colors. The beast drew near and invited her to partake of the forbidden fruit. This somewhat aroused her sense. And she boldly replied, "Nay! IT IS FORBIDDEN!" and a voice answered, "God said, 'the day thou eatest thereof thou shalt surely die.'" "The declaration is untrue," said the voice, "for God doth know that in the day ye eat thereof, then your eyes shall be opened; and ye shall be as gods, knowing good and evil."

The music charmed her, the magnetic sphere encompassed and pervaded her sensitive being, the mystery astonished her. The Tempter urged. She yielded and partook! Adam having missed Eve, pursued her, and was now with her in the sphere of evil. To him she gave and he did eat! THE DEED WAS DONE!! Nature convulsed. Earth changed its position. The heavens gathered blackness. Wild, tempestuous clouds obscured the sun. Terrific thunders burst upon the world, and rolled their stunning peals over land and sea. The globe shook to its center. Oceans submerged the continents, valleys sank, and extensive plains were transformed into mountain ranges. ADAM AND EVE HAD FALLEN!

Having accomplished their infamous design, the demons, for such they truly were, withdrew to witness the scene. And what insane satisfaction they manifested! He who first presumed upon the government of Heaven, on the severed orb, now chief dictator, vaunted to diabolical excess over the victory he had obtained. And reaching forth his hand, from which streamed a sulphuric flame—the perfection of evil magnetism—he defied his Maker, when a bolt of light from on high struck him and he disappeared.

THE MANIFESTATION OF THE SON OF MAN.

As the tempest subsided, a cloud of effulgence appeared above the garden. From this cloud, the angel informed me, the bolt descended upon Apollyon and his clan, and hurled them to their nether abode. Within, was the manifestation of the Son of Man. Mercy and Justice were in attendance.

CHAPTER X.

THE EXPOSITION.

"WHAT has been revealed concerning the Rebellion prior to Earth's existence," said the Angel, "discloses the cause of the dread consequences which followed the fall of Adam and Eve. But this occurred with them while less mature in body and mind than the angel who rebelled.

"The philosophy of Adam's fall has not therefore been disclosed.

"The fruit of which they ate, as heretofore revealed, directly affected the faculties of generation. Its proper use would have developed, in perfection, the physical being, and prepared it for the offices of earthly existence. But the unripe fruit being taken into the system, while in its tender age, by overacting portions of the functions, induced premature results. Had the body and mind been mutually unfolded the laws of progression would have been observed and man obtained, without physical dissolution, to the immortal state. The process has been revealed in the vision of the severed orb.

"Adam and Eve, in yielding to the Tempter, suffered their minds to deviate from their natural tendency, and as the character of influence was base, it inverted the action of their soul; closed the opening flower and attracted the unfolding essence into the stalk, hence gave the spirit an animal tendency. This overcharged the inferior organs of the mind, and robbed the superior of their natural vitality. At this period, when they gave heed to the first suggestion, their moral nature trembled in balances. They knew their duty, had power to hold the mind upon it, and thus keep the avenues closed through which the temptation affected their sympathies. Still, rather than repel the vile suggestive spirit, they allowed it to arrest the meditation and engage it, and therefore approach the natural affinities. Thus pausing, they became passive. This passiveness induced negativeness to the enticing power, which by this advantage secured the disposition and thence bound the soul. Thus Eve submitted to the magnetism of the seducer. The first favorable thought she gave in the direction of the forbidden fruit, constituted *her transgression.* To guard against that constituted her great duty. It was simple then and could have been easily prevented from incorporating itself into her being; but when once indulged was the means of perverting her soul, and having yielded to the first insinuation, she was readily induced to approach the cloud of enchantment, which encompassed the tree of forbidden fruit. Still the Satanic purpose was not disclosed. Nevertheless, when once within the Tempter's power, and encompassed by his sphere, she became an easy subject of that will and artifice, by which her sense was overcome. Therefore, when the fatal proposition was suggested, although from the memory of Heaven's injunction she recoiled, she could not resist, hence she partook.

"The effect of the fruit, unripe, and at that stage of her development, as well the Tempter knew, operated sensibly upon the nervous system, and inspiring to excess, the faculties of the body wrought therein unhealthy desires. This prostituted the mind and rendered positive the laws of being hitherto negative. Herein consists the cause of man's inclination to gratify his baser propensities; his strength of carnal desire; and the weakness of his love for divine things; hence his moral degradation. Man, then, is the servant of sin, and as such must remain until a stronger shall come, bind him who holdeth the soul's dominion, and rescue the fallen spirit.

"No man can possibly serve two masters, nor incline to good and evil at the same time. No more could Adam and Eve be the subjects of wicked device, lust and revenge, (the very spirit of the Tempter,) and retain their moral purity, and perpetuate their original relation to goodness and heaven. Therefore when they suffered evil to prevail over them their moral nature became diseased, their harmony with the Spirit of Life was disturbed, and sympathy with the divine spheres was lost; it came to pass that the spiritual avenues of their soul withered away, and the passional being increased to undue proportions. And being thus prepared they received undue sympathy from the animal and material realms, thence influx from the spheres of darkness, hence became affinitized with the realms of death. Their affinities were of necessity, henceforth deathward tending. They were then prepared for union with those fallen beings who had seduced them, and whose iufluence they thereafter loved and cherished. And by this means henceforth loving the ways of death or perversion, they had an extreme disrelish for the spirit of life. Moreover, constituted as they were for aspiration and indulgence, which otherwise would have been in the law of obedience, their desire embraced the objects of the baser propensions. This indulgence premature, was in effect a violation of every law of being; and from the violation of law they became debased. Thus was wrought in them all manner of concupiscence, which from that period, has been sadly demonstrated by the children of men. For, to gratify his carnal inclinations man perils every interest of his soul, explores land and sea; urges his body to its destruction, deceives, plunders and assassinates. The secret cause of human woe, then, primarily consisted in bending the upright soul to the insidious suggestions of a lascivious spirit, which perverted the affections, deranged the faculties, changed the intentions of the being from heaven and holiness, to vain and unhallowed pursuits; corrupted the fountains of spirit life, whence should issue the principles of goodness and peace, and rendered man a slave to his passions; shut out the light and joys of heaven. Secondarily, from this perversion followed extreme excitement of the nervous system, which subdued the physical man, reduced the mind to a state of imbecility, thence induced disease and physical death.

"To restore that which was lost, holiness in perfect love, must unite itself with the love of the perverted soul, subdue and cast out the evil and depraved principle, change the nature of the inclinations, purify and exalt the sympathies —the love—and support its new-born desire in its heaven-seeking effort; in fine, restore the affections. Therefore, God hath said in his Word to fallen man, 'Thou shalt love the Lord thy God with all thy heart, and with all thy soul and with all thy mind.' 'Ye must be born again.' 'The wind bloweth where it listeth, and thou hearest the sound thereof, but canst not tell whence it cometh and whither it goeth; so is every one that is born of the Spirit. He that is born of God, is born of love. To be carnally minded is death; but to be spiritually minded is life and peace. Lay not up for yourself treasures upon earth where moth and rust doth corrupt, and where thieves break through and steal; but in heaven where neither moth nor rust doth corrupt, and where thieves do not break through nor steal: for where your treasure is, there will your heart be also.'

"These requirements exist in the nature of the human soul, and its relation to universal law. If the mind aspires after heaven the sphere of its sense and action will from that principle naturally seek the superior, and by attraction, will arise continually in the scale of moral goodness and spiritual worth. But if the inclinations are reversed, declination is inevitable. This philosophy of the soul, the Spirit has ever enforced upon man, which however, his perverted heart rejects. Herein consists the error of the human family. To the Bible thou art referred for a history of the events succeeding the fall, and the promise of redemption. And here the scene must be withdrawn until the time appointed when the spiritual currents, modes, and effects of the invisible sphere proximate to man, throughout his history even to the Consummation, shall be disclosed. Go, then, pilgrim, return to the external plane of human existence. Love the Lord with thy whole heart, serve him with thy might. Let no delusive fantasy lead thee from the way of Truth. Jesus, as thou art taught in the Scriptures, is THE REDEEMER. Trust in him. Watch faithfully thy heart, keep thou thy charge. Endure all things for him who endured the decisive conflict for thee. Exchange not thy inheritance for earth and its bestowments. Be thou faithful, fulfill thy mission; in heaven receive thy crown."

RESTORATION TO THE NORMAL STATE

At the close of the solemn charge, the angel gently retired, the scene was withdrawn, and my external sense awoke to sympathy with the interests of mortal life.

Earnestly I enquired, are these things so? Heaven knoweth! Verily the history and character of man confirm the sentiments of the vision.

REMARKS.

Thus the reader has been presented with a vision as probably true as any of the day. It certainly refutes the idea that all modern visions, revelations, etc., are opposed to the Christian Faith. If the Harmonialists denominate it the reflection of undeveloped minds, its system, graphic description, and depth of thought, when compared with their claims is against such conclusions. To account for it as the result of an excited imagination, involves all so-called modern developments in equal difficulty. To regard it as a communication from bigoted spirits, who still retain their prejudices, subjects others, also, to like criticism. However viewed, it is not easily disposed of by Harmonial Spiritualists, and is as much to the discredit of their doctrines as the visions they adduce can be to the disparagement of the Bible.

SPIRITUALISM.

PART I.

CHAPTER I.

MOST ANCIENT SPIRIT MANIFESTATIONS.

The idea of spiritual existence can have no bounds. It embraces the beginning of all things, the manifestation of all intelligence, the eternity of duration:—all thought, happiness or misery. Mind without it has no meaning, and eternity, would be one vast void of inconceivable nonentity.

Whether man possesses a combination of attributes, essences and functions, capable of everlasting duration, is *the* question which has been tried by human sense throughout all time. It is a problem never yet solved to the full satisfaction of the race. Millions have lived and died professing doubt in the reality of future existence. Millions more have lived in the faith of life to come, and with rejoicing in hope of a blissful immortality, have bid adieu to the world of external realities.

Many periods in the history of man have been enlivened, and especially stamped with phenomena acknowledged by multitudes as the indubitable manifestation of intelligences denominated spirits or angels; and in many instances, as the absolute Revelation of the Spirit of the Lord. Those who acknowledge a future state of existence differ as widely as the capacity of the human mind will possibly admit relative to the character of that existence; and also what influence this life may have upon the future state of the soul. This, however is divided into two grand theories. I. The belief that nature, without especial aid, unfolds the human spirit into angelic capacity, and a state of beatific rest. And, II. The theory of immortality based upon the doctrine of man's special creation with spiritual endowments, by the Lord;—of human depravity—the effect of Adam's transgression; and of Redemption from evil through the Mediatorship of Jesus, in whom the Divine Spirit was revealed. This, renders future happiness dependent upon the merciful provisions of the Gospel, and the sinner's repentance toward God and faith in the Lord Jesus—that, upon the progressive laws of nature, unassisted by the Divine Spirit.

The history of these opposing principles is traceable to a period as ancient as the days of Adam. One acknowledges the existence and Truth of the Lord Creator, the other charges the God of the Bible with falsehood and deception of the basest character. In Gen., 2 : 16–17, we read: "And the Lord God commanded the man, saying, of every tree of the garden thou mayest freely eat: but of the tree of knowledge of good and evil, thou shalt not eat of it: for in the day thou eatest thereof thou shalt surely die."

In this passage, reference is had to a law to which Adam was amenable. It indicated his ability to violate the divine requirement; and in the plainest manner informed him that consequences of a malignant character would attend its violation. The opposing spirit is said (Gen., 3: 1–5) to have mocked and contradicted the Lord in the following language. "Yea, hath God said, ye shall not eat of every tree of the garden? And the woman said, We may eat of the trees of the garden: but of the fruit of the tree that is in the midst of the garden, God hath said, Ye shall not eat of it, neither shall ye touch it lest ye die. And the serpent (*Nachash, or khanas, devil,*) said unto the woman, Ye shall not surely die; for God doth know that in the day ye eat thereof, then your eyes shall be opened; and ye shall be as Gods, knowing good and evil."

In these passages, the opposing principles are clearly revealed. It is not, therefore, a new thing that the Spirit which enjoins obedience to

God's laws should be set at naught, the counsels of Heaven be disregarded, and the consequences of disobedience denied. It may be well to remark, that the sequel proved God true, and the opposing spirit a liar. This holds good in every age and test. Moreover, as in modern times the two principles are clearly manifest with men; one urging faithfulness to injunction, and the other contemning it; and as the consequence of trifling with that law brings evil results, therefore, the works of men as well as the primitive history demonstrate and confirm the truth of the Bible statement, and the falsity of the denial—the opposition. Such are the most ancient records concerning "Spirit Manifestations." Nor can their correctness be disproved; but rather, subsequent revealments serve to establish them as faithful accounts.

Here then we fix our data and commence the Record of Spiritualism. This account reveals a malicious opposition to the Supreme Spirit whose Being is declared in the Scriptures; and contempt for his law. And we premise that the same spirit of opposition is traceable down through time, and that modern Harmonial Spiritualism is the legitimate descendant through an unbroken lineage: or is prompted by the same spirit that attempted to *reason* away the Law of the Almighty. If such is the truth, what will remain for discussion is, which is the true principle, that which tempted Eve into sin, or that which taught obedience to divine requirement?

Again: The Lord counseled Adam to control his inclinations, and admonished him against gratifications which might expose him to unfavorable consequences; advised him to a habit of self-government. This is in harmony with divine law. Every organism in the universe is dependent for health, use and development, upon the competency and judicious exercise of some supreme controlling power. Without this, the members of the physical universe would wander confusedly until their order and existence would cease to be. Even so with the mind: there must be government or the most fatal consequences will attend its movement. Nations, circles and families require governmental policy; the exercise of correct determination. In like manner every separate intelligence requires fixedness of purpose—self-control. The Bible informs us that the Lord revealed to Adam the character and tendency of this first and supreme principle. As, therefore, the prohibition harmonized with eternal law, and was adapted to Adam's condition, it follows that the doctrine of its divine origin is a truth. But without this manifest adaptation, the consequences that followed the violation prove the wisdom and righteousness of the command. The Tempter's position was the opposite. He urged self-gratification, and therefore had no respect for the first principle, the great criterion of Adam's being. No government could exist under such an administration. The law of equity, purpose, justice, and of mental, spiritual and moral government was set aside by him; and impulse, passion and appetite instituted in their stead. Consequently, his counsel savored of discord and death, and was opposed to life, harmony and peace. Such was the character of that spirit, which, according to the Scriptures set at naught the counsels of heaven, has made perpetual war upon the servants of God and the Divine Law. Facts prove it the principal actor in the present effort against the Bible—that it is now feeling for the pillars of the House of God. Its magic hands are seeking the candlesticks of the holy Temple, and its spiritual messengers are stealing into the domestic circle and most sacred places. The power, like an invisible cloud, overhangs the earth, and distills its God-opposing spirit into the human soul. It comes as angel whispers, spiritual melody, ghostly visages, and the multitudinous forms of Magnetism, Biology and Necromancy—by clairvoyance, spirit-seeing, writing, rapping, and the disturbance of material bodies. It speaks of heaven and harmony, and while charming with circean song, with its death fingers clutches at the Bible. Its infuriated heart, surcharged, is impatient for the period to arrive when it can belch its venom like a flood, upon those who adhere to the doctrine of the Inspired Word and have faith in the Lord Jesus. The manifestation has varied according to the sense of the device. At times it has, as nearly as possible, imitated the character of divine Inspiration, and in some instances it has been difficult for benighted man to distinguish it from the true, until the effect removed the veil and exposed its perverse and wicked nature.

CHAPTER II.

BIBLE HISTORY OF THE OPPOSING SPIRIT.

IMMEDIATELY succeeding the first transgression, the evil, malicious, and God opposing spirit assumed especial form in the murder of Abel, whose pious soul offered acceptable sacrifice before God. This the evil spirit could not endure, and therefore meted out its hate for holy things upon the meek victim.

Abel was the first of unnumbered martyrs to the Cause of Heaven. And his blood issued first from the fountain thus opened because of the spirit of opposition to the religion known as the religion of the Bible.

However varied the form of manifestation, it has been the humble believer in the doctrine of divine Inspiration, sacrifice, and devout worship of the Lord of heaven and earth, the I AM, who has suffered. And it has been a proud tyranizing spirit which has inflicted pain and death upon those who *would* serve the invisible God, though earth and hell oppose.

Deep-designing, the evil genus sought, by cutting off Joseph, to prevent the salvation of Israel through whose lineage the Messiah, the Conqueror should come. It therefore inspired his brethren with revenge because of his prophetic spirit. And they finally sold the innocent lad a slave into Egypt. But the very means employed to defeat the Spirit of Life was overruled to the greatest and most glorious ends. For a season Joseph suffered. And because his trusty and upright soul could not be tempted into sin, but resisted, by false accusation he was cast into prison. In this also, God defeated the enemy, and by means originating in that affliction, exalted Joseph to a position wisely adapted to the purpose of his Mission—the salvation of the house of Jacob. Gen., 37.

The same evil inspiration at the time of the birth of Moses, the servant of the Most High, caused Pharaoh to purpose the sacrifice of all the males born to the Hebrews. By so doing, the agent of Heaven would have been cut off. This God also overruled to his own glory. For by the inspiration of Wisdom, Moses was saved. And when, after three months, the mother could no longer conceal him, "she took for him an ark made of bulrushes, and daubed it with slime and pitch, and put the child therein; and laid it in the flags by the river's brink. And the sister stood afar off to wit what would be done with him. And the daughter of Pharaoh came down to wash at the river; and her maidens walked along by the river side; and when she saw the ark among the flags, she sent her maid to fetch it.

"And when she had opened it, she saw the child; and behold, the babe wept. And she had compassion on him, and said, This is one of the Hebrew children. Then said his sister to Pharaoh's daughter, Shall I go and call thee a nurse of the Hebrew women, that she may nurse the child for thee? And Pharaoh's daughter said to her, Go. And the maid went and called the child's mother. And Pharaoh's daughter said unto her, Take the child away, and nurse it for me, and I will give thee wages. And the woman took the child and nursed it. And the child grew, and she brought him unto Pharaoh's daughter, and he became her son. And she called his name Moses: and she said, Because I drew him out of the water." Exodus, 2.

What stronger evidence of God's especial Providence could be given than this case affords? And yet it is called a myth. And why? Is it irrational? In what? The narrative is simple: no incident recorded transcends the possibility of actual occurrence. The King's decree is in no way improbable. The concealment of the babe is perfectly natural. The heart of every true mother would respond to hers who clandestinely preserved her child; and their judgment approve her course. Is, then, the case such as naturally suggests doubts of its truth? Is it more inconsistent to believe than that the dead return to earth, and prescribe for the sick? make music on tambourines, accordeons, violins, and the piano? Play a reveille on bass and tenor drums? and cause stands, tables, bedsteads and bureaus to dance like puppets? carry ribbons and penknives across the Atlantic? bake griddle cakes? or manufacture hands and feet and perform midnight wonders by them? If these modern phenomena be true, is it unlikely that the circumstances said to have attended Moses' birth ever transpired, and that the account is founded in truth, and not in fiction? Yea, are there not strong evidences that the spirit which sought to destroy Moses and by so doing to defeat the object of his mission, having failed in that attempt has since opposed, by every imaginable device, those who have had faith in that and succeeding events connected with the Hebrews and pertaining to the belief in especial manifestations of the Lord? Nevertheless, as in the case of Joseph, who was sold into Egypt, by whom God preserved the Patriarchal family; so in that of the attempted sacrifice of the Hebrew children, the Divine Spirit overruled the evil intention to the salvation of the enslaved Israelites.

Moses being found by Pharaoh's daughter, was, therefore, adopted into the Royal family.

By this means, he was educated into the knowledge of the king's policy, the jurisprudence of Nations; and the means employed by Pharaoh's Chief Magistrates to execute his designs. Thus brought up, he was advised of the modes of government and the character of those nations and tribes through which he passed with the children of Israel, while journeying from Egypt to the Promised Land. Thus prepared, at the appointed time God called him. He obeyed, and the Lord, through him, delivered his people.

The next important effort against the Spirit of Truth, consisted in an attempt to suppress the divine influence, by subduing and holding in abject servitude the people through whose descendants the Word of God was to be revealed. Hence when Moses and Aaron appeared before Pharaoh, with the message of the Lord, and in the name of the God of Heaven plead for the freedom of the oppressed Hebrews, he said, "Who is the Lord, that I should obey his voice, to let Israel go? I know not the Lord, neither will I let Israel go."

There are those now saying, like Pharaoh, Who is the Lord, the God of the Hebrews? We know not the Lord: Nature is our God: we cannot obey, neither regard the counsels of the God of the Bible. Such, in substance, is the language of N. D. Revelations, and of Harmonialism.

In reply to Pharaoh, Moses and Aaron said, "The God of the Hebrews hath met with us: let us go we pray thee. And the king of Egypt said unto them, Wherefore do ye, Moses and Aaron, let the people from their works? Get ye unto your burdens. And Pharaoh said, Behold, the people of the land now are many, and ye make them rest from their burdens. And Pharaoh commanded the same day the task-masters of the people, and their officers, saying, Ye shall no more give the people straw to make brick, as heretofore: let them go and gather straw for themselves. And the tale of bricks which they did make heretofore, ye shall lay upon them; ye shall not diminish aught thereof: for they be idle; therefore they cry, saying, Let us go and sacrifice to our God. Let there more work be laid upon the men, that they may labor therein; and let them not regard vain words.

"And the task-masters of the people went out, and their officers, and they spake to the people, saying, Thus saith Pharaoh, I will not give you straw. Go ye, get you straw where ye can find it: yet not aught of your work shall be diminished. So the people were scattered abroad throughout all the land of Egypt, to gather stubble instead of straw. And the taskmasters hastened them, saying, Fulfill your works, your daily tasks, as when there was straw. And the officers of the children of Israel, which Pharaoh's taskmasters had set over them, were beaten and demanded, Wherefore have ye not fulfilled your task in making brick both yesterday and to-day, as heretofore?

"Then the officers of the children of Israel came and cried unto Pharaoh, saying, Wherefore dealest thou thus with thy servants? There is no straw given unto thy servants, and they say to us, make brick: and behold thy servants are beaten; but the fault is in thine own people. But he said, Ye are idle, ye are idle: therefore, ye say, Let us go and do sacrifice to the Lord. Go therefore, now, and work; for there shall be no straw given you, yet shall ye deliver the tale of brick."

Thus Pharaoh, who did not know the God of Israel, disregarded the desire of the people to worship according to their own faith. And to prevent it bound them with still stronger bonds.

As shown in the "Review of A. J. Davis," Anti-Pantheist, Vol. I. the spirit of the Harmonial philosophy denies the Hebrew faith, and urges its banishment from the world. Is it not the spirit of Pharaoh? And taking the case under consideration, as an example, what but servitude, or that which might be worse, could the christian expect, if the spirit of the times should prevail? The doctrines are the same. I know not your God. Go, ye have no need to offer sacrifice, nor to worship a phantom. Worship by gathering your own straw and manufacturing your own brick. "Worship, with the hand of industry," said the great propounder of Harmonialism, in 1854. "He who attends his daily toil, performs his task, is the true worshiper. The idler wishes to offer sacrifice." "Go make brick without straw," said Pharaoh, "ye are idle, ye are idle: therefore ye say, let us go and sacrifice to the Lord." One might suppose Pharaoh had arisen, for the spirit of the two declarations are much in harmony. The modern acclaim is, "Nature is the Temple in which to worship." Adore with the hand of toil."

Both the sentiment of Pharaoh and modern philosophy conflict, yea are, by placing external care first, opposed to the doctrines of Divine Inspiration. Jesus said, "Seek first the kingdom of God, and his righteousness." That is, set not your heart on things below, but on those which are from above. And then lest idleness be encouraged, it also is written, "Do good unto all men. Visit the widow and the fatherless in their afflictions, and keep yourselves unspotted from the world. But if any provide not for his own, and especially that of his own house, he hath denied the faith, and is worse than an infidel." 1 Tim. 5, 8. How clearly the contrast is revealed. One seeks "a building of God, a house not made with hands, eternal in the heavens." 2 Cor. 5, 1. The other says, do sacrifice with the chisel and saw. That is, love and serve the world. The Hebrews' God we know not. Go make brick. Pharaoh denied the God of Israel and mocked his requirements for a season, but he and his people subsequently learned that in blind selfhood he stretched out his hand against God, and strengthened himself against the Almighty. Pharaoh disregarded the petition and afflicted the petitioners. In this he waged war directly with the Spirit who declared himself the Lord, even JEHOVAH. Thence ensued that conflict which engaged the Magicians of Egypt, by whom the works of the Divine were by effort, imitated, and an attempt was made to compete with the Spirit of God before Pharaoh and his host.

The demand made of Pharaoh to release the Israelites, was in fulfillment of a covenant the Spirit made with Abram to give to his seed the land of Canaan. If Abram had not been deceived, it was God who had thus covenanted. Upon a mount in that land Abraham had offered his son Isaac, and there the Messiah must appear through his seed. To defeat the return of the children of Israel, and by bondage and affliction destroy them as a people, would be to prevent the fulfillment of the promise and obtain the victory over the Spirit. The engagement, therefore, on the part of the opposing spirit was one of moment. And to succeed would apparently remove the seed of the true church from the world; close the sacred Canon ere it had assumed form, and submit the world to the power which seduced Adam and Eve. From this cause the opposition was engaged, and the conflict commenced. Moses, Aaron and the children of Israel were the chosen agents in the external through whom God was to perfect his purpose. The magicians were the agents of the spirit of evil now contending with the Spirit of Goodness.

Pharaoh had refused to let the people go, and the Spirit of the Lord spake unto Moses, and said, "I am the Lord. And I appeared unto Abraham, unto Isaac, and unto Jacob, by the name of God Almighty; but by my name JEHOVAH was I not known to them. I have also established my covenant with them to give them the Land of Canaan, the land of their pilgrimage, wherein they were strangers. I have also heard the groaning of the children of Israel, whom the Egyptians keep in bondage; and I have remembered my covenant. Wherefore, say unto the children of Israel, I am the Lord, and I will bring you out from under the burdens of the Egyptians, and I will rid you out of their bondage, and I will redeem you with a stretched out arm, and with great judgments: and I will take you to me for a people, and I will be to you a God: and ye shall know that I am the Lord your God, which bringeth you out from under the burdens of the Egyptians. And I will bring you in unto the land, concerning the which I did swear to give it to Abraham, to Isaac and to Jacob; and I will give it you for a heritage. I am the Lord." Ex. 6.

Long had Israel suffered and hoped for the fulfillment of God's promise to Abraham. And now, it was renewed. God through Abraham sware once to his people. And in this renewal he also commands Moses to proceed to the work of his mission.

Whether there was any especial importance attached to the location God had appointed it, had covenanted it to the children of Israel, and now called upon them to prepare for their Exodus from the land of bondage to that of Canaan, their rightful heritage. Around this clusters the immortal interests of Bible religion. In the name of JEHOVAH the promise was given. Upon that depended all things in future connected with the Faith of Abraham and the promised

Redemption, then Pharaoh determined that the children of Israel should not depart. The Spirit commanded them to prepare.

CHAPTER III.

THE COMMAND AND THE CONFLICT.

"Go in," said the Spirit, "speak unto Pharaoh, king of Egypt, that he let the children of Israel go out of his land." Moses felt his inefficiency: he knew the stubbornness of Pharaoh, and he replied, "Behold, the children of Israel have not hearkened unto me; how then shall Pharaoh hear me, who am of uncircumsized lips?"

And the Lord spake unto Moses and unto Aaron, and gave them a charge unto the children of Israel, and unto Pharaoh king of Egypt, to bring the children of Israel out of the land of Egypt. And Moses and Aaron did as the Lord commanded them.

By miracles God proposed to reveal his power, and he said to Moses: "When Pharaoh shall speak unto you, saying, Shew us a miracle for you: then thou shalt say unto Aaron, Take thy rod, and cast it before Pharaoh, and it shall become a serpent."

It is because of the importance attached to this scene, the fulfillment of determination, the effort and partial success of the magicians to imitate the power of the Lord; the final victory, obtained by the Children of Israel, and its analogy with modern events, that we are thus precise in introducing the history.

The two principles herein revealed, with their nature and effects, are now active in the world. One is heralding the doctrine of salvation through Jesus, the Savior; the other is seeking to counteract it, and to move the human mind by manifestations claimed equal to those offered in support of the Inspired Word.

According to command, "Aaron cast down his rod before Pharaoh, and before his servants, and it became a serpent. And Pharaoh also called the wise men and the sorcerers: now the magicians of Egypt, they also did in like manner with their enchantments. For they cast down every man his rod, and they became serpents: but Aaron's rod swallowed up their rods." Ex. vii, 10–12.

Herein consists the Law, the Principle, the Test, by which Scriptural doctrine is exalted to the Divine, and its opposite overcome. This power alone can demonstrate and confirm the superior nature of Bible religion, and render it worthy of its claims. If the christian Religion is truly of God, and the antagonistic spirit from perversion and evil, then it is capable of victory in every important test. To this we invite the reader's attention, as the principle herein involved is the great criterion connected with external manifestation. And we especially emphasize, because, when considering modern spirit manifestations we shall recur to it again.

As the spirit of the Lord gave commandment, the waters were turned into blood. And the magicians of Egypt did the same with their enchantments. "And the Lord spake unto Moses, Say unto Aaron stretch forth thine hand over the streams; and Aaron stretched out his hand over the waters of Egypt; and the frogs came up and covered the land of Egypt. And the magicians did so with their enchantments, and brought up frogs upon the land of Egypt." But the magicians failed to bring forth the loathsome parasitic insect. Neither could they imitate in the succeeding grievous plagues: nor stand before Moses.

At the command of the Lord, a fierce and destructive storm of hail came upon the land. For as "Moses stretched his hand toward heaven, the Lord sent thunder and hail, and the fire ran along the ground. So there was hail, and fire mingled with the hail very grievous, such as there was none like it in all the land of Egypt since it became a nation. And the hail smote throughout the land of Egypt all that was in the field, both man and beast; and the hail smote every herb of the field, and brake every tree of the field. Only in the land of Goshen, where the children of Israel were, was there no hail." Ex. ix, 23-26.

This was the work of the Almighty. The materialist or magician, could turn water into blood, and entice frogs from their viscous pools, but could not give life, create the thunder tempest, cause the lightnings to leap from the clouds, mingle with the hail, and flash along the ground. And most of all, could not condense the tempest upon Goshen, spare the Egyptians and afflict the children of Israel. Presumptuous mortals! how frail their power! Envious spirit, how short his arm, and how soon subdued when Jehovah proceeded to execute his purposes.

When the magicians failed, and the judgments were heavy, Pharaoh was humbled, and entreated Moses to pray to God for mercies. But the blessings, when granted, were misimproved and converted to selfish ends, thereby his heart was hardened. And with determinate obstinacy he resisted until the Angel of destruction slew of the Egyptians the first-born throughout the land. "And Pharaoh rose up in the night, he and all his servants, and all the Egyptians; and there was a great cry in Egypt: for there was not a house where there was not one dead. Then he called for Moses and Aaron by night, and said, Rise up and get you forth from among my people, both ye and the children of Israel; and go serve the Lord, as ye have said. Also take your flocks and your herds, as ye have said, and be gone; and bless me also." Thus, subdued, he hastened the people forth. Nevertheless, when it was told him that the children of Israel had truly fled, he made ready his chariot, and took warriors and pursued until lost with his host in the Red Sea; while Moses and Aaron with the released captives stood upon the other shore and gave God thanks for their salvation.

Thus closed one of the most eventful scenes connected with the race of man, and in a manner to glorify and exalt that Divine Principle by which God's chosen people were distinguished and set apart for a special end. As the Lord had promised, Israel was taken from the power of their oppressors and led beyond the sea, in the way to Canaan, the land of Promise. And like victory has attended every important trial to this day, when God has been defied and his people faithful.

CHAPTER IV.

DAVID AND GOLIAH.

IN the days of Samuel the Prophet, some five hundred years subsequent to the Exodus of the Children of Israel from Egyptian bondage, when "the Philistines gathered together their armies to battle at Socoh, and Saul and the men of Israel were gathered together, pitched in the valley of Elah, and set the battle in array against the Philistines; and the Philistines stood on a mountain on the one side, and Israel stood on a mountain on the other side: then went out a champion of the Philistines, named Goliath, of Gath, whose height was six cubits and a span. And he had a helmet of brass upon his head, and he was armed with a coat of mail; and the weight of the coat was five thousand shekels of brass. And he had greaves of brass upon his legs, and a target of brass between his shoulders. And the staff of his spear was like a weaver's beam; and his spear's head weighed six hundred shekel's of iron: and one bearing a shield went before him. And he stood and cried unto the armies of Israel, and said unto them, Why are ye come out to set your battle in array? Am not I a Philistine, and ye servants to Saul?

Choose you a man for you and let him come down to me. If he be able to fight with me, and to kill me, then will we be your servants, but if I prevail against him, and kill him, then shall ye be our servants, and serve us. And the Philistine said, I defy the armies of Israel this day; give me a man that we may fight together."

Here again the battle is set. Israel, however they may have erred in individual and domestic character, proclaimed the name of the Lord Most High. Him they adored. They bore the ark of the covenant. God had chosen them from the nations of the earth, and set them apart, a people through whom to record his law; and unfold his merciful manifestations to man—through whom the Messiah should appear. Therefore in defying the armies of Israel, the Philistine defied the Divine Spirit whom the Israelites worshiped as the living God.

Again, then, the wicked spirit sought to defeat the purposes of the Divine Being, by cutting off the chosen people, thereby preventing the fulfillment of the promise made to Abraham, saying, "In thee and in thy seed shall all nations of the earth be blessed." Through the House of Israel, the Stronger was promised. Even the Lion of the Tribe of Judah, the bright and Morning Star, the Conqueror. Hence the evil spirit foresaw that through the seed of Abraham God had determined the manifestation of THE SPIRIT, in the person of Jesus. Nor did he fail to exert his power and device to destroy the children of Israel, and by their extermination defeat the Divine Purpose. In the person of Goliath the chosen people, and in them, their God was defied. How frail is man! how weak his faith! God had saved Israel by his power in every emergency, and yet, "When Saul and all Israel heard those words of the Philistines, they were dismayed, and greatly afraid."

Upon the mountain the Spirit had been fitting a shepherd boy, by and through whom this external medium of evil should fall. Not by might nor by power, but by my Spirit, saith the Lord. Therefore, to reveal his Glory, the trained hosts were permitted to feel their weakness, to tremble and be afraid before the bold blasphemer; and a lad bearing a sling and shepherd's bag, containing five smooth stones from the brook, was inspired to enter the alarmed camp.

The Philistine drew near morning and evening, and presented himself forty days. "And David rose up early in the morning, and left the sheep with a keeper, and took, and went as Jesse had commanded him; and he came to the trench, as the host was going forth to fight and shouted for the battle. For Israel and the Philistines had put the battle in array, army against army. And behold, then came up the champion, the Philistine of Gath, Goliath by name, out of the armies of the Philistines, and spake according to the same words: and David heard them, and said, Who is this uncircumcised, that he should defy the armies of the living God? And he said to Saul, Let no man's heart fail because of him; thy servant will go and fight with the Philistine. And Saul said, thou art not able. And David said, Thy servant when attacked by both the lion and the bear, slew them; and this uncircumsized Philistine shall be as one of them, seeing he hath defied the armies of the living God. The Lord that delivered me out of the paw of the lion, and out of the jaw of the bear, he will deliver me out of the hand of this Philistine.

"And he took his staff in his hand, and chose him five smooth stones out of the brook, and put them in the shepherd's bag, (vessel) and his sling was in his hand: and he drew near to the Philistine. And the Philistine came on and drew near unto David: and the man that bare the shield went before him. And when the Philistine saw David he disdained him, for he was but a youth; and said, Am I a dog, that thou comest to me with staves? And the Philistine cursed David by his gods. And said, Come to me, and I will give thy flesh to the fowls of the air, and to the beasts of the field.

"Then said David to the Philistine, Thou comest to me with a sword, and with a spear and with a shield: but I come to thee in the name of the Lord of Hosts, the God of the armies of Israel, whom thou hast defied. This day will the Lord deliver thee into my hand: and I will smite thee, and take thine head from thee; and I will give the carcasses of the hosts of the Philistines this day unto the fowls of the air, and to the wild beasts of the earth; that all the earth may know that there is a God in Israel. And all this assembly shall know that the Lord saveth not with the sword and spear: for the battle is the Lord's, and he will give you into our hands."

In this history the two principles are clearly manifested. Nothing could render them more so. Goliah is the chosen medium for the conflict, and proudly defies the people through whom God had covenanted to bless the world; and the issue was brought at a period when Israel manifested little of the spirit and power of Godliness.

The Hebrews gathered upon an eminence over against the Philistines, in warlike manner, stood as the external representatives of the Spirit of Truth. Goliath defied; Israel trembled. Days and weeks passed lingeringly away, bringing no change, until David from the care of his father's sheep went to the distracted army. And hearing the armies of Israel defied, he advanced in defence of that name. Though a simple youth, he there appeared the absolute representative of Israel's God, and boldly reproved the daring agent of unrighteousness. The two armies had paused, stood transfixed and rapt in amazement. Goliah the Great, burdened with his armor, inflated with the breath of the false spirit, and inspired with the pompous song of the Philistine hosts, descended behind his shield-bearer, and drew near to David. David, strong in the Lord, proceeded to decide the conflict. In the name and fear of Jehovah he submitted himself and the cause in whose defence he was engaged, to the Spirit thus inspiring him. "The battle," he said; and his words echoed along the armies, "The battle is the Lord's: this day will he give you into our hands. And it came to pass, when the Philistine arose, and came and drew nigh to meet David, that David hastened, and ran toward the army to meet the Philistine. And David put his hand into his vessel, drew thence a stone, and slang it, and smote the Philistine in the forehead; and he fell upon his face to the earth. So David prevailed over the Philistine, and slew him." I. Sam. xviii.

At the fall of their chieftain, the Philistines

fled. Again Israel was delivered, and victory fully obtained over the enemy of God's chosen people. Do not modern Harmonialists defy the God of Israel, in presuming to overcome the influence of the Christian Faith, and break in pieces the power of Bible Religion. Like Goliah, the proud media advance and challenge the external Church to meet them in combat.

Goliah was a man inspired with the spirit of defiance. He mocked Israel, day after day, and vainly supposed the victory won, when in an unexpected manner, and by means in themselves unimportant, God, who was thus defied, removed Goliah, the external agent of the opposing power, and set his people free.

The church, the external representative of the Spirit of Life, this modern Ism is mocking, and challenging to combat daily. But God will deliver the true Israel, and exalt his Name. He who saveth not by the sword or spear knoweth the means: he provideth for the emergency, and in the day appointed will bring salvation.

CHAPTER V.

ELIJAH AND THE FALSE PROPHETS.

"AND it came to pass, when Ahab saw Elijah, that Ahab said, Art thou he that troubleth Israel? And he answered, I have not troubled Israel, but thou and thy father's house, in that ye have forsaken the commandments of the Lord, and thou hast followed Baalim. Now, therefore send, and gather to me all Israel unto Mount Carmel, and the prophets of Baal four hundred and fifty, and the prophets of the groves four hundred, which eat at Jezebel's table. So Ahab sent unto all the children of Israel, and gathered the people together unto Mount Carmel. And Elijah came unto all the people and said, How long halt ye between two opinions? If the Lord be God follow him: but if Baal, then follow him. And the people answered him not a word.

"Then said Elijah unto the people, I, even I only remain a prophet to the Lord; but Baal's prophets are four hundred and fifty men. Let them, therefore, give us two bullocks; and let them choose one bullock for themselves, and cut it in pieces, and lay it on wood, and put no fire under: and I will dress the other bullock, and lay it on wood, and put no fire under: and call on the name of your gods, and I will call on the name of the Lord: and the God that answereth by fire, let him be God. And all the people answered and said, It is well spoken." 1 Kings, 18.

Here again, the opposing principles met: but the order was changed. The prophet of the Lord called upon Baal's prophets to demonstrate the truth of their claims by manifestations indicative of the character of a God. Claiming that the Lord of hosts could send fire and consume the sacrifice. Meantime he said that the God who answered by fire should be acknowledged the true God.

"And they took the bullock that was given them, and they dressed it, and called on the name of Baal from morning even unto noon, saying, O, Baal, hear us. But there was no voice, nor any that answered. And they leaped upon the altar which was made.

"And it came to pass at noon that Elijah mocked them and said, Cry aloud: for he is a God; either he is talking, or he is pursuing, or he is in a journey, or peradventure he sleepeth, and must be awaked. And they cried aloud and cut themselves, after their manner with knives and lancets, till the blood gushed out upon them. And it came to pass when mid day was past, and they prophesied until the time of the offering of the evening sacrifice, but there was neither voice, nor any to answer, nor any that regarded."

Those prophets of Baal could produce wonders in the plane of human life; but when required to secure an answer from their gods which should supercede the power of the finite they failed; thus proving their want of harmony with superior spheres, and devotion to the Lord of hosts. Even so with the modern prophets. They can unfold from unfamiliar realms; can disclose the hidden mysteries of the earth sphere. Can demonstrate their theory to the satisfaction of the amazed spectator, but when have they drawn water from a deeper fountain than known before, or than what springs from the recesses of the human soul.

The prophets of Baal, when successfully opposed, became enraged, leaped upon the altar, and afflicted themselves. Manifestations somewhat similar have been developed in modern times. Media when confronted and charged with falsehood, have leaped upon the accusers, beat them with their fist, gnashed upon them with their teeth; raged and blasphemed. And when the christian in the name of Jesus has rebuked the foul and Bible-opposing spirit, the medium has been thrown into convulsions, and raved as if possessed with the demon of madness. This, we have abundant means to sustain, but refrain farther remarks until reviewing the phenomena of the day.

When the prophets of Baal had broken down the altar, cut themselves, and plead until the time of the evening sacrifice, "Elijah said unto all the people, Come near unto me. And all the people came near unto him. And he repaired the altar of the Lord that had been broken down. And Elijah took twelve stones, according to the number of the tribes of the sons of Jacob, unto whom the word of the Lord came, saying, Israel shall be thy name: and with the stones he built an altar in the name of the Lord: and made a trench about the altar as great as would contain two measures of seed."

Elijah erected the altar so as to distinguish it from that made by Baal's prophets; also to convince the multitude by the demonstration that the God of heaven was the God of true Israel. Success, therefore would bring full confirmation of Elijah's faith and the Divinity of the Hebrew Religion.

When the altar was built, Elijah "put the wood in order, and cut the bullock in pieces, and laid him on the wood, and said, Fill four barrels with water, and pour it on the burnt sacrifice, and on the wood. And he said, Do it the second time. And they did it the second time.

And he said, Do it the third time. And they did it the third time. And the water ran round about the altar: and he filled the trench also with water. And it came to pass at the time of the offering of the evening sacrifice, that Elijah the prophet came near, and said, Lord God of Abraham, Isaac and of Israel, let it be known this day that thou art God in Israel, and that I am thy servant, and that I have done all these things at thy command. Hear me, O Lord, hear me, that this people may know that thou art the Lord God, and that thou hast turned their heart back again.

"Then the fire of the Lord fell, and consumed the burnt sacrifice, and the wood and the stone and the dust, and licked up the water that was in the trench. And when all the people saw it, they fell on their faces: and they said, The Lord he is the God: the Lord he is the God." 1 Kings, xviii.

Here is the distinction. The prophet's of Nature, of Baal, or the Sun, had led the people astray, by their soothsaying, and demonstrations of inferior laws. Elijah had protested against them; proclaiming that Baal was not the true God. Jezebel had sacrificed all the Lord's prophets that could be found. Elijah had fled to the mountains and remained until the day when the false prophets were to be subdued. In the name of the God of Abraham the exiled prophet returned and alone met Ahab and his prophets: having no trust but in the Spirit who called him. The altars were built, the prayers offered; the prophets of Baal failed; but God answered Elijah.

Thus the inefficiency of that spirit which has ever afflicted man was revealed; that which is of nature and nature adoring; while the Spirit of Truth, of Life, of God, was honored before the mocking multitude. One was a spirit of feasting, and merriment; the other self-denying: but God was present to sustain the humble and despised prophet in his day of trial. How analogous the philosophy and tendency of Baal's prophets to that labored in Nature's Divine Revelations—of Harmonial Spiritualism. The modern manifestation is arrayed against the Bible; that was directly opposed to the prophets who wrote the Old Testament Scriptures. The prophets of Baal employed enchantment, soothsaying, and necromancy. Do not modern spiritualists who are so opposed to the christian religion, reflect the spirit of their ancient prototype? Yea, verily, as the analysis of the phenomena will reveal.

We here introduce an historic statement from the "Religious Encyclopædia," directly upon the subject of Baal worship.

"Baal, or Bel, (*governor, ruler, lord,*) a god of the Phœnicians and Canaanites. Baal and Astaroth are commonly mentioned together: and as it is belived that Astaroth denotes the moon, Calmet believes that Baal represents the sun. Bishop Munster as quoted by Professor Robinson, supposes that this was the case, *originally;* and that the fundamental idea of all oriental idolatry—which also may be traced from India to the north of Europe—is the *primeval power of nature,* which divides itself into the *generative* and the *conceptive* or productive power. He supposes the sun and moon to have been worshiped as the representatives of these powers, under the names of Baal and Astaroth. But Cyrenius supposed these appellations to signify the planets Jupiter and Venus. Be this as it may, it is certain that the name Baal is used in a generic sense, for the superior God of the Phœnicians, Chaldeans, Moabites and other people, and is often confounded with the name of some other gods; as Baal-Peor Baal-Zebub, Baal-Gad, Baal-Zaphon, Baal-Beroth. Baal is the most ancient god of the Canaanites, and, perhaps, of the East; and the Hebrews too often imitated the idolatry of the Canaanites, in adoring him. They offered human sacrifices to him, and erected altars to him in groves, on high places, and on the terraces of houses. Baal had priests and prophets consecrated to his service; and many infamous actions were committed in his festivals.

"Some learned men have maintained that the Baal of Phœnicia was the Saturn of Greece and Rome; and certainly there was great conformity between their services and sacrifices. Others are of the opinion that Baal was the Phœnician (or Syrian) Hercules, an opinion not inconsistent with the other; but it is generally concluded that Baal was the Sun; and on this admission, all those characters which he assumes in Scripture may be explained. The great luminary was adored throughout the East, and is the most ancient acknowledged among the heathen.

"The Hebrews sometimes called the sun *Baal-Shemesh;—Baal the sun.* Manasseh adored Baal, planted groves, and worshiped all the hosts of heaven; but Josiah, desirous to repair the evil introduced by Manasseh, put to death the idolatrous priests that burnt incense unto Baal, to the sun, and to the moon, and to the planets, and to all the hosts of heaven. He commanded all the vessels that were for Baal, and for the grove, Ashreh or Astaroth, and for all the hosts of heaven, to be brought forth out of the Temple. He took away the horses that the kings of Judah had given to the sun, and burnt the chariots of the sun with fire."

The Great Positive Mind, it will be remembered, in Nature's Divine Revelations is said to be the living principle or active essences of an illimitable Ocean of Liquid Fire, which is a vortex of Intelligence. (See A. P., vol 1, p. 46, etc.) Also, the Sun of the Divine Mind. This immense Ocean of fire is presented as the Beginning, the Univercœlum from which emanated all things. This is then the God of Harmonialism. According to the best authority, the ancients worshiped precisely such a God as our modern prophets are proclaiming to the world. What else then, but sun-worshipers are the Harmonialists? And the Seers and media of that 'Ism,' are they not the prophets of Baal? By devoting a little time to the history of Baalism and by comparing that doctrine with the principles of Harmonialism, it will be readily discovered that the modern appellation is but a new name for the same kind of religion. This presents the subject in quite a different light from what our Progressionists (?) are wont to do; nevertheless, they profess, and herald the doctrines of a natural religion. Their phrase, applied to nature, "One body of one immortal soul," comprehends all things with them. Their Deity is the Positive Power, or law in Nature, the Motive Force, the active agent, divine Principle. It is co-existent with matter, is the essence or soul of matter. Who can define the difference between the sentiment of these modern Prophets and that of the prophets of Baal? Each makes nature Deity and denies the God of the Hebrews —of the Christian church. The variation, if any, consists in different degrees of transcendentalism. The ancient sun worshipers had idols as representatives of their gods. The modern nature-worshipers deitize "*affinities*," worship at the shrine of "*attractions*," and make themselves more consequential.

The other main pillar of this Harmonial edifice or temple of natural religion, is that of spiritual communication. This, also, constituted the life of Baal worship. "Manasseh did that which was evil in the sight of the Lord, after the abominations of the heathen, whom the Lord cast out before the children of Israel. For he built up again the places which Hezekiah his father had destroyed; and he reared up altars for Baal, and made a grove, as did Ahab, king of Israel: and worshiped all the hosts of heaven and served them. And he built altars for all the hosts of heaven in the two courts of the house of the Lord. And he made his son pass through the fire, and observed times, and used enchantments, and dealt with familiar spirits and wizards." 2 Kings, xxi. In old Testament times, then, Harmonial Spiritualism was in vogue.

And the prophets of Baal were the media it employed. What is Anti-Bible Spiritualism but the revival of that religion whose power was tested by the prophets before Elijah? The Baalite encouraged, while the Inspired Word condemned consulting familiar spirits, those which denied the God of Israel and encouraged the worship of Nature. This doctrine is clearly identified, and the nature of the influences defined in Deut. xviii. 10–11. "There shall not be found among you any one that maketh his son or his daughter to pass through the fire, or that useth divination, or an observer of times, or an enchanter, or a witch or a charmer, or a consulter of familiar spirits, or a wizard, or a necromancer. For all that do these things are an abomination to the Lord." That is, such seek to destroy faith in the doctrine of God's covenant with Abram; hence, the principle upon which Abram went forth, Isaac was offered, the house of Israel set apart; and in the Being and attributes of Jehovah, and the doctrines of the Decalogue. Those who caused their sons and daughters to pass through the fire were followers after Baal—were idol, sun, or nature-worshipers.

"And the spirit of Egypt shall fail in the midst thereof; and I will destroy the counsel thereof: and they" (who deny my Name) "shall seek to the idols, and to the charmers, and to them that have familiar spirits, and to the wizards." Isa. xix. 3. "And when they shall say unto you, Seek unto them which have familiar spirits, and unto wizards that peep and mutter; should not a people seek unto their God? To the law and to the testimony; if they speak not according to this word, it is because there is no light in them. And they shall pass through it hardly bestead and hungry: and it shall come to pass, that when they shall be hungry shall fret themselves, and curse their king and God, and look upward. And they shall look unto the earth, and behold trouble and darkness, dimness of anguish: and they shall be driven to darkness." Isa. viii. 19-22.

"And they took away the horses that the kings of Judah had given to the sun at the entering in of the house of the Lord, by the chamber of Nathanmelech the chamberlain which was in the suburbs, and burned the chariots of the sun with fire. And the altars that were on the top of the upper chamber of Ahaz, and the altars which Manasseh had made in the two courts of the house of the Lord, did the king beat down, and break them down from thence, and cast the dust of them into the brook Kidron." 2 Kings, xxiii. 11-12.

Those familiar with the movements, and doctrines of Harmonial spiritualism cannot fail to notice the conformity between ancient idolatry connected with consulting familiar spirits, whence originated hostility to the Hebrew faith, and modern Bible-opposing manifestations. It is quite evident from results, that recent phenomena connected with Mesmerism, Biology, etc., are no less than the spirit of ancient heathenism then manifested in unnumbered forms, embracing immolation, fetishism, theurgy, hecatomb, sorcery, fascination, etc., modified in mode however, by the usages of the times, and rendered more spiritual by the transcendental tendency of the age. So fascinating was the ancient system, that it frequently obtained to a very great extent even with the Israelites. Wherever it prevailed the God of Abraham was denied and Blasphemed. Wherever it now prevails its effects serve to engender criticism upon the Bible and weaken faith in its validity and reverence for him who is therein denominated the Supreme Being, Jehovah.

It is clear therefore that nothing new under the sun has come to pass in these last days; but that at periods, the power now at work with the people, and against true christianity, has arisen in its might and swept over the world like monsoons. And what renders the system more effectual with the religious world is the incorporation of reflex truth, of the Gospel. By this means multitudes are led at first to believe it the very Gospel.

Moreover, as it is ever liable to be with erring man, many absolute inconsistencies are appended to, if not interwoven with the more external manifestations of the church. These as in ancient days, are, by the opposers, magnified, and presented as the signet of the great underwriter of christianity. And from the very apparent inefficiency of these errors, the plan of salvation through Jesus the Crucified, is proclaimed a fraud. Herein, as connected with the undefinable, incomprehensible and magic movement of the laws of magnetism, Harmonial spiritualism, etc., consists the power of the invasion upon the Inspired Word, now so mighty in its goings forth.

CHAPTER VI.

ESTHER BEFORE THE KING.

THE Old Testament is replete with demonstrations of a similar character to those already noticed. Indeed it is a history of like manifestations; those in which Divine Inspiration is opposed and the especial messengers of Heaven pursued with dread vindictiveness and frequently subjected to the severest trials. It matters little whether the opposition and suffering be from Cain, Pharaoh, the Prophets of Baal, Soothsayers, consulters of familiar Spirits, the fiery furnace, lions' den, Cross, faggot, Mesmerism, Harmonial spiritualism, the purpose and disposition seem the same. The opposed and afflicted, though Abel, Moses, Elijah, Mordecai, Job, Shadrach and his companions, Daniel, JESUS of Nazareth, his apostles, the Martyrs of the middle ages, or the true Christian of the Nineteenth Century, are the external agents, the ambassadors of Heaven, the advocates of Theocracy, Divine Inspiration, and the gospel of the Crucified Redeemer.

Pursuing the ancient history and omitting many important and confirmatory events, we pause to briefly consider the case of Mordecai and Queen Esther. Their trial was with the malicious Haman, whose manifestations class him with the agents of that heaven opposing power which has ever afflicted the faithful servants of God. In that scene, enacted ages long since passed, the proud malicious spirit of evil sought the extirpation of the Jews in the dominion of Ahasuerus the king; but was foiled in a most remarkable manner; and the consequences intended for the worshipers of God, fell upon the head of the medium of the evil device. Most insidious was the scheme to cut off God's people and prostrate the purposes of heaven through them.

Haman as above noticed, was the medium of evil, Mordecai was the point of revenge, while Esther was the means employed for the rescue; the manner of whose exaltation appears to have been the result of divine Wisdom, and for that especial purpose. That from which the conflict arose, consisted in an effort to compel Mordecai to bow down to Haman, a requirement which directly affected his religion. The true Hebrew worshiped God, and him only would he serve. But the decree went forth. "And all the king's servants that were in the king's gate, bowed and reverenced Haman, for the king had commanded concerning him. But Mordecai bowed not, nor did him reverence." How could he bow before man, since the Lord, whom he adored had commanded his people to have no God before him. "And when Haman saw that Mordecai bowed not, nor did him reverence, then was Haman full of wrath. And he thought scorn to lay hands upon Mordecai alone: wherefore Haman sought to destroy all the Jews in the kingdom of Ahasuerus, even the people of Mordecai."

This exceeded personal revenge. Mordecai, alone, had offended; and adequate redress did not require the sacrifice of a people. Nevertheless, his resolution to withhold servile reverence from Haman, was made an occasion against all the Jews in the king's dominion. And Haman's plea before Ahasuerus, plainly discloses an enmity to that scattered and already afflicted race; a disposition to remove them from among men, which disposition has too frequently been evinced by the foe of the true Israelite and devout christian. "And Haman said unto king Ahasuerus, There is a certain people scattered abroad and dispersed among the people of all the provinces of thy kingdom; and their laws are diverse from all people; neither keep they the king's laws: therefore it is not for the king's profit to suffer them. If it please the king, let it be written that they may be destroyed. And I will pay ten thousand talents of silver to the hands of those who have the charge of the business, to bring it into the king's treasures. And the king took his ring from his hand, and gave it unto Haman the son of Hammedatha the Agagite, the Jews' enemy. And the king said unto Haman, The silver is given unto thee, the people also, to do with them as it seemeth good to thee."

The decree was written in the king's name, and sealed with his seal, and sent forth through all the land. "And the king and Haman sat down to drink. But the city of Shushan was perplexed." Again the God of heaven, in his people is mocked and defied; and that spirit which wantonly slew Abel because he offered acceptable sacrifice before the Lord, once more seeks to vent his wrath upon the worshipers of the true God.

How manifest the disparity between the faithful servant of the Lord and the carnal man! how dissimilar in character the two controlling principles! And how marked their distinguishing qualities, when from time to time revealed in important trials. One discloses a deep and genuine devotion to heavenly requirements; the other a disposition to gratify the baser propensions. The natural man indulges in human pleasure, pride, ambition; and if occasion requires, extreme cruelty; while the Heaven-revering soul is cross-bearing, and the victim of maltreatment from the world-serving.

The history states that, "When Mordecai perceived all that was done, he rent his clothes, and put on sack-cloth and ashes, and went out into the midst of the city, and cried with a loud and bitter cry. And came even before the king's gate: for none might enter the king's gate clothed with sackcloth. And in every province, whithersoever the king's commandment and his decree came, there was great mourning among the Jews, and fasting and weeping and wailing; and many lay in sackcloth and ashes." Thus while the king and Haman were reveling and indulging in passional excess, the despised Jews were fasting and mourning in sackcloth and ashes. In this also the characters of the two principles are manifested.

"When the thing came to Esther, the Queen, she was grieved, and sent raiment to Mordecai, and to take away his sackcloth from him: but he received it not; but sent a copy of the writing to Esther, and charged her to go unto the king and importune with him for her people. Esther returned answer, That it was well known that whosoever, whether man or woman, should go unto the king into the inner court, one law of his was to put them to death, except to whom he held out his scepter. Mordecai replied that *her house* would also suffer in the massacre. Moreover said he, "Who knoweth whether thou art come to the kingdom for such a time as this?"

Then said Esther, "Go gather together all the Jews that are present in Shushan, and fast ye for me, and neither eat nor drink three days, night or day: I also and my maidens will fast likewise; and then will I go in unto the king, which is not according to law, and if I perish, I perish."

A day of awful moment was now approaching. The earthly inheritance and life of Esther and her people trembled as if suspended upon a mortal breath. But what appeared in the external world as poising upon one human thought, the decisive thought of the King in the moment of trial, was meager compared with the interior conflict, and the consequences of the inclination of one frail mind. The law once passed could not be repealed and the king's monarchical dignity be preserved. How to rescue the victims from the storm of death already hanging over them was not for man to devise. This Esther full well knew. She therefore proposed to fast three days and nights with all her people, and then she would go before the king which was not according to law. She could but perish, and peradventure the king would be propitious.

Mourning and lamentation arose from the host who were suspended over the yawning sepulchre of death. Multitudes lay day and night in sackcloth and ashes. And can it be supposed that they did not present their cause before the God of Sabaoth whose laws they kept, and for which they now, as a people, were doomed to destruction? Did they not remember his promise to Abraham? his blessings upon Isaac? and his power displayed in the Exodus of the children of Israel from Egyptian bondage? The unnumbered demonstrations of God's providential care bestowed upon his people must have arisen before their afflicted minds. And with agony too deep for tears, they must have uttered as the voice of one: "Thou God of Abraham, Isaac, and Jacob, remember now thy people who are bowed before thee. Because obedient to thy law, ourselves and our little ones are doomed by a mortal to the cruel slaughterer. Our ways are known to thee. Though we have erred, thou art merciful. For thy Name's sake, for the sake of the world buried in iniquity, for the sake of unnumbered generations yet unborn, break thou the power of the foe of heaven, of good, of man. Turn the heart of the king. Let Esther, thy handmaiden, find favor in his sight: and O, thou Eternal Spirit, who art from everlasting to everlasting, thou who upholdest the vast universe, and givest light to all, rescue thy people, and let the evil one, and the nations round about, and succeeding ages, know, that thou art God, and hearest prayer, and answerest thy people when in righteousness and humility they call upon thee."

On the day set apart, and after Esther and her maidens and the Jews had fasted, "It came to pass that Esther put on her royal apparel, and appeared in the inner court according as she had determined. And while the king sat upon his royal throne, in his royal house over against the gate of the house, she drew near." The trial had come, Esther stood before the king! It was a moment in which her fate and that of her people must be sealed, a moment fraught with interests that should affect nations yet unborn. Motionless as a statue she stood in the suppliant's attitude, and paused for the eventful decision. But Esther was not alone in the king's court. The God whom she and her people served, had commissioned the Angel of the Covenant, and with the Spirit of Salvation that Angel also drew near. The king's heart felt the softening influence of the heavenly sphere which pervaded the royal palace. His soul was inclined to the Queen, and lo, his hand moved and the golden sceptre was held out! The Divine power prevailed, Esther approached, touched the scepter, and made known her mission. "If it seem good unto the king," she meekly said, "let the king and Haman come this day unto the banquet I have prepared for him."

"In those days, while Mordecai sat in the king's gate, two of the king's chamberlains, Bigthan and Teresh of those who were wroth, and sought to lay hands upon the king, Ahasuerus. And the thing was known to Mordecai, who told it unto Esther the queen; and Esther certified it to the king thereof in Mordecai's name. And when inquisition was made of the matter, it was found out, therefore they were both hanged on a tree. And it was written in a book of chronicles before the king."

Mysterious to man are the ways of providence. How little mortals understand the consequences of a single act. Mordecai's loyalty and faithfulness to the king was recorded upon the pages of his private history. There it remained unnoticed, until after the king and Haman came to the banquet that Esther had prepared. But "On that night could not the king sleep."

Adam Clarke in his notes upon Ch. vi., remarks: "The Targum says the king had a dream, which was as follows: 'And the king saw one in the similitude of a man, who spoke these words to him: Haman desireth to slay thee, and to make himself king in thy stead. Behold, he will come to thee early in the morning to ask from thee the man who rescued thee from death, that he may slay him: but say thou unto him, What shall be done for the man whose honor the king studieth? And thou wilt find that he will ask nothing less from thee than the royal vestments, the regal crown, and the horse on which the king is wont to ride." Troubled, the king could not sleep. How manifest that providence which encompassed the chosen race! And how prominent the answer to the prayer of the burdened Jews! God, however, made choice of the means to accomplish the end.

Disturbed and anxious, the king commanded to bring the book of records, of the chronicles: and they were read before the king. And it was found written that Mordecai had told of the conspiracy and saved the king. And he said, What honor and dignity hath been done to Mordecai for this? Then said the king's servants who ministered unto him, there is nothing done unto him.

"And the king said, Who is in the court? Now Haman was come into the outer court of the king's house to speak unto the king to hang Mordecai upon the gallows that he had in his pride and haste prepared for him." How vain! He could not endure until the day of execution, but must seek to hang the innocent Mordecai, for his presence annoyed him. The gallows was prepared; it was fifty cubits high. "And the king's servants said unto him, Behold, Haman standeth in the court. And the king said, Let him come in. So Haman came in." Haman's heart was enlarged with the spirit of triumph. The only spot upon his coronet of fame, the only corroding element in his sensual bliss, was Mordecai. True he would perish at the hand of the assassin on the day set apart for the legalized murder of the Jews: but to suffer his presence until then he could not. He resolved therefore to have him hung upon the gallows. Haman's former success insured in his mind, the sanction of the king to that which would be the finishing stroke of his ambitious eclat. "Live forever, O, king," as a prelude to his petition, quivered on his lips, impatient for utterance, when the king said, What shall be done to the man whom the king delighteth to honor?" More glory, even, than Haman's sordid soul had anticipated, now awaited him. The object of his mission was sure since the king was about to add new honors to his increasing renown. "He thought in his heart, To whom would the king delight to do honor more than to myself?" And he answered, "For the man whom the king delighteth to honor, let the royal apparel be brought, which the king useth to wear, and the horse that the king rideth upon, and the crown royal which is set upon his head: and let this apparel and horse be delivered to the hand of one of the king's most noble princes, that they may array the man withal whom the king delighteth to honor, and bring him on horseback through the streets of the city, and proclaim before him, Thus shall it be done to the man whom the king delighteth to honor."

Proud heart! how inflated. Little did he know that in his vanity, and while seeking in his own dignity the humility of another, he was dooming himself and family to shame and death, and exalting him for whom he had erected the gallows. But alas, for finite man! When he designeth against God, and seeketh to make himself as God, his foot shall slip in an unexpected moment.

How stunned was Haman when the king said, "Make haste, and take the apparel, and the horse, as thou hast said, and do even so to Mordecai the Jew that sitteth at the king's gate: let nothing fail of all thou hast spoken." Humbled to the last degree must have been the heart of Haman, while crying before all the city to the honor of Mordecai. How fallen his spirit, when the visage of the gallows was changed, and his soul began to fear lest it might suspend his own body in ignominy before all the people.

Mourning and with his head covered he returned to his house. And he told his wife Zeresh and all his friends, what had befallen him. They answered, "If Mordecai be of the seed of the Jews before whom thou hast begun to fall, thou shalt not prevail against him, but shalt surely fall before him. And while they were yet talking with him, came the king's chamberlains and hasted to bring Haman unto the banquet Esther had prepared."

But the evil device was frustrated, the vile genus foiled, the end purposed anticipated, and now the parties might meet. The way of salvation was opened and Esther could prevail.

"So the king and Haman came to banquet with Esther the queen. And the king said again unto Esther on the second day of the banquet of wine, What is thy petition queen Esther? and it shall be granted thee: and what is thy request? and it shall be performed even to the half of the kingdom."

Merciful dispensation! The Jews were but mortals, but the God of Heaven had revealed his purpose to bring salvation to the world through the seed of Abraham. And from that day the prince of evil pursued them. The prophets of the Lord were hunted like the partridge upon the mountain. And, as the fowler seeks his prey, even so the emissaries of Satan pursued the Israel of God. Often had the cloud of impenetrable darkness closed around them. Oft the enemies' infuriated hosts had encamped about them. The taskmasters had urged them to their daily toil until their hearts failed them, the nerve became languid, the blood ran slowly through the vein, and the emaciated muscle relaxed. The chariot and horseman had pursued them: but in every instance when they looked up to God his Might had interposed and his Mercy had saved them. Adorable Providence! How faithfully fulfilled that promise: "*I will never leave nor forsake thee.*"

How every heart of the Jews must have felt the suspense, while Esther was before the king. In God was their hope, and their trust in Esther as the means. Without, the mourning Jews kept silent with their desire upon God, while the conference proceeded.

"Then Esther, the queen, answered and said, If I have found favor in thy sight, O king, and if it please the king, let my life be given at my petition, and my people at my request: for we are sold, I and my people to be destroyed, to be slain, and to perish. But if we had been sold for bondmen and bondwomen, I had held my tongue, although the enemy could not countervail the damage."

What peril! Not liberty, *but life,* was the burden of her prayer. O, thou most unmerciful and wicked foe of Israel! How thou hast multiplied the woes of God's children! And in thy arch designs hast involved as thy agents the fallen world. What is man that thy madness should thus bedew their couch with tears, burden the air with their groans, and pour upon the earth their blood like water?

Surprised at her strange request, "King Ahasuerus answered and said unto Esther the queen, Who is he, and where is he that durst presume in his heart to do so?"

It would appear that the king had been blinded by the influence upon and around him, and therefore had not considered what had been done nor computed the cost, nor considered the consequences of the death-warrant he had sent forth throughout the land. So fascinating and blinding to the sense was the charmer's power that in reality he knew not the character nor measure of his deed. Even so in this day, not one man alone, but multitudes, spell-bound, act scarcely knowing what they do. Deprived of their native thought, and their own determination paralyzed, they proceed impelled by a power they know not, and undertake measures so adverse to their better sense, that should they be aroused they would abruptly ejaculate, even as did Ahasuerus, "Who? He? This one, and where? What? Who hath filled his heart to do this?" (Original.)

And Esther said, "The main adversary and enemy is this wicked Haman."

What a cloud must have rolled from the king's mind when the charm was broken. The infamous plot arose in all its diabolical form before him.

"And the king arising from the banquet in his wrath, went into the palace garden: and Haman stood to make request for his life to Esther the queen: for he saw that there was evil determined against him by the king."

The scale was changed. The power that had urged him on, having failed, forsook the vile agent in his hour of trial. Against God Haman had been designing, and therefore he was left to the consequences of his course. Each movement sank him still deeper in the quicksands of his ruin. Even his prayer for mercy was the most fatal of all his deeds, and was converted in the king's mind to a most heinous crime. He fell! and was hanged upon the gallows he had erected for Mordecai. Strange reversion! But the Purpose with which his designs contended was the Purpose of God, and Omnipotent, therefore unfailing. Hence Haman's fall was inevitable.

THE COUNTER DECREE.

"And Esther spake yet again before the king, and fell down at his feet and besought him, with tears, to put away the mischief of Haman the Agagite, and his device that he had devised against the Jews. Then the king held out the golden sceptre toward Esther. So Esther arose and stood before the king, and said, If it please the king, and I have found favor in his sight, and the thing seem right before the king, and I be pleasing in his eyes, let it be written to reverse the letters devised by Haman the son of Hammadetha, the Agagite which he wrote to destroy the Jews which are in all the king's provinces: for how can I endure to see the evil that shall came upon my people? and how can I endure to see the destruction of my kindred?"

The final plea of Esther availed. But as the former writing might not be revoked, by order of the king, it was written and sent in haste throughout the king's provinces, from India unto Ethiopia, an hundred and twenty-seven provinces, unto every province according to the writing thereof, and to every people after their language, and to the Jews according to their writing and according to their language. It was written in Ahasuerus' name, and sealed with the king's ring. Wherein the king granted to the Jews which were in every city to gather themselves together and to stand for their life upon the day previously set apart for their slaughter. In this manner, the former decree was countermanded.

The Jews gathered upon that day and became a terror to all the people, so that no man laid hand upon them. Thus thy were preserved, and

Esther and Mordecai were exalted to power. No unprejudiced mind can fail to discover in this event, the hand of divine Providence in the salvation of the Jews and the defeat of the opposing power. And that the same characteristics which had hitherto been manifested by the two principles were there most prominently disclosed. Nor is it needful further to exemplify to reveal the great truth of God's purpose in the Jews; and the determination of evil to overthrow them in order to contravene the end designed in their election.

CHAPTER VII.

THE DREAM AND ITS INTERPRETATION.

"AND the king" (Nebuchadnezzar) "spake unto Ashpenaz, the master of his eunuchs, that he should bring certain of the children of Israel, and of the king's seed, and of the princes; children in whom there was no blemish, but well favored, and skilled in all wisdom, and cunning in knowledge, and understanding science, and such as had ability in them to stand in the king's palace, and whom they might teach the learning and the tongue of the Chaldeans. Now among them were of the children of Judea, Daniel, Hananiah, Mishael and Azariah: unto whom the prince of the eunuchs gave names: for he gave unto Daniel the name of Belteshazzar; and to Hananiah, of Shadrach; and to Mishael of Meshach; and to Azariah, of Abed-Nego."

These are the elect, and they are as men qualified, naturally, for the king's purpose. And hence no native defect can expose them to trial with their king or his princes. Moreover, God had brought Daniel into favor and tender love with the prince of the eunuchs. But Daniel had purposed in his heart that he would not defile himself with the portion of the king's meat, nor with the wine that he drank: therefore he requested of the prince of the eunuchs that he might not defile himself.

"As for these four children, God gave them knowledge in all learning and wisdom: and Daniel had understanding in all visions and dreams.

"And in the second year of the reign of Nebuchadnezzar he dreamed dreams wherewith his spirit was troubled and his sleep brake from him. Then the king commanded to call the magicians, and the astrologers, and the sorcerers, and the Chaldeans, for to show the king his dreams. So they came and stood before the king. And the king said unto them I have dreamed a dream, and my spirit is troubled to know the dream. Then spake the Chaldeans to the king in Syriac, O, king, live forever: tell thy servants the dream, and we will show the interpretation. The king answered and said to the Chaldeans, The thing is gone from me: if ye will not make known unto me the dream, with the interpretation thereof, ye shall be cut in pieces, and your houses shall be made a dunghill. But if ye shew me the dream and the interpretation thereof ye shall receive of me gifts, and rewards and great honor: therefore shew me the dream and the interpretation thereof. The Chaldeans answered before the king, and said, There is not a man upon the earth that can shew the king's matter, except the gods, whose dwelling is not with flesh. For this cause the king was angry and very furious, and commanded to destroy all the wise men of Babylon. And they sought Daniel and his fellows to be slain. Then Daniel answered with counsel and wisdom to Arioch, the captain of the king's guard, which was gone forth to slay the wise men of Baylon; and he said, Why is the decree so hasty from the king. Then Arioch made the thing known to Daniel. Then Daniel went in and desired of the king, that he would give him the time and that he would show him the interpretation. And then made it known to his brethren that they would desire mercies of the God of heaven concerning this secret; that Daniel and his fellows might not perish with the rest of the wise men of Babylon."

Again we are recounting scenes of immortal worth to the christian. The king's wise men are brought to the trial which involves life. They are required to do what the Astrologers, Soothsayers, etc., declare man cannot do, and none but the gods who dwelt not in flesh could bring to pass. And with all their wisdom, the policy of natural endowments, and their chicanery, they yielded, with the decree still echoing in their hearing: "If ye will not make known to me the dream and the interpretation thereof, ye shall be cut in pieces. Ye have prepared lying and corrupt words to speak before me until the time be changed." They could trifle, and play upon incidents and minor demonstrations, but when test equal to their profession was required, they confronted the king, saying, "It is a rare thing the king requireth."

Daniel and his fellows had not been counseled, nor even informed of the king's trouble until the decree was passed, and the captain of the guard, while going forth to slay the wise men, sought them as sharers in the fate of the unfortunate victims. As though every hope must be cut-off, every earthly means rendered unavailable before the Hebrews should be apprised of their danger.

Daniel appealed unto the God of heaven for deliverance, confident, if it was for God's glory he could give answer. The lives of the faithful servants of the Lord were most rashly jeopardized. Nor shall we, considering the history of these Hebrews, distort the circumstances into unnatural features, by charging the scheme as the plot of interior evil: and that the tragedy was designed in order to cut off those Hebrews, especially Daniel, with whom God's designs were connected; and who constituted an important link in the chain of events terminating in the advent of the Messiah. The position he occupied in that age, and the display of God's grace connected with him rendered his existence necessary to the uses of that period. His prophetic visions, and the prediction of the Spirit: "Go thy way, Daniel; for the words are closed up and sealed till the time of the end: go thy way, until the end be: for thou shalt rest and stand in thy lot at the end of the days," render him an especial object of evil design. Therefore the conclusion is rational that, to prevent God's purpose in him, the spirit of darkness instituted the plan of massacre under consideration. But in this, also, the Enemy of righteousness was doomed to fall before the Spirit of Truth. For in a night vision the secret was revealed to Daniel; and he blessed the God of heaven. Upon God he called, in him he relied, and when the secret was revealed, to him he gave the glory. Those Hebrews were, therefore, of that faith ever opposed by Satanic power, by sun, moon and star worshipers, and now, by Harmonial Spiritualists—advocates of a religion of Nature. Mark Daniel's declaration; observe his doctrines! "And Daniel answered and said, Blessed be the name of God forever and ever: for wisdom and might are his: and he changeth the times and seasons: he removeth kings and setteth up kings: he giveth wisdom unto the wise, and knowledge unto them that know understanding: he revealeth the deep and secret things: he knoweth what is in the darkness, and the light dwelleth with him.

"I thank thee and praise thee, O, thou God of my fathers, who hast given me wisdom and might, and hast made known unto me now, what we desired of thee: for thou hast now made known unto me the king's matter."

No one will presume to deny that the spirit Daniel manifested was identical with that revealed by the Patriarchs, and all the Lord's Prophets antecedent to him. His reliance was the same, his mode of action also was in perfect conformity with all before him who worshiped the God of Abraham. Around him, therefore, clustered the incidents of invaluable worth in the line of prophetic descent and divine unfoldings. God who had at sundry times and in divers manners revealed his purpose and disclosed his merciful designs unto the children of men; God whose ear is ever open to the prayer of his people; and who is almighty to save;—even the God of heaven shielded Daniel and his fellows, and confirmed the validity of his covenant with Abraham, and fulfilled his promise to regard all who in spirit and truth call upon his name.

"Therefore Daniel went in unto Arioch, whom the king had ordained to destroy the wise men of Babylon: he went and said thus unto him; destroy not the wise men of Babylon: bring me in before the king, and I will shew unto the king the interpretation."

How, but by the Spirit, did Daniel know he had the dream and could shew the interpretation? His confidence was in the God of heaven, not in men nor familiar spirits. Upon God he had called, and was assured that by his will the secret had been revealed to his mind. And now, in that faith he is ready to go before the king."

"Then Arioch brought in Daniel before the king in haste, and said thus unto him, I have found a man of the captives of Judea, that will make known unto the king the interpretation. The king answered and said unto Daniel, whose name was Belteshazzar, art thou able to make known unto me the dream which I have seen, and the interpretation thereof? Daniel answered in the presence of the king, and said, The secret which the king demanded cannot the wise men, the astrologers, the magicians, the soothsayers shew unto the king; but there is a God in heaven, that revealeth secrets, and maketh known to the king Nebuchadnezzar what shall be in the latter days. Thy dream, and the vision of thy head—upon thy bed, are these; As for thee, O, king, thy thoughts came *into thy mind* upon thy bed, what should come to pass hereafter: and he that revealeth secrets maketh known to thee what shall come to pass. But as for me, this secret is not revealed to me for any wisdom, that I have more than any living, but for their sakes that shall make known the interpretation to the king, and that thou mayest know the thoughts of thy heart."

How unlike the spirit of the carnal heart were the spirit and motives of Daniel? How precautionary, that the king should not accredit him with the wisdom, but that his mind should be directed to God as the Author and Giver. How meek and overflowing with the spirit of gratitude and reverence, and how careful to give God the glory. His humble soul delighted in that acknowledgement which at once precluded him from all importance in the matter, save that as God's servant he had sought unto him with all his heart, and submitted himself as the humble instrument of the Spirit.

Then said Daniel, "Thou, O king sawest and beheld a great image. This great image, whose brightness was excellent, stood before thee: and the form thereof was terrible." (See Daniel, xi., 31—44.) "And whereas thou sawest iron mixed with clay, they shall mingle themselves with the seed of men; but they shall not cleave one to another, even as iron is not mixed with clay. And in the days of those kings shall the God of heaven set up a kingdom which shall never be destroyed, and the kingdom shall not be left to other people, but it shall break in pieces and consume all these kingdoms, and it shall stand forever. Forasmuch as thou sawest that the stone was cut out of the mountain without hands, and that it brake in pieces the iron, the brass, the clay, the silver and the gold: the great God hath made known to the king what shall come to pass hereafter: and the dream is certain, and the interpretation thereof sure."

The dream and its interpretation being revealed to the king, greatly humbled him, and he answered unto Daniel, and said, "Of a truth it is that your God is a God of gods, and a Lord of kings, and a revealer of secrets, seeing thou couldst reveal this secret."

Although the preliminary circumstances, to all human appearance, greatly endangered Daniel and his fellows, the result disclosed one of the most important prophecies on record. And thus God again revealed his power and wisdom; also, the remembrance of his promise to Abraham that he would preserve his seed, and through them bless the nations of the earth.

CHAPTER VIII.

THE FIERY FURNACE.

BUT the trial of their faith, who worshiped the Living God, was not yet complete. A darker day awaited them. More subtle still were the evil machinations that conspired against them; and more dreadful the conflict purposed, by the Foe of all righteousness. For "Nebuchadnezzar the king made an image of gold, whose height was three-score cubits, and the breadth thereof six cubits: he set it up in the plain of Dura, in the province of Babylon. Then the king sent to gather together the princes, the governors and the captains, the judges, the treasures, the counselors, the sheriffs, and all the rulers of the provinces, to come to the dedication of the image which Nebuchadnezzar had set up, and when gathered together they stood before the image. Then a herald cried aloud, To you it is commanded, O people, nations, and languages, that at the time ye hear the sound of the cornet, flute, harp, sacbut, psaltery, dulcimer, and all kinds of music, ye shall fall down and worship the golden image that Nebuchadnezzar the king hath set up: and whoso falleth not down and worshipeth shall the same hour be cast into the midst of a burning fiery furnace. And at the time when the people heard the music, all the people, the nations, and the languages, fell down and worshiped the golden image. Wherefore certain Chaldees came near and accused the Jews, saying, O king, live forever. Thou hast made a decree that all at the sound of the music shall fall down and worship the image. There are certain Jews whom thou hast set over the offices of the provinces of Babylon, Shadrach, Meshach and Abed-Nego: these men, O king, have not regarded thee: they serve not thy gods, nor worship the golden image which thou hast made. Then the king in his rage and fury commanded them to be brought, and they brought these men before the king: and the king said, Is it true, O Shadrach, Meshach and Abed-Nego? do ye not serve my gods, nor worship the golden image which I have set up? Now if ye be ready that at what time ye hear all kinds of music to fall down and worship the image I have made, well; but if ye worship not, ye shall be cast the same hour into the midst of the burning fiery furnace: and who is that God that shall deliver you out of my hands?"

Thus is recorded another issue between the powers of darkness and the servants of God. The king, confident in his own sufficiency, menacingly enquires what God could save them when he purposed their destruction. He admitted no power above his, no authority equal. It was therefore presumptuous for any man, or number of men to attempt the infraction of his law. To do it was to blindly rush into the distended jaws of destruction.

Had the Jews, three in number, considered the consequences? What did they know of Abraham's God? Would he surely deliver them? To do so would require a miracle, and that the king and his wise men, soothsayers, astrologers, etc., considered contrary to nature, an infringement upon her laws, a violation of principles eternally fixed: and verily they deemed it the perfection of folly to entertain the remotest idea of its possibility, and a mark of insanity to believe in its probability. Hence the king according to his philosophy, could naturally say, The furnace is mine, my servants will readily heat it: the free and untrammeled thought of the dignitaries congregated unite with me in this principle, there can be no rescue, for surely no power in earth or heaven can save them. Will nature transcend her own laws? Never? It is preposterous for these bigoted Jews to resist my purpose, or seek to evade the fatal consequences of their stubbornness.

Guided by the evil genius displayed in former attempts to pervert the harmonious current of the divine Oracles, we can plainly perceive through the gauzy external, that fiend-like visage which mocks Divinity. The king and his hosts are the media, and the combined powers intent upon crushing the humble advocates of Divine Requirement, seek first to intimidate them by enhancing the probabilities against them, and beclouding their vision of faith, enshrouding the promises of God in doubt, and finally frustrating their confidence in the Abramatic Covenant. But being steadfast and immovable they, without faltering, repulsed the command. Neither were they moved by his threats, nor dismayed by the pomp of the royal acclaim which as the multitudes bowed and worshiped the image, filled the heavens with the prolonged utterance of the idolatrous chant. Their heart was fixed upon God; they loved his law, and would not bow down before the image or likeness of any thing that is in the heavens above, or in the earth beneath, or in the waters under the earth. Therefore, they answered the king, "O Nebuchadnezzar, we are not careful to answer thee in this matter. If it be so, our God whom we serve is able to deliver us from the burning fiery furnace, and he will deliver us out of thine hand, O king. But if not, be it known unto thee, O king, that we will not serve thy gods, nor worship the golden image which thou hast set up."

This was an earnest trial of faith. Their only hope was in God. He alone could save them. Still they indulged no misgivings, or inclination to consider the king's decree. They were resolved. In keeping that resolution they could but perish. If God was best glorified in their death, that was their choice. God had commanded, and obedience to his law was their first thought. Hence, in view of the heated furnace, and before the multitude they declared, in une-equivocal terms, their immovable determination, "If our God see not fit to deliver us, be it known unto thee, O king, we will not serve thy gods, nor worship the image which thou hast made." Do with us as thou seest fit, if we perish we perish.

"Then the king was filled with fury, and the form of his visage was changed toward them; therefore he commanded that they should heat the furnace even seven times more than it was wont to be heated."

This history reveals in the proceedings of the king the same spirit which has been traced throughout the annals of the Church. A spirit of affliction, of effort to extinguish the light of truth being revealed in the faithful Israel. Now the inspiration was against Shadrach, Meshach and Abed-Nego, whose religion prohibited their obedience to the king. Still the decree was that all should bow before the image, and whosoever refused should be cast into the fiery furnace. The Jews disregarding the king and his edict rendered themselves obnoxious. The multitude, like some bending forest, bowed before the image. But as the mass of human beings lay low in the dust, three forms, firmly erect, silently defied the majesty of the king, and scorned the servile show. Statue-like they entered their protest against the heaven-daring sin, and regardless of the consequences, vindicated the law of God, and were therefore, the agents of the divine Spirit through whom the Power of the Lord was to be revealed.

Obedient to the cruel and most rash edict, the three "were bound in their coats, their hosen, and their hats, and their other garments, and were cast into the midst of the burning fiery furnace." But the heat was so intense that it slew those men that cast them into the furnace. "And as the men fell down bound into the furnace, the king was astonished, and rose up in haste and spake and said, Did we not cast three men bound into the midst of the fire? Lo, I see four men loose, walking in the midst of the fire, and they have no hurt; and the form of the fourth is like the Son of God."

If this history be correct, (and who shall be able to disprove its authenticity,) this was a supernatural interposition: a suspension of a natural law. And the presence of the fourth, having the appearance of a God, is a spiritualism that is truly available, reliable, and absolutely useful. Moreover, it was a manifestation in opposition to the maxim of progressionists, "*nature must have her course.*" It would have been natural for the fire to have consumed the men: otherwise was unnatural. Therefore this is verily a supernatural manifestation. And this one instance is sufficient, of itself, to break in pieces the image of clay now revealing its colossal stature; on whose brow is inscribed "Nature's Divine Revelations," "Great Harmonial," "Natural Religion," "Harmonial Spiritualism," "Friends of Progress," etc., etc. In whose right hand is a human form, bound by and the instrument of mesmerism; and from whose mouth issues many words, as if from the Divine, which being interpreted is, "Let all the world revere the Organ." In its left hand is a vase, containing many relics, some gathered from the land and some from the seas.

Upon the breast is a cloudy mirror, reflecting, in unmeaning order, the vestiges of the past. These uniting, seek to disclose the Beginning, Unfolding and End of all things. The body is Pantheism; over its brow is a hazy atmosphere, called Progressive or Harmonial Spiritualism.

It denies the supernatural, yet wreathes about its temples illusive appearances, bedecked in fantastic order with fugitive gems from the supernatural realm. Though when superficially viewed, resembling a structure massive and strong, its body, when analyzed, is found to be of perishable, unreal and unsightly parts; hence the manifestation above considered, and which is recorded in the book of Daniel, Ch. iii., breaks it in pieces. For it is recorded that Nebuchadnezzar the king, when "Coming near to the mouth of the burning fiery furnace, said to Shadrach, Meshach and Abed-Nego, Ye saints of the most high God, come forth and come hither. When they came forth from the midst of the fire, and the princes, governors, and captains, and the king's counselors, being gathered together, saw these men, upon whose bodies the fire had no power, nor was a hair on their head singed, neither were their coats changed, nor the smell of fire had passed on them."

This surely excels modern manifestations, at least any that have come before the public. What are the "rappings"—producing a few intonations—or performances upon musical instruments, revealing hands and feet; writing, speaking, or pouring forth language in torrents, through well-trained and long-experienced media;—yea, what are all the manifestations of the age, when compared with this? Are there, or could there be, greater and more ample manifestations? What though the Rev. Dr. ——, the Hon. Mr. ——, the highly respectable Ed. ——, etc., etc., assure the public, that in their presence, and to the satisfaction of their senses, a spirit medium was mysteriously actuated—and that a book was written in prose or rhyme in an incredibly short space of time, and some unknown facts were most astonishingly revealed, or event disclosed, ere it had by other means, come to light?

Do any or all of these exceed the vision and its interpretation, by Daniel? or the Presence in the fiery furnace? Nay, verily, all modern phenomena sink into dim shadows, when compared with this. And it is a manifestation strictly Biblical, being, by incorporation, a part of the Bible. It is one opposed to all isms, notions, or creeds which deny the God of Abraham, and the truth of Divine Inspiration. In the light, and by the aid of disclosures from the eternal and invisible world, the Bible is sustained as true, and by the infinite superiority of the character of the manifestation, it is exalted to a plane far above that of recent developments, and therefore its doctrines are established as truths. Hence all opposition from Spiritualism is powerless, and the Bible endures the Ordeal of the Nineteenth Century, like pure gold. Truth may be discarded by the multitudes still it abides, since founded in eternal reality, and those who reject it suffer loss. Is the narration under consideration classed with legends and therefore doubtful? Why? Is it not sustained by unimpeached testimony? Is it less reliable because of ancient date? All history may be erased upon the same principle, and man left without any knowledge of the past. And succeeding generations might be led to regard the present in like manner. This would make time a blank—a void. Have important results attended modern spiritualism, such as inducing men to change their opinions and modes of thought? Note the effect of the ancient manifestation upon the king.

"Then Nebuchadnezzar spake and said, blessed be the God of Shadrach, Meshach and Abed-Nego, who hath sent his angel, and delivered his servants that trusted in him, and have changed the king's words, and yielded their bodies, that they might not serve nor worship any god, except their own God. Therefore I make a decree, that every people, nation and language, which speak any thing amiss against the God of Shadrach, Meshach and Abed-Nego, shall be cut in pieces, and their houses shall be made a dunghill; because there is no other God that can deliver after this sort." Has the like been produced in modern times.

For spiritualists to denounce this account is worse than folly. And until they can at least equal it, in vain they condemn its doctrines, and by works infinitely inferior seek to establish an opposing theory. What though a man or a number of men who have doubted the immortality of the soul, are in opinion changed by the modern demonstrations? By one test, a king reversed his decree, acknowledged the existence of the true God, his power to save, and declared that by no other means the like effect could have been produced. Let therefore, Bible-opposing spiritualists call to their aid equal power, and disclose before the world at midday, as astounding facts; then may they demand acknowledgement to their opposing theories; but by virtue thereof can only expect equal credit with the Bible relative to the great question of Religion. But until then, it were better and more consistent by far, that they dismiss their efforts against the Inspired Word.

Do professed believers in christianity, who are being led into doubt respecting the Divine Origin of the Bible, by modern "Spiritualism," "Mesmerism," "Biology," etc., do they realize the meagerness of the present phenomena in their highest phases, and their insignificance when compared with those revealed in the Scriptures of Truth? Let the christian pause ere he takes the fatal step, lest he at last be found to have exchanged the Divine and Infinite, for a frail, exceedingly vague and imperfect cause. "And why should the heathen rage and the people imagine a vain thing?" As well might the fugitive leaf from some dwarfed shrub deny the origin of gathered fruit, or the existence of the tree that bore it: and while fluttering in the changing breezes boast of its ponderous worth and its progressive tendency to the foliage of celestial bowers.

CHAPTER IX.

THE SMITTEN TREE.

NEBUCHADNEZZAR the king unto all people, nations, and languages, that dwell in all the earth; Peace be multiplied unto you. I thought it good to shew the signs and wonders that the high God hath wrought toward me. How great are his signs! and how mighty are his wonders! his kingdom is an everlasting kingdom, and his dominion is from generation to generation. I Nebuchadnezzar, was at rest in mine house and flourishing in my palace: I saw a dream which made me afraid, and the thoughts upon my bed and the visions of my head troubled me. Therefore I made a decree to bring all the wise men of Babylon before me, that they might make known unto me the interpretation thereof. Then came the magicians, the astrologers, the Chaldeans and the soothsayers: and I told the dream before them; but they did not make known the interpretation thereof."

Again, those who put their trust in nature, genius, and the magic movement of sympathetic laws, have failed. To play upon the mysterious, to excite the marvelous and awe the unlearned and inexperienced were not difficult, but to coin truth from the unbroken mine, or even from reflections, determine the cause and thence the results, was beyond their philosophy.

"But," says the king, "at the last Daniel came in before me, whose name was Belteshazzar, according to the name of my god, and in whom is the spirit of the holy gods; and before him I told the vision, saying, Thus were the visions of mine head in my bed; I saw, and beheld a tree in the midst of the earth, and the height thereof was great. The tree grew and was strong, and the height thereof reached unto the heaven, and the sight thereof to the end of the earth: the leaves thereof were fair, and the fruit thereof much, and it was meat for all: the beasts of the field had shadowed under it, and the fowls of heaven dwelt in the boughs thereof, and all flesh was fed of it. I saw in the vision of my head upon my bed, and behold a watcher and a holy one came down from heaven; he cried aloud and said thus, Hew down the tree, and cut off the branches, shake off his leaves and scatter his fruit: let the beasts get away from under it, and the fowls from his branches: nevertheless, leave the stump and his roots in the earth, even with a band of iron and brass, in the tender grass of the earth: and let it be wet with the dews of heaven: and let his portion be with the beasts in the grass of the earth: let his heart be changed, and let a beast's heart be given unto him. This matter is by decree the decree of the watchers, and the demand by the word of the holy ones: to the intent that the living may know that the Most High ruleth in the kingdom of men, and giveth it to whomsoever he will.

"This dream I, king Nebuchadnezzar, have seen. Now thou, O Belteshazzar, declare the interpretation thereof, forasmuch as all the wise men of my kingdom are not able to make known unto me the interpretation: but thou art able for the spirit of the holy gods is in thee." Daniel, ch. iv.

From demonstration, the king proves his wise men unable to reveal the secret or interpret the dream, thence for the solution he is compelled to seek Daniel, who was a worshiper of the God of heaven, with whom he declares the spirit of the holy gods to be. In other words, he acknowledges Daniel in communion with the spirit of Holiness and divine Wisdom. It is observable, also, that the astrologers and soothsayers depended upon a power whose existence was in a sphere more immediately connected with the natural, for Daniel's God, the opposite of theirs, was declared the God of heaven. From this it is certain that the king understood Daniel's profession to differ widely from that of his wise men and to embrace the Divine. Moreover, the king proves his inclination to seek wisdom from the astrologers, etc., for he first gave them the dream, nor did he call upon Daniel until compelled by necessity. When he saw Daniel his consciousness prompted his frank acknowledgement of the presence of the Divine with the Hebrew. The history, therefore, has a direct bearing upon the question at issue. And when viewed in their several aspects, the circumstances afford an exposition of the two principles thus far traced.

After hearing the dream "Daniel was astonished for one hour, and his thoughts troubled him." As his soul was in sympathy with divine Truth, and as heaven had purposed to shake the king and his dominion unless he (having so much light) repented, he saw the dark cloud which encompassed the king, and his soul was troubled. But the king said, Belteshazzar, let not the dream, or the interpretation thereof trouble thee. Belteshazzar answered, The tree thou sawest, strong, luxuriant, and laden with fruit, whose boughs were a habitation for the fowls of the heaven, and a shelter for the beasts of the field. It is thou, O king, that art grown and become strong. (See Daniel, iv., 22, 23.) This is the interpretation, O king, and this is the decree of the Most High, which is come upon my lord, the king: that they shall drive thee from men, and thy dwelling shall be with the beasts of the field, and they shall make thee eat grass as oxen, and they shall wet thee with the dew of heaven, and seven times shall pass over thee, till thou know that the Most High ruleth in the kingdom of men, and giveth it to whomsoever he will. And whereas they commanded to leave the stump of the tree roots; thy kingdom shall be secure unto thee, after that thou shalt have known that the heavens do rule. Wherefore, O king, let my counsel be acceptable unto thee, and break off thy sins by righteousness, and thy iniquity by showing mercy to the poor; if it may be a lengthening of thy tranquility.

"All this came upon king Nebuchadnezzar. At the end of twelve months he walked in the palace of the kingdom of Babylon. And while boasting of his power and dominion, there fell a voice from heaven, saying, O king Nebuchadnezzar, to thee it is spoken; the kingdom is dedeparted from thee, and they shall drive thee," etc. "The same hour the thing was fulfilled, and he was driven from men, and did eat grass as oxen, and his body was wet with the dews of heaven, till his hairs were grown like eagles feathers, and his nails like birds' claws. And at the end of the days I, Nebuchadnezzar, lifted up mine eyes unto heaven, and mine understanding returned unto me, and I blessed the Most High, and I praised and honored him that liveth forever and ever, whose dominion is an everlasting dominion, and his kingdom from generation to generation: and all the inhabitants of the earth are reputed as nothing: and he doeth according to his will in the armies of heaven, and among the inhabitants of the earth: and none can stay his hand, or say unto him, What doest thou?

"And at the same time my reason returned unto me; and for the glory of my kingdom, mine honor and brightness returned unto me; and my counselors and my lords sought unto me; and I was established in my kingdom and excellent majesty was added unto me."

The strength of this vision, its interpretation and fulfillment, according to the principle declared by Daniel, is so apparent and so applicable that it needs little comment. 1. It was a reproof, a solemn admonition. 2. Being from the divine sphere, the natural man could obtain no light upon it, his material mind was capable of no adequate or even legitimate conceptions of its true character or interest. 3. It was only interpreted by means of him whose hope and trust was in the living God. 4. To obey the heavenly injunction was contrary to the king's inclination. 5. Its fulfillment only echoed the interpretation —both harmonized. To record the events in the retribution, only required the repetition of the language employed in its interpretation. 6. Its effects, when verified by actual occurrences, served to humble the proud monarch, according to indication. 7. When the king acknowledged his frailty, and that of all flesh; the power, wisdom and goodness of God, he was restored and abundantly blessed. 8. And finally, the ultimate effect was to cause the king to exalt the name of the Most High, as the King of heaven, and to proclaim all his works, Truth. Therefore, the events amply sustain the doctrine of the Inspired Word, expose the worthlessness of all manifestations, or dependence, which in any way conflict with the fundamental doctrines of the Bible. And also, that the arm of nature is paralyzed whenever an attempt is made to substitute it for the power of God; and that the God of Abraham, of the Hebrews, of the true Christian, is the Lord Almighty, the only Safety in the day of trouble.

CHAPTER X.

THE MYSTERIOUS WRITING.

THE sad scene now introduced is of the deepest interest, one to which modern spiritualists often refer, and which is by them claimed as evidence in their favor. And since by them employed as argument fovorable to their cause, it follows, most assuredly, that they endorse it as true. If, therefore, this is admitted into the catalogue of authentic facts, which no one conversant with the arguments of spiritualists will deny, the Book of Daniel must be admitted true. Either circumstance, then, recorded in Daniel cannot be denied by the spiritualists. And they prove the Harmonial theory false. If Progressionists claim what was called God's works in those days to have been only the "manifestation of spirits" in accordance with modern profession, they do so in the face of opposing facts, for in those days there were, as already shown, the two spheres. One the natural, or human; and the other instituted claims equal to the Christian's doctrine of the Nineteenth Century, respecting the Supreme Being. The ancient ideas of God's character, attributes, and also his dealings with men, are still those of the true Church. From the Bible accounts of Divine and Angelic manifestations, the Christian Faith is derived. Therefore, to admit the truth of one incident in "Daniel" is to admit all, and to concede the actual occurrence of those manifestations is to sanction the Christian doctrine; and such concession blasts the philosophy of Bible-opposers.

With these remarks we proceed to the investigation and application of this manifestation, which is so frequently adduced as strong evidence in the behalf of spirit writing, hand and feet manufacturing, etc.

In Daniel, ch. v., it is recorded, that "Belteshazzar, the king, made a great feast to a thousand of his lords, and drank wine before the thousand. And while he tasted the wine, he commanded to bring the golden and silver vessels which his father Nebuchadnezzar had taken out of the temple which was at Jerusalem; that the king and his princes, his wives and his concubines might drink therein. Then they brought the golden vessels that were taken out of the temple of the house of God which was at Jerusalem. And the king and his princes, his wives and his concubines, drank in them. They drank wine, and praised the gods of gold, and of silver, of brass, of iron, of wood and of stone."

The religion of the king and his guests cannot be mistaken. They were nature-worshipers. Not quite so spiritual perhaps as modern nature worshipers, still they saw the god they adored only in the material. The true Israelites looked above the material for his dwelling place whom they worshiped as the I Am. The distinction is clear. Belteshazzar acknowledged no God but Nature.

"In the same hour" (while they drank and worshiped their idols) "came forth fingers of a man's hand, and wrote over against the candlesticks, upon the plaster of the wall of the king's palace: and the king saw the part of the hand that wrote. Then the king's countenance was changed, and his thoughts troubled him, so that the joints of his loins were loosened, and his knees smote one against another."

Again the astrologers, Chaldeans and soothsayers, are called; and wealth and honor proffered to whosoever would read and interpret the writing. But as on former occasions they could not read or make known the interpretation. And why? The answer is obvious: They were altogether in their earth and natural sphere, while the hand that wrote was from heaven and the supernatural sphere. Otherwise, why did they not read and interpret?

"Then the king was greatly troubled, and his

lords were astonished. Now the queen by reason of the words of the king and his lords, came into the banquet house: and the queen spake and said, O king, live forever: let not thy thoughts trouble thee, nor let thy countenance be changed: there is a man in thy kingdom in whom is the spirit of the holy gods; and in the days of thy father light and understanding and wisdom, like the wisdom of the gods, was found in him: whom the king, Nebuchadnezzar, thy father, I say, thy father, made master" (exalted above) "of the magicians, astrologers, Chaldeans, and soothsayers. Now let Daniel be called and he will shew the interpretation. Then was Daniel brought in before the king. And the king spake and said unto Daniel, Art thou that Daniel which art of the children of the captivity of Judah, whom the king, my father, brought out of Jewry? I have even heard of thee that the spirit of the gods is in thee, and that light and understanding, and excellent wisdom is found in thee. And now the wise men, the astrologers have been brought in before me, that they should read this writing, and make known unto me the interpretation thereof: but they could not show the interpretation of the thing."

Here is another instance, wherein the wisdom of the earth-sphere, and the wonder-workers in the natural realm, are proclaimed by a monarch incapable of deciphering what was even partially revealed from the supernatural. And Daniel, who is of the Theocratic Sect, a believer in the direct and special aid of the Lord in matters pertaining to the kingdom of God on earth, is called, his faith acknowledged, and he is exalted infinitely above the naturalist.

"I have heard of thee," said the king to Daniel, "that thou canst make interpretations, and dissolve doubts: now if thou canst read the writing, and make known to me the interpretation thereof, thou shalt be clothed with scarlet and have a chain of gold about thy neck, and thou shalt be the third ruler in the kingdom."

Accustomed to dealing with unregenerate men, the king thought to inspire the greater effort on the part of Daniel by offering gifts and honor. But mark the spirit of Daniel, who answered and said, "Let thy gifts be to thyself, and give thy rewards to another; yet I will read the writing unto the king, and make known to him the interpretation."

"My kingdom is not of this world," said Jesus; and also, "Lay not up for yourselves treasures upon earth where moth and rust doth corrupt," etc. Throughout all history, sacred and profane, it is recorded of the true and faithful believer, the humble and Heaven-adoring, that they seek not the honors or wealth of this world, but a kingdom of righteousness; fellowship with the Father of Spirits. Daniel revealed the spirit of meekness. It would not flatter him to have it recorded and proclaimed to the world, that by and through him most remarkable disclosures had been made. Never! His was not a time serving spirit. How little the king's rehearsal of Daniel's good qualities, united with his liberal offers affected him. "Give thy rewards to another," said the meek medium of Divine Disclosures. "I will read the writing unto the king, and make known the interpretation." Not for gold or earthly honor, but by the will of the Spirit and for the glory of God. Then in the most solemn manner he addressed Belteshazzar, saying, "O thou king, the most high God gave Nebuchadnezzar, thy father, a kingdom, and majesty, and glory, and honor: and for the majesty he gave him, all people, nations and languages trembled and feared before him: whom he would he slew; and whom he would he kept alive: and whom he would he set up; and whom he would he put down. But when his heart was lifted up, and his mind hardened in pride, he was deposed from his kingly throne, and they took his glory from him, and he was driven from the sons of men; and his heart was made like the beasts, and they fed him with grass like oxen, and his body was wet with the dew of heaven; until he knew that the most high God ruled in the kingdom of men, and that he appointeth over it whomsoever he will. And thou his son, O Belteshazzar, hast not humbled thine heart, though thou knewest all this; but hast lifted up thyself against the Lord of heaven: and they have brought the vessels of his house before thee, and thou and thy lords and thy wives and thy concubines have drunk wine in them; and thou hast praised the gods of silver, of gold, of brass, iron, wood and stone, which see not, nor hear, nor know; and the God in whose hand thy breath is, and whose are all thy ways thou hast not glorified; then was the part of the hand sent from him; and this writing was written." Note the distinction still kept up. The God of heaven had not been served; but gods of nature.. Moreover, the God of all the earth had been mocked, defied, in that they drank in honor to gods of wood, stone, etc., from those vessels consecrated to the invisible Jehovah. But note the result of this presumption!

"This," continued Daniel, "is the writing that is written, MENE, MENE, TEKEL, UPHARSIN.

"This is the interpretation of the thing: MENE; God hath numbered thy kingdom and finished it. TEKEL; Thou art weighed in the ballances and found wanting. PERES; Thy kingdom is divided and given to the Medes and Persians." Solemn prediction!

"In that night was Belteshazzar, the king of the Chaldeans slain. And Darius, the Median, took the kingdom." Daniel, ch. v.

In these days, by the Progressionists, Harmonial Spiritualists, etc., those who are believers in the Scriptures and advocate the doctrine of their Divine origin,—those whose faith is like Abraham's, Moses', Elijah's and Daniel's, are called "the unprogressed." It is quite likely that the king's wise men, said even so, in spirit, of Daniel. They might have looked upon him as the medium of undeveloped and bigoted spirits, those who had not escaped the dogmas of their mundane education. But which in the test revealed the most wisdom? Daniel believed in the same God that the christian does. The wise men were men of a natural religion. They believed in nature, and no doubt greatly ridiculed the illiberal and restricted notions of the Hebrews. But in the trial, how did they appear? Each test exposed the fallacy of their theory. But God was with the lone captives who trusted in his name. He unfolded his Wisdom and displayed his power before all men, and thus sustained the faith of his people.

CHAPTER XI.

DANIEL WITH THE LIONS.

BUT Daniel's final trial drew near. His faith and determination must be exposed to still severer tests. Is his heart established? The gathering storm will reveal his true character. Is there a God who is able to save? And will that God regard the devotion of a finite mortal? Daniel's opposers, or rather the spirit of opposition to the kingdom of heaven will not rest. God has wrought wonders through humble means, but so virulent is the opposition that the God of eternal Truth must interfere and prevail, or Daniel will be cut off. "He was preferred above the presidents and princes, because an excellent spirit was in him; and the king" (Darius) "thought to set him over the whole realm. Then the presidents and princes sought to find occasion against Daniel concerning the kingdom; but they could find none occasion or fault; forasmuch as he was faithful, neither was there any error or fault found in him.

"Then said these wise men, We shall not find any occasion against this Daniel, except we find it against him concerning the law of his God." How earnestly the emissaries of error seek to thwart the influence of Truth! In every age and clime this spirit has been manifested against those by whom the law of God is especially maintained, and the infinite contrast between Divine Revelations and those of the finite and unreal rendered prominent. Nor is it necessary to resort entirely to the history of the ancients, to discover the evil designing against the Truths of heaven. Every age from Adam to the present, is stamped with unmistakable demonstrations. And who, familiar with the religious history of the Hebrew or christian, will presume to attribute the cause to man alone? The conflict is with the law of God. The heralds of Divine Truth, of God's revealed Will, the advocates of Holy Inspiration, are the objects of revenge. Upon them sorrows have been multiplied. And for what? Why should communities and even nations combine, and labor for the destruction of individuals whose position renders them the specific manifestation of Heavenly Purpose? If their inspiration is unreliable it must fail. If their doctrines are founded in error, they must pass away. Why then this evil strategy which has revealed its insidious form in every important period and combined its forces to suppress the principles of the Word of God? Daniel's religion did him no harm. He was wise above all others of the king's court;

blameless and useful withal. Why then seek his destruction? No answer can be given, save that which charges the purpose upon the malicious being who first seduced the race to sin.

The plot against Daniel epitomizes the natural movement of perverted sense. Whoever reads cannot fail, if divested of prejudice, to recognize the deceptive and invidious nature of that element which is ever operative against the religion of the Bible. The king, without the remotest thought of the end of the scheme, was drawn into an act which terminated upon Daniel. His professed friends, therefore, betrayed him. They presented an object before his mind, best calculated to mislead and render him, through base intrigue and from his confidence in them, most unexpectedly the agent of a nefarious plan. Mark their hypocrisy. "Then these presidents and princes assembled together to the king, and thus said unto him, King Darius, live forever." How like Judas: "Hail Master, and betrayed him with a kiss." Little did they respect the king's welfare, if they could only effect their purpose. Satanic characteristic most manifest by those Heaven-daring and God-opposing agents of Diabolism. They continued to plead with Darius, saying, "All the presidents of thy kingdom, the governors, and the princes, the counselors, and the captains, have consulted together to establish a royal statute." Where was Daniel? The devil was a liar from the beginning. "Ye are of your father, the devil, whose works ye do," said Jesus. How truly confirmed by those who contend with divine Truth! Does a natural religion require such base concealment? such an hypocritical countenance? such a false tongue? Facts, both ancient and modern, shall answer these important inquiries. The multitudes thronging the king, and the tumult consequent upon such an occasion, rendered it improbable that he would enquire after each of his prime-counselors, etc.; therefore they said, "all have consulted together to establish a royal statute, and to make a firm decree, that whosoever shall ask a petition of any god or man for thirty days, save of thee, O king, shall be cast into the den of lions. Now, O king, establish the decree and sign the writing, that it may not be changed, according to the law of the Medes and Persians, which altereth not." (How flatteringly introduced, and how cautiously and assiduously guarded.) "Wherefore king Darius signed the writing."

What conspiracy! and against an individual! Who cannot in this perceive the ghastly visage of infernal design? How plainly revealed the fallen spirits who behind the screen prompted the external actors! "Now, when Daniel knew that the writing was signed, he went into his house, and his windows being open in his chamber toward Jerusalem, he kneeled upon his knees three times a day, and prayed, and gave thanks before his God as he did aforetime." But Daniel could not have misunderstood the decree. Each time he kneeled before his God he endangered his life. The law was like that of the Medes and Persians, unalterable. Therefore he must choose to abide the consequences rather than refrain from or even conceal his devotion. Observe that single servant of the Most High. His was a faith, a religion, that in very deed affected the heart. He loved his law who had revealed himself to the Patriarchs in the glory of Divine bestowments. His soul delighted in prayer. God was his hope, and in him he put his trust. No earthly potentate or demoniac tactic could induce him astray or move him from his purpose. He therefore proceeded according to his accustomed manner, and to God submitted himself. Heaven could deliver, if for the glory of God. If to suffer was the most effectual means by which his mission in the world would be fulfilled, with meekness he submitted. He prayed not to king Darius, but to the King of kings,—the Disposer of events.

"Then these men assembled and found Daniel praying and making supplication before his God."

Whereupon they reminded the king of his decree, saying, "Hast thou not signed a decree that any man that shall ask a petition of any god or man within thirty days, save of thee, O king, shall be cast into the den of lions? The king answered and said, the thing is true, according to the law of the Medes and Persians, which altereth not. Then answered they and said before the king, That Daniel, which is of the captivity of Judah regardeth not thee, O king, nor the decree that thou hast signed, but maketh his petition three times a day. Then the king when he heard these words was sore displeased with himself, and set his heart on Daniel to deliver him; and he labored until the going down of the sun to deliver him."

Not until the dread crisis arrived did the king know or conceive the character of the plot. And when he awoke it was too late; for as he toiled to save Daniel, his enemies assembled unto the king and said, "Know, O king, that the law of the Medes and Persians is, that no decree or statute which the king establisheth may be changed."

The king could do no more; he was powerless; the decree was fatal, the end accomplished. Daniel had prayed to God and must make his bed with the wild and ferocious lions. For him earth had no hope to offer. No hope was written in the decree! No hope ruled the design, and there was no hope in all created things. Daniel was doomed. Alas for man! Because the Judean captive prayed to God he must suffer all the evil that could multiply upon him in this fallen world. "Then the king commanded, and they brought Daniel and cast him into the den of lions. Now the king spake and said unto Daniel, Thy God, whom thou servest continually, he will deliver thee." So palpable was the maliciousness of Daniel's enemies, that the king was made sensible of their wickedness. And the contrast was so great between their spirit and that of Daniel that the king was led to believe his God the true and living Lord, and hence he hoped for his preservation. "And a stone was brought and laid upon the mouth of the den, and the king sealed it with his own signet and with the signet of his lords, that the purpose might not be changed concerning Daniel."

Imagine the Satanic jubilee that moved the dark realms of perverted and fiendish spirits as the innocent victim was shut in; and the lords and counselors how they rejoiced with exceeding great joy. Each moving breeze was received by them as a messenger of gladness, and the echo of uttered agony from Daniel in the jaws of the hungry lion. And as the wine went round, and Bacchus reigned, the glee rose higher still. The dance in magic form swept along the halls, while the victors' acclaim chimed with the phantom notes of hell.

"But the king went to his palace, and passed the night fasting; neither were instruments of music brought before him." His heart was on Daniel, the Lord's Prophet.

The den of lions presents another scene. There slumbers the servant of the Most High. Like lambs the lions lay around him. "Then the king arose very early in the morning, and went in haste to the den of lions. And when he came to the den, he cried with a lamentable voice unto Daniel: O, Daniel, servant of the living God, is thy God, whom thou servest continually, able to deliver thee from the lions?" Question of the deepest interest. It involves all natural religion, of whatever name or nature. Answered and demonstrated in the affirmative, and Pantheism, with its unending schemes, united by sophistic concatenations of masterly device, crumbles, like the disintegrated parts of the falling temples, and the Hebrew religion is confirmed and established in everlasting truth. The king's words descended into the den, and deep in the subterraneous vault broke upon the ear of Daniel. Why disturb the calm and humble sleeper? Lo! the lions, like comforters, lay around him, and protect him from the cold, damp night air of the habitation of the wild digitigrade. But the king's lamentation aroused him, and in language of consolation he answered, "O, king, live forever. My God hath sent his angel, and hath shut the lions' mouths, that they have not hurt me; forasmuch as before him innocency was found in me," (blessed boon! what a solace in trouble!) "and also before thee, O king, I have done no hurt.

"Then was the king exceedingly glad for him, and commanded that they should take Daniel up out of the den. So Daniel was taken up out of the den, and no manner of hurt was found upon him, because he believed in his God.

"And the king commanded, and they brought those men which had accused Daniel, and they cast them into the den of lions, them, their children, and their wives, and the lions had the mastery of them, and break all their bones in pieces or ever they came at the bottom of the den."

What a lamentable retribution! Clear as truth in its untarnished glory the contrast is revealed, heavenly grace magnified, and the evil, in its malice and recklessness, exposed. God is glorified in the confirmation of his Word.

By the revelation of God's sovereign mercy, and the demonstration of his power, another king is induced to issue a proclamation in honor of the Hebrew religion. "Then king Darius wrote unto all people, nations, and languages, that dwell in all the earth: Peace be multiplied unto you. I make a decree, That in every dominion of my kingdom men tremble and fear before the God of Daniel; for he is the living God, and steadfast forever, and his kingdom that which shall never be destroyed, and his dominion shall be even unto the end." The permanency of that grace in which Daniel trusted, the king saw: first in the firmness of Daniel, and second in the rescue. Therefore his conviction was that the Immutable God was with the captive. Such effects attended those divine dispensations understood as God's dealings with man. But Darius continues: "He delivereth and rescueth, and worketh signs and wonders in heaven and in earth, who hath delivered Daniel from the power of the lions."

Again and in our concluding comments upon the Book of Daniel, we remark: In the Nineteenth Century it is deemed sufficient evidence that the Bible is not worthy of public confidence if a table tip by means not externally visible, and the sentiment of the mind-sphere encompassing it culminates in the denunciation of the Scriptures. If a medium is impelled to utter incoherent rhapsodies, or poetic strains, while in some abnormal state, it is proclaimed equal or superlative to Bible revelation and literature; or if the evidences render it probable that the spirit of some departed friend communicates from the spiritual to the external sphere, it is heralded forth as parallel with or of greater consequence than the evidences of Christianity. If sensitive persons, after years of experience, and arduous effort and untiring application, become efficient in transcendental arts, they are exalted as gods and proclaimed "the Oracles." If a bell is made to ring without hands, or musical instruments played by the inexperienced, or rattled without physical contact, the marvel-stricken spectators exclaim, "Those who performed the works recorded in the Bible, and attributed to the Almighty Lord, are now removing the darkness which shuts the glory and being of spirit spheres from mortality, revealing greater light than the Scriptures afford, and by disclosing their true nature, are demonstrating that all the Christian claims as the supernatural, the Work of the Divine Spirit, can easily be excelled by earth's departed, and therefore human spirits were the Bible communicators. Hence arises that form of anti-Christ, which determines upon the overthrow of true Christianity. But until the Harmonialists and their spirits unfold principles more profound, and disclose greater and more efficient laws than have yet attended their works, no evidence is afforded worthy of comparison with those means God has ordained and brought to light with the race, and substantiated by his Almighty Power; by the bestowments of his Mercy, the gracious disclosures of his Wisdom, and the efficacy of his Grace. The proposition of the christian Religion, is that, God, the Lord and Creator, by means of divine appointment, in the Spirit of Heavenly Benefaction, provides for the salvation of man from his deplorable condition, and the record of God's dealings accord therewith. The professions of anti-Christian spiritualism is high and extensive; let the demonstration be paramount to the claims or let the claim descend to the ability manifested.

CHAPTER XII.

NEW TESTAMENT INCIDENTS.

EIGHTEEN hundred years ago, in Bethlehem of Judea, and in the days of Herod the king, JESUS was born. "When Herod heard thereof he was troubled, and all Jerusalem with him. And when he had gathered all the chief priests and scribes of the people together, he demanded of them where Christ should be born. And they said unto him, In Bethlehem of Judea, for thus it is written by the prophet: And thou Bethlehem, in the land of Judea, art not the least among the princes of Judah, for out of thee shall come a Governor, that shall rule my people Israel.

"Then Herod, when he had privily called the wise men, inquired of them diligently what time the star appeared. And he sent them to Bethlehem, and said, Go and search diligently for the young child, and when you have found him bring me word again, that I may come and worship him also."—Mat. ch. ii.

This was another evil device against the Spirit of Truth, for the context and sequel prove that Herod disguised his purpose in the charge given to the wise men. "When Herod had heard these things he was troubled and all Jerusalem with him." Not because he desired to worship; that need not beget fear or perplexity. Had he been a true Israelite, the Mesiah's advent would have given him joy and tranquility. His proceeding evinced his consciousness that Christ, when he came, would possess a spirit adverse to his. Jerusalem was also troubled. But had she been actuated by the true principle, the star would have been hailed as the prelude of a most glorious day to them.

By examining the history of that event, it will be found that former conflicts between the Spirit of Truth and the Principle of Evil were only types of this their legitimate ante-type, and that in the spiritual history of man this was the Great Centre Epoch and Period when the heavenly Grace was to seal the Covenant and make an end of Oblations. To prevent the consumating Offering the Prince of Darkness seems to have been preparing his agents at Jerusalem, and so adjusting the external government that when the trial should come, as by magic the forces of wickedness might be arrayed against the Savior. But God provided for the emergency. Hence, the wise men having found the young child acknowl edged him. Being warned of God in a dream not to return to Herod, they departed into their own country another way. "And an angel of the Lord appeared to Joseph in a dream," (Will Harmonial *Spiritualists* deny this? By what authority?) "saying, Arise, and take the young child and his mother and flee into Egypt, and be thou there until I bring thee word, for Herod will seek the young child to destroy him.

"When he arose, he took the young child and his mother by night, and departed into Egypt, and was there until the death of Herod."

As the wise men did not return, and Herod not being able to find and identify the child whom he feared, he caused all the children to be slain that were in Bethlehem, and in all the coasts thereof, from two years old and under, according to the time he had diligently enquired of the wise men.

From this time Jesus was pursued until he made the final Offering upon the cross. The following record reveals the cause of this opposition to Jesus, and also unmistakably proves the malicious author to have been the same who from the days of Adam had afflicted the people of God, and contended with Theopneustic principles.

"Then was Jesus led up of the Spirit into the wilderness to be tempted of the devil. And when he had fasted forty days and forty nights, he was afterward an hungered. And when the tempter came to him he said, If thou be the Son of God, command that these stones be made bread."

In answer, Jesus introduced the superior necessity of the soul, saying, "Man shall not live by bread alone, but by every word that proceedeth out of the mouth of God."

Can he who denies the divinity of the Scriptures, the design of evil spirits, and of Redemption through the Lord and Savior Jesus Christ, define the cause of this distinction, and so prominently revealed along the descending ages from Adam even to Christ? Whether men may or may not be able to quiet their own minds upon this subject, the account (and it cannot be impeached,) informs us that the tempter met Jesus and in him sought to contravene the law of Truth and Righteousness, and hence suppress the principles of immortal joy.

Again, having presented the kingdoms and glory of the world, the tempter said, "All these things will I give unto thee if thou wilt fall down and worship me."

The tendency of perverted sense is, to exalt the creature, deify Nature and weaken respect for the Creator. Could Satan persuade the Nazarine, through whom God had promised to bruise the serpent's head, that is, destroy demoniacal power with man, to magnify Nature and acknowledge himself worthy of adoration, of reverential regard, then he would hope to hold human hearts in perpetual bondage, as sympathizers with himself in sin. He had succeeded with Adam, but God's promise to subdue him at last through the seed of Abraham, had been an insurmountable barrier to his universal reign on earth. He had failed in every important attempt since that covenant, and as the lineal descent could not be broken, resolved to unite his forces, and direct his energies against the man Christ Jesus. Meeting the Savior, he personally sought to tempt him by saying, "Command that these stones be made bread." Again he endeavored to induce him to a presumptuous act. "If thou be the Son of God cast thyself down; for it is written, He shall give his angels charge concerning thee; and in their hands they shall bear thee up, lest at any time thou dash thy foot against a stone." Jesus said unto him, "It is written again, Thou shalt not tempt the Lord thy God."—Matt. iv. 6, 7. He then sought to excite vanity; not by saying, "The day thou eatest thou shalt be as God," but "If thou wilt fall down and worship me—be at my command, I will give unto thee the kingdoms of earth; I will exalt thee to an earthly throne which shall rule over all other thrones; I will cause thy government to extend to the ends of the earth, and there shall be none like thee. I hold the hearts of men, and will give them and their possessions into thy hands if thou wilt submit to my dictation; accept my counsel and honor me before man." But Jesus said, "Get thee hence Satan, for it is written, Thou shalt worship the Lord thy God and him only shalt thou serve. Then the devil leaveth him, and behold angels came and ministered unto him."

Thus, at a period by no means so remote as to render the history doubtful, the two principles were fully disclosed. And since that trial harmonized with those of the Old Testament times, and since like characters are now revealed, it is most rational to conclude the Biblical account authentic.

What then is Harmonial Spiritualism but the manifestation of that spirit of evil, that soul-deceiving principle which led Adam into sin — which opposed the ancient Israel of God — contended with Jesus, and has persecuted the Christian since the days of the Apostles; finally, that is now exciting the world against the disciples and doctrines of the Lord?

Not able to divert the Nazarene from the divine purpose by personal intercourse, the foe of God and man proceeded to inspire the populace against him, and to create jealousy in the minds of the officers of government respecting his claims.

CHAPTER XIII.

THE MISSION AND DOCTRINES OF JESUS.

"And Jesus returned in the power of the Spirit into Galilee. And there went out a fame of him through all the region round about. And he taught in their synagogues, being glorified of all. And he came to Nazareth, where he had been brought up, and, as his custom was, he went into the synagogue on the Sabbath day and stood up to read; and there was delivered unto him the book of the prophet Esaias; and when he had opened the book, he found the place where it was written, The Spirit of the Lord is upon me, because he hath anointed me to preach the gospel to the poor; he hath sent me to heal the broken-hearted, to preach deliverance to the captives, and recovering of sight to the blind; to set at liberty them that are bruised, to preach the acceptable year of the Lord. This day is this scripture fulfilled in your ears."—Luke iv., 18–21. "No man can serve two masters; for either he will hate the one and love the other, or else he will hold to the one and despise the other. Ye cannot serve God and Mammon. Lay not up for yourselves treasure upon earth, but in heaven. Seek ye first the kingdom of God and his righteousness, and all things shall be added unto you."—Math. vi. "Enter ye in at the straight gate, for wide is the gate and broad is the way that leadeth to destruction, and many there be which go in thereat; because straight is the gate and narrow is the way which leadeth unto life, and few there be that find it.

"Beware of false prophets, which come to you in sheeps clothing but inwardly they are ravening wolves. Ye shall know them by their fruit. Do men gather grapes of thorns, or figs of thistles?" —Math. vii. That is, shall disease and death beget life and health? "Think not that I am come to destroy the law or the prophets. I am not come to destroy, but to fulfill."—Math v., 17. "Love your enemies, bless them that curse you, do good to them that hate you, and pray for them which persecute you. . When ye pray say, Our Father which art in heaven. Hallowed be thy name. Thy kingdom come. Thy will be done in earth, as it is in heaven. Give us this day our daily bread, and forgive us our debts, as we forgive our debtors. Suffer us not to be tempted, but deliver us from evil. For thine is the kingdom, and the power, and the glory for ever. Amen."—Math. vi. "Let not your heart be troubled; ye believe in God, believe also in me. In my Father's house are many mansions. I go to prepare a place for you. Believe me that

I am in the Father, and the Father in me, or else believe me for the very works' sake. If ye love me keep my commandments, and I will pray the Father, and he will give you another Comforter, that may abide with you forever—even the Spirit of Truth, whom the world cannot receive, because it seeth him not, neither knoweth him. He that loveth me keepeth my sayings; and the word which ye hear is not mine, but the Father's which sent me. These things have I spoken unto you, being yet present with you; but the Comforter, which is the Holy Ghost, whom the Father will send in my name, he shall teach you all things. . . . Peace I leave with you; my peace I give unto you: not as the world giveth give I unto you. . . . Hereafter I will not talk much with you, for the prince of this world cometh, and hath nothing in me. If the world hate you, ye know that it hated me before it hated you. If ye were of the world, the world would love its own; but because ye are not of the world, but I have chosen you out of the world, therefore the world hateth you. They hated me without a cause. . . . Nevertheless I tell you the truth—it is expedient for you that I go away; for if I go not away, the Comforter will not come unto you: but if I depart I will send him unto you. And when he is come, he will reprove the world of sin, of righteousness, and of judgment:

of sin, because they believe not on me; of righteousness, because I go to my Father; of judgment, because the prince of this world is judged. In the world you shall have tribulation; but be of good cheer, I have overcome the world. These words spake Jesus, and lifted up his eyes to heaven and said, Father, the hour is come; glorify thy Son, that thy Son also may glorify thee. This is life eternal, that they might know thee, the only true God, and Jesus Christ, whom thou hast sent. O, righteous Father, the world hath not known thee, but I have known thee, and these have known that thou hast sent me. I have declared thy name, and will declare it; that the love wherewith thou hast loved me may be in them, and I in them."—John, chapters xv. xvi. and xvii. "Then Pilate therefore took Jesus, and scourged him, and the soldiers platted a crown of thorns and put it on his head, and put on him a purple robe and said, Hail, King of the Jews! and they smote him with their hands.

"Pilate therefore went forth again, and saith unto them, Behold, I bring him forth unto you, that ye may know that I find no fault in him. Then Jesus came forth, wearing the crown of thorns and the purple robe; and Pilate saith unto them, Behold the man! When the chief priests, therefore, and officers saw him, they cried out, Crucify him, crucify him! Pilate saith unto them, Take ye him and crucify him, for I find no fault in him. Then answered the Jews, We have a law, and by that law he ought to die, because he made himself the Son of God".—John xix.

Such was the spirit indulged toward Jesus, "the Anointed," by whom the Gospel of Salvation was given to man; and the above compend, embracing the declaration of his mission, the purposes thereof, the law of life, revealed through him, the principles of heavenly requirements, the impossibility of fellowship with the world or carnal sphere, while in the way of heaven and righteousness; the union of his Being with the Divine; the certainty that those who loved him would keep his word; the promise of the Holy Ghost—the Comforter, which would be in direct opposition to the carnal man; his prayer; his crucifixtion: these reveal him not of the world; hence his kingdom is unlike that which would unfold from the human heart in its degenerate state. To this end, and for a purpose hereafter to be explained, these passages are thus collected, as well as those of the succeeding chapter, which comprehend the close of his labors before the Ascension, and the fulfillment of his promise by the Spirits' descent on the day of Pentelost. And these passages are quite sufficient to show the want of harmony between the teachings of Jesus and his Spirit, and those of the popular spiritualism of the day.

CHAPTER XIV.

COMMISSION, PROMISE, ASCENSION, DESCENT OF THE SPIRIT, ETC.

"BEHOLD," said Jesus, "I send you forth as sheep in the midst of wolves; be ye therefore wise as serpents and harmless as doves. But beware of men, for they will deliver you up to the councils, and they will scourge you in their synagogues. But when they deliver you up, take no thought how or what ye shall speak, for it shall be given you in that same hour what ye shall speak; for it is not ye that speak, but the Spirit of your Father which speaketh in you. He that findeth his life," (loveth the pleasures of the passional man,) "shall loose it," (shall come short of divine joys and dwell in darkness) "and he that looseth his life," (overcometh sensual gratification and liveth in truth,) "for my sake, shall find it."—Math. x. "But whereunto shall I liken this generation? It is like unto children sitting in the market places, and calling unto their fellows, and saying, We have piped unto you, and ye have not danced; we have mourned unto you, and ye have not lamented: for John came neither eating nor drinking, and ye say, he hath a devil: the Son of Man came eating and drinking, and ye say, 'Behold a man gluttonous, a wine bibber, a friend of publicans and sinners. But wisdom is justified of her children.

"At that time Jesus answered and said, I thank thee, O Father, Lord of heaven and earth, because thou hast hid these things from the wise and prudent, and hast revealed them unto babes." That is, rendered them simple and unadorned, and adapted to the necessities of the meek, though not admired by the wise or self-exalted. "Come unto me all ye that labor and are heavy laden, and I will give you rest. Take my yoke upon you, and learn of me; for I am meek and lowly in heart; and ye shall find rest to your souls."—Math. xi.

"Afterward he appeared unto the eleven as they sat at meat, and upbraided them with their unbelief and hardness of heart, because they believed not them which had seen him after he was arisen. And he said unto them, Go ye into all the world, and preach the gospel to every creature. He that believeth and is baptized shall be saved; but he that believeth not shall be damned. . And these signs shall follow them that believe: In my name they shall cast out devils; they shall speak with new tongues; they shall take up serpents."—Mark xvi. "And he said unto them, It is not for you to know the times or the seasons, which the Father hath put in his own power. But ye shall receive power after that the Holy Ghost is come upon you; and ye shall be witnesses unto me both in Jerusalem, and in all Judea, and in Samaria, and unto the uttermost parts of the earth. And when he had spoken these things, while they beheld, he was taken up; and a cloud received him out of their sight. And while they looked steadfastly toward heaven, as he went up, behold two men stood by them in white apparel, which also said, Ye men of Galilee, why stand ye gazing up into heaven? This same Jesus, which is taken up from you into heaven, shall so come in like manner as ye have seen him go up into heaven." —Acts, ch. 1.

"And when the day of Pentecost was fully come, they were all with one accord in one place. And suddenly there came a sound from heaven as of a rushing, mighty wind, and it filled all the house where they were sitting. And there appeared unto them cloven tongues, like as of fire, and it sat upon each of them. And they were all filled with the Holy Ghost, and began to speak with other tongues, as the Spirit gave them utterance. And there were dwelling at Jerusalem Jews, devout men out of every nation under heaven.

"Now when this was noised abroad, the multitude came together and were confounded, because that every man heard them speak in his own language. And they were all amazed and marvelled, saying one to another, Behold, are not all these which speak Galileans? And how hear we every man in our tongue wherein we were born? Parthians, and Medes, and Elamites, and the dwellers in Mesopotamia, and in Judea, and Cappadocia, in Pontus, and Asia, Phrygia and Pamphylia, in Egypt, and in the parts of Libya about Cyrene, and strangers of Rome, Jews and proselytes, Cretes and Arabians we do hear them speak in our tongues, the wonderful works of God."—Acts, ch. ii.

When modern spiritualists can imitate these demonstrations of spiritual ability, then may they boast of their revelations. But how vain to shout "Progression" if a table tips, a tambourine rattles, a hand jerks and moves in rapid disorder, or even executes the work of written sentences, or if a medium utters incoherent sounds, that a Chinaman may call his tongue? The spiritualism of this day compares with that of New Testament times about as the works of the magicians of Egypt did with the miracles wrought through Moses and Aaron. And it is verily strange that men should forsake the Christian faith for antagonistic teachings, which are supported by Modern Spiritualism, since, when contrasted with those upon which the Bible doctrines are predicated, there is no proper analogy.

Another marvel consists in an effort to palm off the teachings of the recent "communications" as Christian, for all unprejudiced readers of the Bible know that the spirit and tenor of Gospel truths directly conflict with the sentiments disclosed by Harmonialism. This the above passages alone amply confirm. With the Gospel of Jesus and the natural or carnal heart there is no likeness. They have no affinity; nor do the doctrines of Salvation through Jesus compromise divine command or eternal principle. The Truth of Heaven is immutable, and those who enjoy the fruition of heavenly love must abide Divine dictation. Ye cannot serve God and Mammon, is an axiom existing in the nature of mental and moral law.

Divine Inspiration seeks to attract the soul from human pleasures, change the inclinations, and raise the being entirely above a world-serving spirit, or pleasure-loving pursuits, from Nature to Nature's God. "If any man will be my disciple, let him deny himself, take up his cross, and follow me," was the language of Jesus; also, "My kingdom is not of this world." Great is the contrast between this and the tendency of Harmonialism as the doctrines, means of dissemination, effects upon mind, social tendencies, and consequences as far as revealed, together with the subtle workings, when fully analyzed, will show.

CHAPTER XV.

THE OPPOSING SPIRIT.

"AND Stephen, full of faith and power, did great wonders and miracles among the people. And there arose certain of the synagogue, which is called the synagogue of the Libertines, and Cyrenians, and Alexandrians, and of them of Cilicia and of Asia, disputing with Stephen. And they were not able to resist the wisdom and spirit by which he spake. Then they suborned men, which said, We have heard him speak blasphemous words against Moses, and against God." How natural with perverted minds, when other efforts fail to prevent the influence of Divine Truth, to resort to defamation of character, to false accusations, and thence to excite public prejudice against the firm advocates of principles most difficult to overcome by error and sophistry. The enemies of the Gospel having failed to subdue Stephen by an attack upon his principles or himself personally, resorted to the basest means, even that of subornation, in order to prevent him from promulgating the Gospel. Truth needs no such infamous Satanism to sustain it, or overcome its foes; but error must needs resort to deception and calumniation.

To condemn Jesus required false testimony. So also they suborned men who testified that Stephen had blasphemed. But the Spirit was with him, even as Jesus promised, so much so that while accused, "All looking steadfastly on him, saw his face as it had been the face of an angel."

"Then said the high priest, Are these things so? And he (Stephen) said, Men, brethren, and fathers, hearken: the God of glory appeared unto our father Abraham when he was in Mesopotamia, before he dwelt in Charran," etc.—See Acts vii. Stephen was an earnest advocate of the laws and merciful bestowments of the God of Abraham, of the Abrahamic covenant, of Jesus Christ the Messiah, and of Redemption through him. And the natural man persecuted him even unto death.

"Howbeit," he said while pleading before his accusers, "the Most High dwelleth not in temples made with hands; as saith the prophet, Heaven is my throne and earth my footstool: what house will ye build me? saith the Lord; or what is the place of my rest? Hath not my hand made all these things?

"Ye stiffnecked and uncircumcised in heart and ears, ye do always resist the Holy Ghost; as your fathers did, so do ye. Which of the prophets have not your fathers persecuted? and they have slain them which shewed before of the coming of the Just One, of whom ye have now been the betrayers and murderers."

"When they heard these things, they were cut to the heart, and they gnashed on him with their teeth." (Some media of modern times, as we shall show, have manifested a similar spirit.) "But he, being full of the Holy Ghost, looked up steadfastly into heaven, and saw the glory of God, and Jesus standing on the right hand of God. And said, Behold, I see the heavens opened, and the Son of Man standing on the right hand of God. Then they cried out with a loud voice, and stopped their ears, and ran upon him with one accord, and cast him out of the city, and stoned him; and the witnesses laid down their clothes at a young man's feet, whose name was Saul."

Notice that the witnesses, vile perjurers, were foremost to stone him whom they knew innocent. "And they stoned Stephen, calling upon God, and saying, Lord Jesus receive my spirit. And he kneeled down, and cried with a loud voice, Lord lay not this sin to their charge. And when he had said this, he fell asleep.—Acts vii, 48, 60.

Stephen suffered at the hands of wicked deceivers, and for the doctrines of Christianity, the name of Jesus. But he endured meekly, without retaliation, and, like his Savior, prayed for his executioners. Jesus, while on the cross, said, "Father, forgive them, they know not what they do." Stephen prayed, "Lord, lay not this sin to their charge, and fell asleep."

"Then Philip went down to the city of Samaria, and preached Christ unto them. And the people with one accord gave heed to those things which Philip spake, hearing and seeing the miracles which he did. For unclean spirits, crying with loud voice, came out of many that were possessed with them. . . But there was a certain man, called Simon, which beforetime, in the same city, used sorcery and bewitched the people of Samaria, giving out that he himself was some great one, to whom they all gave heed, from the least to the greatest, saying, This man is the great power of God." Need names be mentioned to cite the mind to corresponding incidents which are now transpiring? But the history continues, saying, "And when Simon saw that through the laying on of the Apostles' hands the Holy Ghost was given, he offered them money, saying, Give me also this power." Simon acknowledged his power inferior to that which attended the Apostles; nevertheless he had bewitched the people of Samaria, "all of whom had said, This man is the power of God." But Peter said, "Thy money perish with thee, because thou hast thought that the gift of God may be purchased with money. Thou hast neither lot nor part in the matter; for thy heart is not right in the sight of God. Repent, therefore, of this thy wickedness, and pray God if perhaps the thought of thine heart may be forgiven thee. For I perceive that thou art in the gall of bitterness and in the bonds of iniquity. Then answered Simon, Pray the Lord for me." Thus Heaven's Truth is again vindicated, and the opposing principle rendered vain; and, also, the sorcerer forced to admit his magic and source of skill inferior by far to the power accompanying the Apostles. He first offers to purchase the spirit as an art and failing, solicits prayer for himself: "Pray ye to the Lord for me."—Acts viii, 5–24. Thus was the perverted nature-sphere that had formerly controlled him, and by which the people of Samaria had been deluded, overcome, and its insufficiency exposed by the light of the Spirit of Truth, and he the medium of evil influences brought to see his necessity of God's grace.

The next incident we shall notice is that of a female medium, who was under the influence of a spirit of divination, but which was cast out by Paul. The record says of her: "And it came to pass, as we went to prayer, a certain damsel, possessed with a spirit of divination, met us, which brought her master much gain by soothsaying. The same followed Paul and us, and cried, saying, These men are servants of the Most High God, which shewed unto us the way of Salvation. And thus did she many days. But Paul, being grieved, turned and said to the spirit, I command thee in the name of Jesus Christ to come out of her. And he came out that same hour. And when her masters saw that the hope of their gains was gone, they caught Paul and Silas, and drew them into the market-place unto the rulers, and brought them to the magistrates, saying, These men, being Jews, do exceedingly trouble our city."—Acts xvi, 16-20.

"And the seventy returned again with joy, saying, Lord, even the devils are subject unto us through thy name. . . Notwithstanding, in this rejoice not," said Jesus, "that the spirits are subject unto you; but rather rejoice because your names are written in heaven,"—Luke x, 17–20. There is a name above the name of spirits, and he who trusts therein is able to bid all evil away, and lo! it flees. In that name Jesus denying-spirits are exorcised; it is a terror to them. But he who obtains Divine aid must have the Holy Spirit in his heart. Of this more shall be said in the investigation of the present spiritual phenomena.

The above quotations from Luke are corroborated and confirmed by that just considered from

Acts xvi, 18, as well as many others of like nature recorded of those days. And the opposite is revealed in the following incident, where those whose heart was not the temple of the Holy Ghost attempted to exorcise evil spirits but failed. Thus it is written, Acts xix, 13:

"Then certain of the vagabond Jews, exorcists, took upon them to call over them which had evil spirits the name of the Lord Jesus, saying, We adjure you by Jesus, whom Paul preacheth. And there were seven sons of one Sceva, a Jew, and chief of the priests which did so. And the evil spirit answered and said, Jesus I know, and Paul I know; but who are ye? And the man in whom the evil spirit was, leaped on them, and overcame them, and prevailed against them, so they fled out of the house naked and wounded. And this was known to all the Jews and Greeks also dwelling at Ephesus, and fear fell on them all, and the name of the Lord Jesus was magnified. And many of them also which used curious arts brought their books together, and burned them before all."

No one can mistake the character of the true principles disclosed in these historic facts. Spiritualists, who deny the Christian Faith, admit the presence of spirits as recorded in the Scriptures. They claim that the Patriarchs, Prophets and Apostles held communion with spirits, etc. This confession commits their cause, for the Prophets and Apostles professed a faith directly contrary to that of the Naturalists; moreover, by the name of Jesus evil spirits were exorcised, and the spirits which operated with those of the natural sphere confessed the divinity of Jesus. "Why art thou come to torment us before the time?" was the language of spirits to the Savior. By this they, in the strongest manner, admitted the power of the Lord over them; their consciousness that they could not endure his ,presence, or resist his command. But the evil spirits overcame those who were not the true and faithful servants of the Lord; those who had not the Spirit of Christ. Incidents in perfect accordance with these have transpired connected with modern spiritualism.

Again, it is written, 1 John, iv., 1-3, "Beloved, believe not every spirit, but try the spirits whether they be of God; because many false prophets have gone out into the world. Hereby know ye the Spirit of God: Every spirit that confesseth that Jesus Christ is come in the flesh is of God; and every spirit that confesseth not that Jesus Christ is come in the flesh is not of God; and this is the spirit of anti-Christ, whereof ye heard that it should come, and even now already is in the world."

How plainly the distinction is here expressed.

And how abundant the evidence afforded by history, both sacred and profane, that connected with man are two spheres of spiritual influx; that two classes of influences from the interior or invisible world seek the control of the human heart: one is divine and infinite, and the other sickly, discordant and finite; and that the same spirit which now opposes the doctrines of the Inspired Word was anciently developed.

CHAPTER XVI.

THE CONSUMMATION.

"AND the fifth angel sounded, and I saw a star fall from heaven unto the earth; and to him was given the key of the bottomless pit.. And he opened the bottomless pit, and there arose a smoke out of the pit, as the smoke of a great furnace; and the sun and the air were darkened by reason of the pit. And there came out of the smoke locusts upon the earth, and unto them was given power, as the scorpions of the earth have power. And the shape of the locusts were like horses prepared unto battle," (manifestation of power,) "and on their heads were as it were crowns like gold, and their faces were like the faces of men; and they had a king over them, which is the angel of the bottomless pit, whose name in the Hebrew tongue is Abaddon, but in the Greek tongue hath his name Apollyon. . . . And the rest of the men which were not killed by these plagues yet repented not of the works of their hands, that they should not worship devils, and idols of gold, and silver, and brass, and stone, and wood, which neither can see, nor hear, nor walk."—Rev. ix.

Had the Revelator lived in the Nineteenth

Century, he could not have portrayed Harmonial Spiritualism more perfectly. These, taking the sayings of their Oracle, the Poughkeepsie Seer (whose sentiment is echoed by the sympathizing spirit manifestations,) as the principles of their philosophy, behold their god in gold, silver, brass, stone, and wood; worship nature, etc. The sayings of spirit-media seem to answer all purposes with them, hence they are in fact worshipers of spirits. These Harmonialists do not acknowledge the Christian religion, and hence are not worshipers of the Christian's God, but rather are the denunciators of both. Nature external, and spirits, the departed of earth, are their hope. Even in death they depend upon the spirits of the dead, seemingly unmindful of any higher power.

"And I stood upon the sand of the sea, and saw a beast rise up out of the sea, having seven heads and ten horns, and upon his horns ten crowns, and upon his head the name of blasphemy. And the beast which I saw was like the leopard, and his feet were as the feet of a bear, and his mouth as the mouth of a lion." (Such elements enter into man's composition according to A. J. Davis and the modern philosophy.) "And the dragon gave him his power, and his seat, and great authority. And they worshiped the dragon which gave power unto the beast; and they worshiped the beast, saying, Who is like unto the beast? who is able to make war with him?"

Is not the likeness of this in our land, and in a form and from a source never conceived by expounders of the prophesies? Whatever may be the literal fulfillment of this prophecy, we cannot fail of noticing a striking resemblance in the beast or form of anti-Christ, which combines the teachings of Mesmerism, Clairvoyance, Psychology, Harmonial Spiritualism, etc., whose philosophy, when fully disclosed, is the sum of sensualism, hence culminates in a natural religion, denying the supernatural; and whose votaries ridicule the idea of any successful opposition to the great human leader of the present effort against the Christian Faith. "Who is able to make war with him?" mingles with the hollow laugh that rings as if from brazen lungs and callous hearts.

"And there was given him a mouth speaking great things and blasphemies; and power was given unto him to continue forty and two months. And he opened his mouth in blasphemy against God, to blaspheme his name, and his tabernacle, and them that dwell in heaven."

A. J. Davis is said to be Nature's Oracle, through whom she uttered "Nature's Divine Revelations," and now speaks her "Great Harmonial," etc., and most assuredly nothing could be said more blasphemous, and against the tabernacles of God, and the prophets, apostles and saints that dwell in heaven. Add to this what might be called a lesser beast, Robert Hare, and others of that school, who most daringly blaspheme the name of the God of Abraham, mock Jesus and his teachings, and we have a "mouthpiece" for anti-Christ, for the utterance of Satanic inspiration against the Most High. And who can determine that clairvoyants, anti-Christian media, psychometrists, etc., etc., with their external magnetizers, prompters and defenders, are not the mouth of the beast? speaking great swelling words?

"And it was given unto him to make war with the saints, and to overcome them; and power was given him over all kindreds, and tongues, and nations. And all that dwell upon the earth shall worship him, whose names are not written in the book of life, of the lamb slain, from the foundation of the world."

Do those wedded to the common mode of interpretation dislike our inference, and feel that the scriptures are wrested by the suggestion? Let them pause, for it may be that there is in these things at least a collateral application of those prophecies. "And I beheld another beast coming up out of the earth; and he had two horns like a lamb, and he spake as a dragon." Those who are conversant with modern mesmeric and spirit subjects,need not be told that one, and by no means an inferior class of their works, assumes the name of Christian teachings, but by denying the fundamental principles of the Gospel are absolutely opposing the doctrine of Salvation through Jesus Christ.

"And deceiveth them that dwell on the earth by the means of those miracles which he hath power to do in the sight of the beast," (by the aid or in the name of the spirits, etc.) "saying to them that dwell on the earth that they should make an image to the beast. And he causeth all, both small and great, rich and poor, free and bond, to receive a mark in their right hand or in their foreheads." Submit to affinity, be spiritualized, adopt the physical as the substance, and believe in a natural religion—in the rational: that is, Give us a (so called) intellectual religion—a religion of the senses; and let our power be that of Nature. "And that no man might buy or sell, save he that had the mark, or the name of the beast, or the number of his name." (Not yet fulfilled.) "Here is wisdom: let him that hath understanding count the number of the beast, for it is the number of a man, and his number is six hundred, three score and six."—Rev. xiii.

Aware that these scriptures are otherwise applied, we have merely suggested their likeness, as prophecies, to the events of the day, and submit the thought until we analyze more specifically Harmonial Spiritualism and the teaching and effects of modern anti-Christian philosophers.

"And I looked, and, lo, a lamb stood on the mount Zion, and with him a hundred forty and four thousand, having his father's name written in their foreheads. These are they which follow the lamb whithersoever he goeth. These were redeemed from among men, being the first fruits unto God and to the lamb. And in their mouth was found no guile, for they were without fault before the throne of God. . . Here is the patience of the saints; here are they that keep the commandments of God, and the faith of Jesus."—Rev. xiv.

"And I saw the beast, and the kings of earth, and their armies, gathered together to make war against him that sat on the horse, and against his army. And the beast was taken, and with him the false prophets that wrought miracles before him, with which he deceived them that had received the mark of the beast, and them that worshiped the image. . .

THE END.

"And when the thousand years are expired,

Satan shall be loosed out of his prison, and shall go out to deceive the nations which are in the four quarters of the earth, Gog and Magog, to gather them together to battle, the number of whom is as the sands of the sea. And they went up on the breadth of the whole earth, and compassed the camp of the saints about, and the beloved city; and fire came down from God out of heaven, and devoured them. And the devil that deceived them was cast into the lake of fire and brimstone, where the beast and the false prophets are. . . And I saw a great white throne, and him that sat on it. . . And I saw the dead, small and great, stand before God; and the books were opened, and another book was opened, which is the book of life. And the dead were judged out of those things which were written in the books, according to their works. And the sea gave up the dead which were in it, and death and hell gave up the dead which were in them; and they were judged every man according to their works; and death and hell were cast into the lake of fire. This is the second death."—Rev. xx.

"And I saw a new heaven and new earth, for the first heaven and the first earth were passed away and there was no more sea. . . And I heard a great voice out of heaven, saying, Behold the tabernacle of God is with men, and he will dwell with them, and they shall be his people, and God shall be with them and be their God, and God shall wipe away all tears from their eyes, and there shall be no more death, for the former things are passed away. . . And he said unto me, It is done; I am Alpha and Omega, the beginning and the end. . . He that overcometh shall inherit all things, and I will be his God and he shall be my son."—Rev. xxi.

Such is the consummation as predicted in the Scriptures; and according to Bible spiritualism there has been from the earliest day a conflict between the spirit of Theopneustic doctrine and that which denies the principle upon which the Christian religion is founded. But in the trial of their power in every important event, the Spirit, the Life of Bible religion, has prevailed over the opposition; and in the end of the conflict the prophecy is, that the religion of Abraham, of the Prophets, of Jesus, even the Gospel will prevail, and close the conflict by depriving the Evil of its power and liberty with men. Such is the compend of scripture teachings upon this subject. Hence the Christian believes, and his faith is predicated upon the Word of God, that Jesus, who was despised and rejected of men, a man of sorrow and acquainted with grief, who was betrayed, falsely accused, unjustly condemned, and finally crucified, and who is now denied as Savior, will return, subdue the foe of God, the afflicter of man, and redeem his people. For it is written, "Blessed are they that do his commandments, that they may have right to the tree of life, and may enter in through the gates into the city; and there shall in nowise enter into it anything that defileth, neither whatsoever worketh abomination, or maketh a lie: but they which are written in the lamb's book of life. . . And God shall wipe away all tears, for the former things are passed away. . . And there shall be no night there, and they need no candle, neither light of the sun, for the Lord God giveth them light; and they shall reign forever and ever." Thus saith the scriptures.

Having traced the Bible history of Spiritualism connected with the Spirit of Truth and that of Error; and having discovered the divine nature and utility of the one, and the evil and falsity of the other, we next proceed to consider the COVENANT, its fulfillment and confirmation.

PART II.

CHAPTER I.

THE ABRAHAMIC COVENANT.

AGAIN we invite the reader, and particularly the spiritualist, to the consideration of Old Testament "manifestations;" and, ere we yield the Christian faith for clairvoyant sayings, and the sentiment of anti-Bible spirit communications, we request the "progressed," "exalted," and "illumined" "spirits," their "media" or advocates, to equal by *one* demonstration, those we shall offer them connected with Bible religion.

The first instance we shall notice of heavenly communication with man, is the call of Abraham by the Lord, and the Covenant then made. This is one of the most important to the Christian, and is a "manifestation" quite at war with the naturalist, and one that the opposition should do away, or at least counteract by an equal or superior demonstration from the spirit world. Spiritualists tell us that whatever of the Bible is of spirit origin was given by like spirits to those now communicating, only less developed, and in a manner similar to the present manifestations. In view of this, the following is introduced, and the entire anti-Christian manifestation, embracing mesmerizers, psychologists, prophets, seers, media, poets, and their spirits, all, *all*, are challenged to disclose its equal. Let us, then, examine that communication with Abraham, its profession, promise, and results as far as fulfilled. But be it remembered that the doctrine of Redemption is intimately and inseparably connected with that Covenant. To do away with the Gospel, therefore, it is important to prove the following doctrines unfounded: 1. That of the fall; 2. The Abrahamic Covenant; 3. The doctrine of the Incarnation; 4. The Messiahship of Jesus; 5. His Resurrection; 6. The doctrine of repentance and the forgiveness of sin.

The doctrine of the Fall cannot be disproved by man or spirit, for there are no means adapted to that end. And, moreover, the history of the race corroborates it. But this subject will be considered under a different head, and therefore will not now engage our attention.

With respect to Abram and his communion with the Spirit of God, it is thus recorded, Gen. ch. xii.: "Now the Lord had said unto Abram, Get thee out of thy country, and from thy kindred, and from thy father's house, unto a land that I will shew thee: and I will make of thee a great nation, and I will bless thee, and make thy name great; and thou shalt be a blessing: and I will bless them that bless thee, and curse him that curseth thee; and in thee shall all families of the earth be blessed. So Abram departed, as the Lord had spoken unto him, and Lot went with him; and Abram was seventy and five years old when he departed out of Haran."

The above, if admitted at all by modern spiritualists, is classed by them with the so-called spirit communications of this day. But the history of the succeeding ages crown it with awful grandeur, and connect it with events majestic and mighty in their character. And the Jews have ever been a monument of miraculous worth erected to that single "COMMUNICATION," and are now a living pyramid composed of mysterious attestations of the Divinity of that Promise.

That communication was given some four thousand years ago, and to this day events intimately connected with the covenant then made are exceedingly confirmatory by their demonstrations. Nevertheless man is so constituted, or rather perverted, that he more readily inclines to the rule of false prophets. Hence, though fortunes may be lost in unprofitable speculations prompted by clairvoyants and spirit-media, and also in excavating the earth for buried treasure pointed out by them; and although unnumbered vague and dreamy transcendental rhapsodies, having no direction whatever, may glut the press, the excited multitudes follow on as heedless as the drifting winds. And although failing, times without number, when their skill and power are tested, if they pronounce the ancient record fabulous or unmeaning, their followers shout "Amen," and all in the face of incontrovertible facts which cluster around the history of the past, and with the nation of scattered Jews now living as indubitable demonstrations of the Truth and Divinity of the Abrahamic Covenant.

"And Abram passed," says the account, "through the land unto the place of Sichem, unto the plain of Moreh. And the Canaanite was then in the land. And the Lord appeared unto Abram, and said, Unto thy seed will I give this land: and there builded he an altar unto the Lord, who appeared unto him. And he removed from thence unto a mountain on the east of Beth-el, and pitched his tent, having Beth-el on the west, and Hai on the east: and there he builded an altar unto the Lord, and called upon the name of the Lord. And Abram journeyed, going still toward the south."—Gen. xii., 6-9.

In confirmation of this call of Abram and the promise made to him, and to convey more fully to his mind the principle of mediation and divine life engaged in the work of that Covenant, "Melchizedek king of Salem met Abram, brought forth bread and wine: and he was the priest of the most high God. And he blessed him, and said, Blessed be Abram of the most high God, possessor of heaven and earth: and blessed be the most high God, which hath delivered thine enemies into thy hands."—Gen. xiv.

The law of equity requires the submission of aggressive principles to those of right. A similar law is observable in physics, else no equilibrium could be obtained or perpetuated. In morals it is immutably fixed that when mercy cannot prevent the growth of evil, justice, the law of rectitude, assumes the throne of judgment —not to afflict, but to prevent the consequences which attend the increase of wrong. Otherwise, order could not exist. Justice seeks to prevent the ultimation of evil. "If thy right hand offend thee, cut it off and cast it from thee," said Jesus, "for it is profitable for thee that one of thy members perish, and not that thy whole body should be cast into hell."—Matt. v., 30. This law is self evident, and men seek strenuously to put it into execution; but the nature-worshiper utters "tyranny," when it is said by the Christian to be inherent in the principles of divine government. And if Jehovah, in his Procedure, shall break the worm possessed of the spirit of wickedness, and which, if permitted to continue, would be the agent of unnumbered ills and even annihilate peace, then the Almighty is charged with injustice and revenge. Blind philosophy!

According to the scriptures, Lot had been taken captive, and Abram, pursuing, had rescued him. Abram was in the right. Why, then, should not the God of Justice protect him? Moreover, had he not prevailed over the enemy and returned victor, the same spirit that captured Lot very likely would have destroyed him also, and by cutting him off, the Covenant would have been of no effect. Here is wisdom—the manifestation of Design, and power to execute it. But the magnitude of that communication, given to Abram through Melchizedek the king of Salem, overspans the human race, and reaches to heaven. Simple as it may at first appear to have been, it discloses the law of mediation, in which is revealed Divine Propitiation, and the means by which a God, infinite in his perfections, can restore that which, by sin, is lost. It also revealed to Abram the unchangable truth that his victory over evil, and the success of his seed after him, would depend upon the justice of the cause, the necessity of the action as connected with God's purpose, and, finally, the sanction of heaven. "Blessed be the most high God," said Melchizedek, "who hath delivered thine enemies into thy hand." The sentiment of that communication is fully confirmed in the history of the Hebrews; for when by ambition they went up to battle they sooner or later fell; but when their existence, advance, or the perpetuation of the visible manifestation of the Divine Purpose required it, they moved on overcoming whatever opposed, and, as by Omnipotence, maintained their nationality. "After these things, the word of the Lord came to Abram in a vision, saying, Fear not, Abram, I am thy shield, and thy exceeding great reward. . . And he brought him forth abroad, and said, Look now toward heaven, and tell the stars, if thou be able to number them; and he said unto him, So shall thy seed be."

This promise, it will be remembered, was given when Abram as yet had no heir. But, "he believed the Lord, who counted it to him for righteousness. And he said unto him, I am the Lord that brought thee out of Ur of the Chaldees, to give thee this land to inherit it. And he said, Lord God, whereby shall I know that I shall inherit it? . . And when the sun was going down, a deep sleep fell upon Abram, and, lo, a horror of great darkness fell upon him; and he said unto Abram, Know of a surety that thy seed shall be a stranger in a strange land that is not theirs, and shall serve them; and they shall afflict them four hundred years: and also that nation whom they shall serve will I judge; and afterward they shall come out with great substance: and thou shalt go to thy fathers in peace; thou shalt be buried in a good old age. But in the fourth generation they shall come hither again; for the iniquity of the Amonites is not yet full." Communication most strange to be compared to modern developments! The very character of its expression exalts it above the work of created beings. Its language is like that of One Almighty and Omniscient. Where is the communication of these days worthy of a comparison with this? Verily, the heart sickens at the thought. And yet even some preachers, becoming *intoxicated with "spiritual magnetism,"* seem to have lost sight of the Infinite and to be overwhelmed with that scarcely worthy of the name of the finite.

"And it came to pass," continues the history, "that when the sun went down, and it was dark, behold a smoking furnace and a burning lamp that passed between those pieces. And the same day the Lord made a covenant with Abram, saying, Unto thy seed will I give this land, from the river of Egypt unto the great river, the river Euphrates." . . .

"And when Abram was ninety years old and nine, the Lord appeared unto Abram, and said unto him, I am the Almighty God; walk before me, and be thou perfect. . . And Abram fell on his face, and God talked with him, saying, As for me, behold my Covenant is with thee;

and thou shalt be a father of many nations. . . And I will establish my Covenant between me and thee, and thy seed after thee in their generations, for an everlasting Covenant, to be a God unto thee and thy seed after thee."—Gen. xvii.

This is the "Covenant" upon which depends the Law and the Prophets—the Gospel and the Christian Church. Let spiritualists consider it in all its bearings, and remember that before they can firmly establish their opposing manifestations as more worthy of religious regard, they must either reduce this to the plane of "spirit-rappings," or exalt them and kindred phenomena to this. How shall they accomplish either? Who can give answer?

This Covenant is to man, morally, as a centre sun around which revolves a universe of lesser orbs. Being the pledge and type of the "Incarnation," its position, nature and magnitude render it the external utterance to which are united all subsequent revelations. It was the foreshadowing of the great moral events that have since unfolded from the world of Light. And by its prophetic character it overspans the Consummation. It is infinite in its Spirit, almighty and inexorable in its Purpose, certain in its Procedure, merciful in its Nature, God-like in its Majesty, and eternal in its Ultimation. Its distant reflections overwhelm the light of Nature, and submerge beneath the tide of inspiring Truth the wisdom of man. And to name in its connection, by way of comparison, the substance of clairvoyant and spirit manifestations, from the monosylabic song to the most miraculous revelations (?) and voluminous essays, is to trifle with man's better sense. These conclusions the Covenant, succeeding disclosures, and demonstrations fully suggest and amply sustain.

CHAPTER II.

DIVINITY OF THE COVENANT.

THE following leading ideas are suggested by the above history:

I. It is claimed that the Supreme Being called Abram; hence, that obedient to the purpose and dictation of the Divine Spirit, he journeyed, a stranger in a strange land. No call could, therefore, supercede its authority.

II. It is before the world as a communication from the Supreme Being. No doctrine can claim superior origin.

III. The ASSURANCE, which was a pledge in the name of the Almighty God, to bestow certain blessings, and cause certain grand results ere the ultimate of human existence, which as a divine archetype should finally assume the form of a spiritual kingdom—world without end.

The Promise was threefold:

1. "I will bless them that bless thee, and curse him that curseth thee." That is, through thee and thy seed I have purposed to reveal my glory and redeeming grace to the world, and, therefore, shall sustain thee and thy seed to the fulfillment; hence, who or whatever opposes must fall before the power of the Redeeming

Procedure. A proper knowledge of this divine determination would render less obscure and objectionable to the sceptic very many important passages in the Bible history of Israel. But we must pass this subject with little notice until engaged in the "Exposition of the Scriptures." 2. The Prediction. "In thee shall the families of the earth be blessed." To this the above remarks are also applicable. 3. "And the Lord appeared unto Abram, and said, Unto thy seed will I give this land." This is the *land*, the possession of which has been so much contested by the tribes and nations of men. It was promised, as an external inheritance to his seed, when Abram passed through it subsequent to his call; and although at that time he was but a lone pilgrim, that location has since been the scene of most important and astounding tragedies connected with a people then unborn.—Moreover, each great act of that people has been a link in the chain of events which, united, have been in fulfillment of the above Promise. The promise, then, accepted as from the Almighty, was borne along succeeding ages clothed in majesty. Even unto the days of Christ it was encompassed and guarded by external sacerdotal rights. And since the vail of the temple was rent on the day of crucifixion, it has been enthroned in the heart of the devout believer in the Lord Jesus. The adoption of the divine principle with the true Christian Church is thus expressed by the word of Inspiration: "And if ye be Christ's then are ye Abraham's seed, and heirs according to the promise."—Gal. iii., 29.

How humiliating the thought, that the frail, fluctuating, and dreamy media of these times should be set up as reflectors of greater light, revealers of greater wisdom, and means of greater power than formerly bestowed on man. And most of all should the Christian grieve when those who have been ministers of the Gospel of Jesus descend from their high and holy calling to repeat blasphemies against God and the holy religion of the Cross, at the beck of these sensitive organs of anti-Christ.

To the Covenant made with Abram we call especial attention, as a COMMUNICATION not imitated in the remotest degree by anti-Christian manifestations; 1. Because of the unnumbered incidents flowing from and inseparably blending with that original fountain; 2. Because of the great truth that that covenant and its ultimation has ever been opposed by nature-serving spirits and the carnal man; 3. Because no power has successfully assailed it, or been competent to stand before it; 4. Because the truly faithful to its spirit and requirements have been humble, cross-bearing, and heaven-adoring; 5. Because it has been, yea is the hope of the Christian world; 6. Because to do it away would blast all the purported revelations from the unknown world, and leave man without evidence of future existence; for if the communication with Abram, and those that succeeded it which have been in confirmation thereof, are not genuine, then there is no hope, founded upon tangible evidence, that any are.

Let the reader for a moment contemplate the power and extent of that Covenant. Let him glance at the consequences which have followed it. Let him conceive of the millions which now are moved by its might, and held by its Omnipotence;—and then enquire if it is probable the Being who communed with Abram was the departed spirit of a mortal. It was given to one man, and affected his future life. Bound by its influence, and succeeding communications, he became a stranger and a pilgrim henceforth in the world. All this might have been accomplished without the presence of the Divine Spirit. But he offered his son, obedient to what he believed the Word of the Lord. This, peradventure, might have been the result of delusion; but whence came the ram that was caught in the bushes? Who led the house of Israel into Egypt, and thus preserved them in the days of famine? Even this the sophist might seek to evade. Were these events, all connected with that peculiar prophecy, and had no more demonstrations of divine direction and predetermination been given, the Covenant would have been of little effect. Then might the naturalist more plausibly question the truth of the Christian dependence, and with some excuse seek to eradicate from the human heart faith in the divinity of the Covenant and its fulfillment. But, like the fountain emerging from the bosom of the earth, and thence becoming the majestic river, the divine dispensation has increased in volume, while descending the vale of time, until its disclosures reveal their Infinite Cause, and display the goodness of God in his boundless love to man.

CHAPTER III.

MOSES AND THE MANIFESTATIONS.

CENTURIES after God met Abram, observe a babe in the ark floating amid the rushes, having been thus left by a fond mother to save him from the cruel executioner. Who guided that mother? and who the daughter of the king to save the child? You who mock Bible religion, give answer if ye can. And ye boasting spiritualists equal that communication, which thus rolled its providential wave along the tide of time. Let us follow that babe to manhood. In those days it is said of the seed of Abraham, "And it came to pass in the process of time that the king of Egypt died; and the children of Israel sighed by reason of the bondage;" (they were captives in Egypt,) "and they cried, and there came up a cry unto God," (the God of Abraham, the Spirit who made the Covenant,) "by reason of the bondage: and God heard their groaning, and God remembered his Covenant with Abraham, and with Isaac, and with Jacob, and God looked upon the children of Israel, and God had respect unto them." That is, by reason of his mercy and purpose in them, which purpose was expressed in the covenant, he preserved them. And when, by affliction, they were led to feel there was no hope but in the God of their fathers, and poured forth their supplications to him, he appeared for their relief, and proceeded to provide means for their deliverance. Thence he called the chosen servant to lead them from captivity.

"Now Moses kept the flock of Jethro his father-in-law, the priest of Midian; and he led the flock to the back side of the desert, and came to the mountain of God, even to Horeb."

"And the angel of the Lord appeared unto him (Moses) in a flame of fire out of the midst of a bush; and he looked, and behold, the bush burned with fire, and the bush was not consumed: and Moses said, I will now turn aside to see this great sight, why the bush is not burnt; and God called unto him out of the bush, and said, Moses, Moses; and he said, Here am I; and he said, Draw nigh hither; put off thy shoes from thy feet, for the place whereon thou standest is holy ground. Moreover he said, I am the God of thy father, the God of Abraham, the God of Isaac, and the God of Jacob: and Moses hid his face, for he was afraid to look upon God: and the Lord said, I have surely seen the affliction of my people which are in Egypt, and have heard their cry by reason of their task-masters, for I know their sorrows; and I am come down to deliver them out of the hands of the Egyptians, and to bring them up out of that land unto a good land and large, unto a land flowing with milk and honey; unto the place of the Canaanites," etc. "Come now therefore, and I will send thee unto Pharaoh, that thou mayest bring forth my people, the children of Israel, out of Egypt." Moses, in reply, said, "Who am I, that I should go unto Pharaoh, and that I should bring forth the children of Israel out of Egypt? And he said, Certainly I will be with thee, and this shall be a token unto thee, that I have sent thee: When thou hast brought forth the people out of Egypt, ye shall serve God upon this mountain." Thus, over four hundred years from Abram's call, and at the time appointed, the Lord met Moses, called and commissioned *him* to go to the king, and in the name of the I AM demand the captives.

Agreeable to God's promise, in due time the children of Israel emerged from Egyptian bonds, passed through the Red Sea, and moved over the desert toward the land of Canaan. And why? God had promised the land whither they journeyed to the seed of Abram. When famine threatened them with destruction, quails gathered around their camp for meat, and the heavens rained manna. In the thirsty and parched country, the smitten rock became a fountain. Whatever tribe or nation arose to prevent their progress was cut off. On, on they marched;—and why victorious? God had promised Canaan to the chosen race.

It would be sacrilege to linger around Sinai, witness the awful grandeur that attended the giving of the Law, or to overlook Gethsemane, where Jesus suffered in spirit, and pause on Calvary during the Crucifixion; or stand at the mouth of Joseph's tomb while the body of the Lord slumbered there, and behold the Resurrection, when death was conquered;—we repeat, it would be sacrilege to awake these scenes and offer them by way of comparison with the sickly opposing phenomena of the Nineteenth Century.

Let the spiritualists who deny the divinity of the Bible communications, meet this Covenant with whatever their manifestations afford! Let them invoke their gods to come down and imitate! In vain they shall plead from the morning until the evening sacrifice for an answer.

REFLECTIONS.

To contravene this, as already shown, they must excel it throughout in power, wisdom and effect, by contradictory manifestations; and as they propose to establish a religion of an opposite character, they must disclose a superior prophetic spirit, make and fulfill greater promises. Nor can this be admitted as proof in support of their theory, and in condemnation of the Christian doctrine, until their prophecies of a superior character, extending ages into the future, shall have been fulfilled. Truly that COMMUNION with a single individual (Abram) presents a barrier that our prophets, media, and all spirit dictations will hardly be able to remove during this age.

To seek to evade the test, and weaken the Abrahamic Covenant, by crying Myth, Tradition, Bigotry, etc., is but to concede their inability to contest its truth or stand before its majesty. It absolutely beggars their cause. As one revelation from the Invisible that cannot be touched by the magnetic hand of the age, or equaled by modern phenomena, or overcome by any philosophy, we present that Covenant, and call upon all men and the spirits of anti-Christ to meet it. We offer and defend it as from the Almighty Lord, the Creator of heaven and earth, the eternal Logos.

Spiritualists, cavil not! Ye challenge with many words the Christian: with this we meet that challenge. It is a world of unfolding truth, an unfathomable deep of Infinite and Almighty Design; an inexhaustible fountain of Providential Benefaction. Here is divinity! philosophy! manifestation! Ye who boast of wonderful disclosures, of your natural religion, and unfailing philosophy, launch your fleets upon this sea. Fathom it! Ascertain its boundaries, and bring testimony, tangible, irrefutable, self-evident that ye have reached its distant shore, or even passed into regions hitherto undiscovered and unrevealed.

Ye modern miners for truth, dig deep, sink your magnetic shaft far into the unknown, and undermine the ROCK OF AGES; then bring your trophies forth. Ye who ascend (?) to spheres on high, reach the summit of its lofty dome, and bring a gem from realms superior, one blossom plucked from the heavens over-arching it. The work to overthrow is yours, ye boasters. Grapple with this Truth, ye subjects of opposing powers, ye heaven-daring of this reckless age!

CHAPTER IV.

ELIJAH AND THE MANIFESTATIONS.

MESMERIZERS, psychologists, and media make lofty professions of spiritual and mesmeric power. They claim to equal the works of the Lord, his prophets, and apostles; and, as by the present relief which attends animal magnetism, they have, in many instances, persuaded the subjects and their friends to believe themselves capable of doing what the Christian denominates miracles, we shall consider this phase of the subject before examining modern manifestations. We are aware that when an immovable difficulty arises, these modern teachers cry out, "fables," "legends," "tradition of the undeveloped," but boasting and denunciation is not argument, and although they satisfy superficial minds, magnetic subjects, and the marvelously inclined, it is trifling to the thoughtful and informed. By such methods could they obtain, all history might be blotted from the page of ages, and facts be done away. It seems most probable that there have been true and learned men before the present school; men as well qualified to note what passed before them, and of which they were witnesses, as are those now assuming the teachership, and seeking the absolute control of the mind of this generation.

Elijah, the prophet, of whom this chapter treats, lived some nine hundred years before Christ. He was a native of Tishbe beyond Jordon, in Gilead. Says a distinguished historian, "Elijah was one of the most eminent of that illustrious and singular race of men, the Jewish prophets. Every part of his character is marked by a moral grandeur, which is heightened by the obscurity thrown around his connections and his private history. He often wears the air of a supernatural messenger suddenly issuing from another world to declare the commands of heaven, and to awe the proudest mortals by the menace of fearful judgments. His boldness in reproof; his lofty zeal for the honor of God; his superiority to softness, ease, and suffering, are the characters of a man filled with the Holy Spirit; and he was admitted to great intimacy with God, and enabled to work miracles of a very extraordinary and unequivocal character. These were called for by the stupid idolatry of the age, and were in some instances equally calculated to demonstrate the being and power of Jehovah, and to punish those who had forsaken him for idols. The author of Ecclesiasticus has an encomium to his memory, and justly describes him as a prophet 'who stood up as a fire, and whose word burned as a lamp.' He was a type of John the Baptist."

To afford opposers of Bible truths occasion for the exercise of their boasted power, the following facts, connected with Elijah's history, are introduced, and all the "wonder-workers," now so numerous and active, are invited to equal them by the union of their forces, and whatever means they can bring to their aid:

I. *The Restoration of the Widow's Son.*

"And it came to pass after these things that the son of the woman, the mistress of the house, fell sick; and his sickness was so sore that there was no breath in him: and she said unto Elijah, What have I to do with thee, O thou man of God? Art thou come unto me to call my sin to remembrance, and to slay my son? And he said unto her, Give me thy son; and he took him out of her bosom, and carried him up into a loft, where he abode, and laid him upon his own bed; and he cried unto the Lord and said, O Lord my God, hast thou also brought evil upon the widow with whom I sojourn, by slaying her son? And he stretched himself upon the child three times, and cried unto the Lord, and said, O Lord my God, I pray thee let this child's soul come into him again; and the Lord heard the voice of Elijah, and the soul of the child came into him again, and he revived: and Elijah took the child, and brought him down out of the chamber into the house, and delivered him unto his mother; and Elijah said, See, thy son liveth;—and the woman said to Elijah, Now by this I know that thou art a man of God, and that the word of the Lord in thy mouth is truth."—1 Kings xvii.

This is said by mesmerizers to be a case in which human magnetism was employed to stimulate a child merely fallen into a comatose state by reason of exhaustion. But the account will not admit the interpretation. Moreover, the narrator must have known better, by far, how to relate the facts than men of a period so remote as this from its occurrence. And, besides, the following prominent points in the case reported remove it from the natural sphere: 1. The child fell so sick that there was no breath in him. 2. Elijah prayed to God, not magnetism, to let the child's *soul come into him again.* This language is very clear, and according to all usages can convey no other idea than that the child's body was dead. It must have been, if the absence of breath, the departure of the soul from the body is death. To allow a different construction would render all history useless, and man, nature, and ultimates would be reduced to nondescripts. 3. The account states that the *Lord*, not "nervo-vitality," "nervaura," or the "odd force," *heard* the voice of Elijah's prayer. 4. The soul of the child did not revive but came into him again, and he (the child) revived. 5. The mother bore witness to the truth that it was the Lord's and not Elijah's doings. "I know," said she, "that thou art a man of God, and that the word of the Lord is in thy mouth." Who are most likely to be correct, those immediately connected with the circumstances, or they who, by changing the history from its original and simple meaning into a sophisticated narrative, or by entirely perverting it, seek to exalt themselves, and establish their own theory? Unfold one of like character, ye who assay to compete with the scriptures, and then may ye have somewhat whereof to boast. By awaking the somnambulist, restoring to the normal state the mesmerized, or the self-induced clairvoyant; or to quiet nervous excitement, and relieve physical suffering by pathetism, will not meet the case in hand. Bring back the departed soul, and let breath, which had *left the body, be restored.* Literally, bring life to the dead, ye who boast of power. Again we say, let all the anti-Christian spirits that hover around the living, and all the psychomancists, seers, media, and believers therein, combine, and bid the dead body arise, be animate, and live. By your profession this ye should be able to do, and even greater things, because (ye say) ye are progressed.

II. *Elijah and the Rain.*

Again, it is written of Elijah, even the undeveloped, as "progressionists" conclude the prophets to have been, that upon one occasion he "said unto Ahab, As the Lord God of Israel liveth, before whom I stand, there shall not be dew nor rain these years, but according to my word. . . And it came to pass after a while that the brook dried up, because there was no rain in the land. . . And Ahab said unto Obadiah, Go into the land unto all fountains of water, and unto all brooks; peradventure we may find grass to save the horses and mules alive, that we lose not all the beasts."

"And Elijah went up to the top of Carmel; and he cast himself down upon the earth, and put his face between his knees, and said to his servant, Go up now, look toward the sea. . . And it came to pass at the seventh time, that he said, Behold, there ariseth a little cloud out of the sea, like a man's hand. . . And it came to pass in the meanwhile, that the heaven was black with clouds and wind, and there was a great rain."—1 Kings, xvii. and xviii.

And thus it is written, that at Elijah's *word* the heavens withheld their rain, and again, that as he bowed to the earth a cloud arose and the waters descended. Thus is offered another fact for the trial of the "progressed." Let them cause the heavens to withhold rain and dew, and again bid the elements pour forth their floods upon the world, and let it be *done.*

Elijah trusted in God, was the Lord's servant in very deed; moved and spake by divine dictation, and was therefore a successful agent in the work of the Lord. So saith the Bible, and thus doth the Christian believe. Equal this power and manifestation, if ye are able, ye who condemn the Book of God.

III. *The Translation.*

"And Elijah said unto him, (Elisha) Tarry, I pray thee, here, for the Lord hath sent me to Jordan. And he said, As the Lord liveth, and as thy soul liveth, I will not leave thee; and they two went on. And fifty men of the sons of the prophets went, and stood to view afar off: and they two stood by Jordan. And Elijah took his mantle, and wrapped it together, and smote the waters, and they were divided hither and thither, so that they two went over on dry ground. And it came to pass, when they were gone over, that Elijah said unto Elisha, Ask what I shall do for thee, before I be taken away from thee. And Elisha said, I pray thee, let a double portion of thy spirit be upon me. And he said, Thou hast asked a hard thing; nevertheless, if thou see me when I am taken from thee, it shall be so unto thee; but if not, it shall not be so. And it came to pass, as they still went on, and talked, that behold, there appeared a chariot of fire, and horses of fire, and parted them both asunder; and Elijah went up by a whirlwind into heaven. And Elisha saw it, and he cried, My father, my father, the chariot of Israel, and the horsemen thereof! And he saw him no more; and he took hold of his own clothes, and rent them in two pieces. He took up also the mantle of Elijah that fell from him, and went back, and stood by the bank of Jordan: and he took the mantle of Elijah that fell from him, and smote the waters, and said, Where is the Lord God of Elijah? and when he also had smitten the waters, they parted hither and thither: and Elisha went over."—2 Kings, ii.

The above account states that fifty sons of the prophets witnessed the manifestation of Elijah and Elisha. Moreover, those men sent fifty men to look for Elijah, thinking perhaps he had fallen again to the earth, but after searching three days, they returned unsuccessful.

If half a score, or even less, witness modern manifestations, the believers expect the public to give credit to their report. Yet, the very people who witness most of their astounding scenes in the "dark," and who censure the world for not giving their testimony the fullest credit, are quite unwilling to admit this account as truthful, but "say" it away among legends. As a truth, however, we present it, and demand its like of those who profess to have light superior to that reflected in the days of the prophets. It may be said the account is a fiction, but *the world* cannot prove it such.

CHAPTER V.

ELISHA AND THE MANIFESTATIONS.

"AND when the child was grown, it fell on a day, that he went out to his father to the reapers. And he said unto his father, My head, my head! And he said unto a lad, Carry him to his mother. . . And he sat on her knees till noon, and then died. And she went up, and laid him on the bed of the man of God, and went out. . . And she went and came unto the man of God to mount Carmel.

"And when Elisha was come into the house, behold, the child was dead, and laid upon his bed. He went in therefore, and shut the door upon them twain, and prayed unto the Lord: and he went up, and lay upon the child, and put his mouth upon his mouth, and his eyes upon his eyes, and his hands upon his hands; and he stretched himself upon the child, and the flesh of the child waxed warm. Then he returned, and walked to and fro; and went up, and stretched himself upon him; and the child opened his eyes."—2 Kings, iv.

Here is another and somewhat similar incident: the child is declared *dead*, and restored by Elisha, and in answer to his prayer to God. Can the teachers in Bible opposition, those who deny the divinity of these strange results, imitate them? "By their fruits ye shall know them." The effort to reduce the phenomena disclosed in the days of the Patriarchs, Prophets, and of the primitive Christian Church, disposes of the accounts according to the necessity of the times. The history is not consulted to learn wisdom and arrive at the truth; if so, the facts would be admitted in the character presented by the historian. But such points as serve their interest are taken as literally true, and others, not in harmony with modern developments, are rejected, or said to be the record of imaginative scenes. The Bible, in the plainest terms, says "the child died," and that Elisha prayed to God, etc., and the child lived again. Either the child was dead, or the account, entire, must be fabulous; at least so much so as to render it questionable. But, as already noticed, the Ancient Record cannot be proved untrue. Science may exhume the fossils of the past, and genius may bring from their silent tombs the indices of sunken cities; clairvoyants may seem to read old MSS., and tell therefrom the rise, progress, and fall of tribes and nations, and also to translate the mystic hieroglyphics of past ages; the pre-adamic (?) spirits may speak from trumpets in the dark, and write with spirit-made(?)

hands; media may be reduced to walking ghosts; still that Book, hated by the Prince of *Darkness*, that Record of Heavenly Dispensations, the Inspired Word, can never be proved a compilation of vagaries, of original myths, concocted by the dreamy dupes of ghostly imaginations, traditionally transmitted from generation to generation, and employed by a false and hollow-hearted priesthood to collude the masses into menial servitude. However, scheme after scheme has been devised, evil machinations, sophistry, and every project unfolded and executed, in order to remove the Bible from the world. Still it remains. It has withstood the combined forces of God-opposing powers; been enveloped in the flames perpetuated by infidelic fuel, and yet, as the pure gold in the furnace, it is not consumed.

Elisha and the Syrian Army.

"Then the king of Syria warred against Israel, and took counsel with his servants, saying, In such and such a place shall be my camp. And the man of God sent unto the king of Israel, saying, Beware that thou pass not such a place; for thither the Syrians are come down. And the king of Israel sent to the place which the man of God had told him and warned him of, and saved himself there, not once nor twice. Therefore the heart of the king of Syria was sore troubled for this thing, and he called his servants and said unto them, Will ye not shew me which of us is for the king of Israel? And one of his servants said, None, my lord, O king; but Elisha the prophet that is in Israel, telleth the king of Israel the words that thou speakest in thy bed chamber. And he said, Go and spy where he is, that I may send and fetch him; and it was told him, saying, Behold, he is in Dothan: therefore sent he thither horses and chariots, and a great host, and they came by night and compassed the city about.

"And when the servant of the man of God was risen early, and gone forth, behold, a host compassed the city, both with horses and chariots. And his servant said unto him, alas, my master, how shall we do? And he answered, Fear not: they that be with us are more than they that be with them: and Elisha prayed, and said, Lord, I pray thee open his eyes that he may see." Remember, Elisha prayed to the Lord, not to a spirit or nervaura. "And the Lord opened the eyes of the young man, and he saw; and, behold, the mountain was full of horses and chariots round about Elisha.

"And when they (the Syrian hosts) came down to him, Elisha prayed unto the Lord, and said, Smite this people, I pray thee, with blindnes: and he smote them with blindness, according to the word of Elisha."

Thence Elisha led the people blind into Samaria, and when in Samaria he again prayed, saying, "Lord, open the eyes of these men, that they may see: and the Lord opened their eyes, and they saw; and, behold, they were in the midst of Samaria. And the king of Israel said unto Elisha, when he saw them, My father, shall I smite them? shall I smite them?" This was not done in the dark. "And he answered, Thou shalt not smite them: wouldst thou smite those whom thou hast taken captive with thy sword and with thy bow? Set bread and water before them, that they may eat and drink, and go to their masters. And he prepared great provisions for them; and when they had eaten and drunk, he sent them away, and they went to their master. So the bands of Syria came no more into the land of Israel."—2 Kings, vi.

With this, we conclude our present reference to Old Testament manifestations; not, however, without reminding opposing philosophers of the importance of their unfolding from the interior, from nature, or spirits, some evidence of equal ability, ere they hope to swerve the true Christian and establish "magnetism," "spiritual affinity," etc., etc., as worthy of man's hope; more reliable in the day of trouble, and a more sure guide to everlasting peace, than the Inspired Word, and the religion it teaches.

It is well, also, to notice that spiritual blindness will not be a parallel with that by which the Syrians were smitten. No one will question that their natural vision was closed, because they were not conscious of being in Samaria until Elisha prayed unto the Lord, and the Lord opened their eyes, when, lo, they were in the midst of Israel. Therefore, although the multitude may be led, spiritually blind, by a false religion, the case calls for a different effect, one that shall close the natural vision—shut out the material world. That magnetism, psychology, soothsaying, and psycomancy weave more closely the veil obscuring the sunlight of the moral heavens, and make darker still the night of man's spiritual gloom, we will not deny; nor that thousands may be thereby pursuing an object adverse to that intended. This the wild, indefinite, and vacant eye of the spiritualist, especially the media, fully reveals. But let the psychologist control an army, at once, by his nature-power, and lead them whither he will. Hosts may be led by the power of influence, by excitement, or their regard for a leader. But Elisha was not an object of their admiration, and besides, they were struck blind, and again their eyes were opened; after which they ate and drank; then returned to their master. Ye progressed, learned, and skillful in your sciences and arts; we still admonish you to bring forth corresponding manifestations while claiming, not only equal but superior ability to that which was conferred through God's ancient servants, and which is deemed by Christians as the work of the Divine Spirit.

CHAPTER VI.

NEW TESTAMENT MANIFESTATIONS.

"And when Jesus was entered into Capernaum, there came unto him a centurion, beseeching him, and saying, Lord, my servant lieth at home sick of the palsy, grievously tormented. And Jesus saith unto him, I will come and heal him. The centurion answered and said, Lord, I am not worthy that thou shouldst come under my roof; but speak the word only and my servant shall be healed. And Jesus said unto the centurion, Go thy way; and as thou hast believed, so be it done unto thee. And his servant was healed in the selfsame hour." Matt. viii.

"This is holy ground," said the Lord to Moses, as he drew near the burning bush. With what spirit should we approach this subject? May Heaven forgive us for contrasting the work of Jesus with the vague, lingering and incomplete deeds of opposing spiritualism. Need we enquire what medium or charmer of this age, has revealed ability worthy of the comparison? Nay, verily, so far short of an imitation are all their works when best revealed that no language can express the diversity. At the *word* of the Lord, the sick of the palsy was healed.

It was not necessary for Jesus to take up his

abode with the centurion and pathetize the disease away. Moreover, it was the *palsy* and not merely a nervous weakness under which the servant was laboring, and from which he was restored.

Again it is written, Matt. xvii: "And when they were come to the multitude, there came to him a certain man, kneeling down to him, and saying, Lord, have mercy on my son for he is a lunatic, and sore-vexed: for oftimes he falleth into the fire, and oft into the water. And I brought him to thy disciples, and they could not cure him. And Jesus rebuked the devil, and he departed out of him; and the child was cured from that very hour. Howbeit," said Jesus to his disciples, "this kind goeth out but by fasting and prayer."

This is a case of mental derangement occasioned by an evil spirit, and which, although it withstood the disciples, did not contend with the Lord, but fled from his presence. The Savior instructed the disciples, that such went out only by fasting and prayer. Thus he evinced a nature unlike that of his disciples. He healed by his word, while they must fast and pray,—must present the case before God, and invoke his immediate aid to overcome like stubborness. The doctrine of Jesus conflicts with modern philosophy, for it is not necessary to fast or pray in order to psychologize. At least such seems not to be the habit of Mesmerisers. Nervo-vitality does not require religious devotion in order to be invoked, and we believe it is not customary for "operators" to ask the Lord to vouchsafe his aid, but rather, they feel their own importance in the case and declare themselves equal to JESUS. It is also worthy of notice, that, although the nervously debilitated, and sometimes those partially deranged, may be at times relieved; and there are multitudes of professors in the art, yet the ratio of the insane has not been much diminished by their benevolence and the exercise for good of the mesmeric power. In view of this profession, may we not enquire why psychologists and mediums do not enter our asylums and bid the sufferers go forth in their right mind; and thus applying their skill and displaying their philanthropy, remove the need of asylums, and make happy and cheerful many homes now desolate. The answer is obvious.

"And it came to pass, that as he came nigh unto Jerico, a certain blind man sat by the wayside begging. And hearing the multitude pass by, he asked what it meant. And they told him that Jesus of Nazareth passeth by. And he cried, saying, Jesus, thou son of David, have mercy on me. And Jesus stood and commanded him to be brought unto him; and when he was come near, hs asked him, What wilt thou that I shall do unto thee? And he said, Lord that I may receive my sight. And Jesus said unto him, Receive thy sight, thy faith hath saved thee. And immediately he received his sight, and followed him, glorifying God. And all the people when they saw it, gave praise unto God." —Luke xviii

All the people saw this blind man restored to sight; and it was not simply strengthening weak eyes or relieving ophthalmia by magnetism and the application of remedial agents; but Jesus *said*, "Receive thy sight," and the *blind* man saw. Go and do likewise, ye minglers in the intermediate realms, ye who take the magic hand of mysterious law, and guide the current of nervauric power. Heal the palsy, cure the leprosy, open the eyes of those born blind, loose the tongue, cause the dumb to talk, and the really deaf to hear. And when ye have accomplished all this, go to the tombs, call forth those bodies slumbering in the cold arms of death. Then, nor until then, have ye cause to compare your works with those of the Savior's, or counsel the christian from his faith in Jesus.

Finally: The following manifestations, through the apostles of the Lord, are suggested as worthy of imitation by those who seem "the exalted" in their relation to supermundane spheres.

And if their professions are founded in truth, it should not be difficult for them to demonstrate it.

1. We propose as a test the case of a man who was lame from his birth, "and who was laid daily at the gate of the temple which was called Beautiful, to ask alms of them that entered the temple, who seeing Peter and John about to go into the temple, asked an alms. And Peter, fastening his eyes upon him with John, said, Look on us. And he gave heed unto them, expecting to receive something of them. Then Peter said, Silver and Gold have I none; but such as I have give I thee: In the name of Jesus Christ of Nazareth rise up and walk. And he took him by the right hand, and lifted him up: and immediately his feet and ancle bones received strength. And he leaping up stood, and walked, and entered with them into the temple, leaping, and praising God. And all the people saw him walking and praising God. And they knew that it was he which sat for alms at the Beautiful gate of the Temple; and they were filled with wonder and amazement at that which had happened unto him."

2. "And there sat a certain man at Lystria, impotent in his feet, being so from his mother's womb, who never walked. The same heard Paul speak, who steadfastly beholding him, and perceiving that he had faith to be healed, said

with a loud voice, Stand upright on thy feet. And he leaped and walked. And when the people saw what Paul had done, they lifted up their voices, saying in the speech of Lycaonia, "The Gods are come down to us in the likeness of men." And when the people would have offered sacrifices, the apostles, Barnabas and Paul, said, "Why do ye these things. We also are men of like passions with you, and preach unto you that you should turn from these vanities unto the living God, which made heaven, and earth, and the sea, and all things that are therein."—Acts xiv.

The Apostles wrought miracles by the spirit of the Lord; otherwise: God revealed his power through them. To God they gave the glory.—But modernists occupy a different sphere, and manifest a different spirit, while their works are sickly when compared to the above.

CONCLUSION.

Here we close the Bible history of Spiritualism, and proceed to notice its perpetuation from the days of the Apostles, and to offer some propositions for the consideration of Bible opposers, thence shall proceed to the analysis of modern Spiritualism.

Against all forms of philosophy and religion which are antagonistic to, or deny the divine origin of the Inspired Word, we oppose that

Word, nature, reason, and the facts connected with human existence. We also maintain that whatever manifestations have been, or may now be, bordering upon spiritualism, whether professedly opposed to or in harmony with the scriptures, are in confirmation thereof, either by disclosing divine truths from the sphere of holiness, or of the principles of evil, both of which accord with the teachings, doctrines and predictions, or are fulfilling their prophecies. This position the reader cannot mistake. In the illustration and defence thereof we have engaged whatever ability God and Nature may have bestowed upon us. "To the law and to the testimony." If they speak not according to this, it is because there is no light in them. In Jesus we behold the Divine Logos; hence in him God manifest in the flesh: not as in any and every man, but by direct Incarnation, and for the purpose of redeeming the world from sin. Accordingly we affirm man fallen, and hence that by repentance towards God and faith in the Lord Jesus alone he can be saved. To this end it is written, and in faithfulness, "Let the wicked forsake his way and the unrighteous man his thoughts, and let him return to the Lord, who will have mercy upon him, and to our God, who will abundantly pardon."

Add to these doctrines those of the resurrection of the dead; the final judgment, and a compend of the principles in whose defence this work is undertaken, is expressed in such a manner as to render our faith and object clear. We, therefore, reject as false any so-called philosophy, doctrine, or manifestation of whatever nature, which conflicts with the above principles. Not because they may be said to constitute our system of theology, but because they are the true principles of divinity, of nature as now manifest, and of existing facts; and the only principles that cause and sequence unfold and sustain; and because they are incorporated in the elements of reason—are the *rationale* connected with man.

PART III.

CHAPTER I.

THE INTERIM.

From the apostolic age until the present time the conflict between the Israel of God and the powers of darkness has been perpetuated. We shall not, however, trace the history from thence, for it is not needful to introduce farther testimony upon the subject respecting the past. But lest opposers should attempt to evade our conclusions by an effort to weaken confidence in the Bible account, we introduce the following passages from an article written by William Fishbough, one of the earliest and strongest advocates of modern spiritualism. Much of the sentiment is applicable to the question at issue. The article to which reference is had, appeared in the *Spiritual Telegraph*, vol. 2, number 37, (New York, 1854,) and was headed, "Ancient Christian Spiritualism." From the tenor of the argument the writer evidently intended to prove spiritualism no new phenomenon; but in his remarks, and by the passages introduced from history, he has firmly established the existence of evil spirits, embracing the doctrines taught in the Scriptures of Truth, and particularly that which awards to the prophets and apostles power, through divine aid, over evil and unclean spirits.

From the character of the writer, his established erudition, relation to mesmerism, (having been the scribe and compiler of "Nature's Divine Revelations,") his knowledge of the rise and progress of spiritualism, connection therewith, etc.; and also from the fact that the article appeared before the world in the most popular spiritual organ, no believer will for a moment question its authority. In his remarks he observes:

"Let us now glance at some of the numerous historical testimonies as to the post-apostolic perpetuity of spiritual gifts and intercourse in the Christian Church. The learned Dr. Mosheim, in treating the history of the Church during the second century, says, "It is easier to conceive than to express how much the *miraculous powers and the extraordinary divine gifts* which the Christians exercised on various occasions contributed to extend the limits of the Church. The gift of foreign tongues appears to have gradually ceased as soon as many nations became enlightened with the truth, and numerous churches of Christians were everywhere established, for it became less necessary than it was at first. But the other gifts with which God favored the rising Church of Christ were, as we learn from numerous testimonies of the ancients, still conferred upon particular persons here and there." * Dr. Murdock, the translator of Mosheim, sanctions these statements with emphasis, adding a long note, in which he argues the point, and refers to numerous passages in the ancients to establish it." . . . "Notwithstanding there appears to have been a gradual decline and final cessation of *heathen oracles* after the establishment of the Christian Church, (and we might show strong reasons for believing that these oracles were actual spiritual communications, as both heathens and Christians believed them to be,) there seem to have still been among the heathens some mediums for spirits (or the alledged gods) for a long time after the apostolic age. Between these spirits and their mediums on the one hand, and the Christian prophets on the other, there was generally an open hostility; but wherever a trial of powers occurred, the heathen spirit was forced to give way, showing the existence still in the Church of that power conferred by Jesus upon his disciples to "cast out devils." Hence we find Tertullian, in his "Apology for the Christian Religion," boldly challenging all heathendom to a trial of their

Mos. Eccl. Hist., B. I. Cent. II. Part I. Chap. I. § 8.

patron spirits and divinities, who were accustomed to possess and speak through the bodies of certain men. "Hitherto," says he, "we have used words; we will now come to a demonstration of the very thing, that your Gentile gods are no one of them greater than another. For a decision of the point, let any one that is judged to be possessed by a devil be brought into open court before your tribunals; when that spirit shall be commanded by a Christian to speak, he shall as truly confess himself a devil there, as elsewhere he falsely claims to be a god. Or let one equally be produced who is among you Gentiles judged to be *inspired of God*, who waits at your altars, and is esteemed a sacred person by you; nay, though he be acted by one of your most venerated deities, be it Diana the heavenly virgin, or Esculapius that prescribes your medicines, and who pretends to relieve the dying, yet these, or any others, when they are summoned, if they dare to lie unto the Christian summoning, and if they do not confess themselves openly to be devils, then let that reproaceful Christian's blood be spilt by you on the spot." . . . "Tertullian died about the year 231." . "Indeed, Mosheim informs us that in the third century the office of exorcist, as a special office, was created in the churches, it being the duty of the one holding it to cast out these subtile and un-

Christian spirits from the bodies of such as were infested by them, and which they did by a process similar to that employed by the apostles."!

No spiritualist will presume to deny the above statements. What, then, do they establish but the great truth maintained throughout the Bible, viz.: that a Satanic power opposes the government of God with man? and that by the Spirit of the Lord evil spirits are subdued and cast out of the possessed. *It is important to regard this fact*, 1. Because the sentiment is called in question by the "anti-Christ" of this age, and indeed the denial is important to the life of Harmonialism and all other "isms" which conflict with the Gospel; 2. Because it constitutes *one* strong point at issue between the Biblicist and Naturalist; 3. Because by the application of this principle (Divine power) the Christian faith is confirmed and also distinguished from the imitations thereof, by false and deceptive beings, and because it is a Bible doctrine; 4. Because there is a power actively engaged with men, assuming the form and name of mesmerism, spirit manifestations, etc., which denies the divine authenticity of the Bible, the fall and depravity of man, the divinity of Christ; also redemption through Jesus, and therefore utterly rejects the doctrines of the Gospel, whose necessity depends upon the existence of absolute evil; 5. Because this power heralds its determination to remove the Christian Church from the world; 6. Because the Opposition to Christianity demands, like the ancient Philistines, the issue; and its Goliath, with shield and armor-bearer, appears before men, boldly defying the God of Israel.

The religious world may deem this subject unworthy their consideration; nevertheless, a power is at work with the hearts of men that, unless checked, shall shake the external church and try every soul, and test the faith of every believer in the Lord Jesus. We are thus emphatic upon this subject because when analyzing the present phenomena we shall have occasion to disclose, define and elucidate these principles. We only add, that Zion's watchmen have occasion to guard well those avenues through which these invidious influences approach the souls of men. Nor is it from fancy, as the sequel will determine, that these thoughts are suggested.

CHAPTER II.

PROPOSITIONS FOR SPIRITUALISTS, ETC.

As the anti-Christian spiritualists proclaim their system of so-called "Rational Religion" as the true religion, and as they profess to have power equal or even superior to that which accompanied the Prophets, Jesus of Nazareth, and the Apostles, we invite them to bring a parallel to the following incidents of the Old and New Testament times. As they complain much of those who deny the spiritual origin of their works, and who seek to change the character of the manifestation by rendering other reasons for their origin than those set forth by the advocates, we suggest to spiritualists that by their own law they are bound to admit the ancient Records, and especially since they have no means to disprove their authenticity and the correctness of their claims. If they deny their validity, they sanction arguments against themselves and condemn their own theory.

Progressionists denominate those "bigots" who adhere to Bible theology in this age of light and reason, (?) and particularly those doctrines not endorsed by "the spirits." Therefore they teach that the Bible should receive credit only so far as corroborated by clairvoyants and media. To establish their claims the present phenomena should, 1. Surpass in power and effect those whose teachings they condemn. 2. Should excel all former manifestations in wisdom. 3. Should be better adapted to man's necessity, and in their use to his purity. 4. They should beget greater harmony with the believers. 5. Should be a more firm support to the principles of right. 6. Should more abundantly confirm their mental equilibrium and moral goodness. 7. Should render them more heaven-like, more angelic, hence 8. Should beget more charity, brotherly kindness, and forgiveness for the erring. 9. Should cause them, particularly the media, to excel the true Christian in loving their enemies, and in their efforts for the restoration of the wanderer. 10. Their influence should excite more perfect union between men, and make more peaceful and happy the restless, troubled mind. 11. They should unfold divine qualities superior to the conceptions of the dormant soul, and of all former revelations; and 12. They should carry the devotee to a plane above that which stimulates the inferior qualities of sensuous beings;—should make them God-like, heavenly, divine, according to their professions.

Such results should attend the works of modern reformers (?) if they are the recipients of purer and more perfect light than has previously been given to man. Yea, and greater works should accompany them than these, if their theory of progression, and their ideas of the advanced condition of the present generation are established in truth; and more particularly, if the exalted inhabitants of spiritual realms descend to instruct and illumine them, and through external media disclose the light of diviner spheres.

No lover of truth, no philosopher, no christian, yea, no mortal can be so indifferent to his own interest, to his present and future well-being as not to desire any additional *light* upon a subject so important as that connected with the immortality of his being. Men may be sectional in matters of minor moment, they may indulge contracted feelings upon subjects of earthly duration, but the mind must prefer truth respecting the future state? But because it is *said* that a great light has appeared and that declaration is attended with no adequate demonstration, if the Christian does not heed it, shall he therefore be denounced a bigot and unwilling to learn? Verily not! It is therefore consistent, that, ere the Christian submit his soul to the moulding of an opposite principle to that of his faith, he requires the evidence of its superior origin, character and ability. In material arrangements value is closely considered in the exchange of commodities: how much more should that be of religion? With the proper understanding of this subject, and with the exalted and glorious character of the Inspired Word before our minds, let us gradually descend to the plane of Spiritualism as reflected upon the present age.

CHAPTER III.

SUGGESTIONS FOR BIBLE OPPOSERS.

1. Every important era has its corresponding mode and means of introduction. And these must embrace the principles by which results are obtained.

2. In a religion, whether true or false, the nucleus primarily revealed is the type of *its* succeeding degrees. Wherever it obtains, leading characteristics, (the manifestation of the archetypal,) distinguish it from all other religions, and relates it, unmistakably, to its prototype; and when the original ceases, that religion is no more.

3. Different circumstances may require and admit varying modes; yet no condition can make void first principles, for unless they are retained and disclosed, the appearance a deceptive shadow, is accepted for the cause.

4. ILLUSTRATION: Bible religion could not be so transformed as to be mistaken for Mahomedanism; nor the spirit of christianity for carnality—lasciviousness. Being opposites, one could not

so merge into the other as to loose its original characteristics.

5. False appearances may be assumed, but the spring of action must remain unchanged however varied and graduated may be the order of manifestation.

6. The prelude, by its likeness to that which it is to succeed, indicates its existence, nature and movement.

7. John the Baptist "was not the Light, but was sent to bear witness of that Light." He was the foreshadowing. But his mission must have been by the inspiration of that Light, or he could not have been the Forerunner.

8. A confirmed Mahomedan by a name and corresponding ceremony might pass for a believer in the Lord Jesus; still he would be a Moslem. Assumption would not make him a christian.

9. These laws extend throughout all the relations and proceedings of men, and are truly applicable to the subject before us.

10. EVERY REVELATION must emerge from its unknown or unrevealed state by the use of adapted means, those in harmony with its nature and useful to the end indicated.

11. The idiotic brain could not be the medium for intellectual and exalted disclosures.

12. The uncultivated, but properly organized

cerebrum might be inspired by a superior mental sphere; but if it was destitute of the organ adapted to the use of the centre or leading thought, no inspiration could induce proper utterance.

13. Neither can a cause reveal itself in a form antagonistic to its nature, or employ means unadapted to its use.

14. The dove would hardly consign its young to the vulture for brood and succor, or the shepherd the lamb to the wolf.

15. No more would Heaven employ as embassadors of Truth, those who reject divine counsel, deny the existence of those principles upon which the embassy is predicated and labor to overthrow the government whence they were commissioned.

15. The air balloon would not be employed to transport the burden of the freighted ship, nor the iron steamer to navigate the aerial realms. These principles are also applicable to the philosophy in question.

17. As the heavens are higher than the earth, even so must the dwellers in the celestial be above the groveling in this sickly world.

18. Therefore, were the likeness of the heavenly daguerreotyped upon the heart of man, it would not reflect the portraiture of the human, but the divine. This can self-evidently apply to modern spiritualism.

19. If the Holy and Divine descends to, and in mercy pervades the perverted and unholy, the effect will be to incline them to the plane of moral goodness. Thus will be revealed the contrast between the pure and impure, the infinite and the finite.

20. Good may be removed by evil, but can never conform to it.

21. Right may be invaded by wrong, but can never comply with its dictation.

22. Means originally adapted to useful ends, *may* be perverted, overcome and forced as agents of opposing principles.

23. Goodness is a quality, a distinguishing principle.

24. Man is good when his moral nature is unaffected with evil.

25. Error is opposed to truth, and therefore exists in its absence.

26. If evil obtain possession of the soul, goodness retires.

27. Evil may be overruled for good, but of itself, can never engender it.

28. Principles have palpable characteristics, and beget their likeness, and reduce to their nature that over which they prevail.

29 Laws cause to converge what constitutionally affinitize.

30. Hence, principles in their procedure dis-

seminate their spirit or essences throughout proximate and unconfirmed material; absorb affinities; bring to their sphere, or repel opposites.

31. Bodies formed by, and around the principles of error, are attracted and held by improper, and therefore, unreliable adhesion; hence are subject to disintegration.

32. Such bodies not being sustained and conducted by eternal law, move indifferently, and drift by the preponderance of whatever current may chance to reach them to which they happen to incline, or into which they, by oscillation, dip.

33. Truth and Right being immutable and eternal, shall prevail; hence error and wrong shall be subdued.

34. Therefore, the Kingdom of Righteousness will overcome the realms of discord and unrighteousness.

35. Heaven is Love and Unity.

36. Dwellers upon the earth are carnal, selfish and repugnant.

37. The family of man is, thence, inharmonious, unlike heaven, and therefore the opposite.

38. Cause cannot sublevate its effects to a plane more exalted than it occupies.

39. Hence the elements of the earth-sphere by their native ability, and unaided from on high, cannot exalt themselves to a state above the apex of their nature.

40. Therefore earth cannot transform itself into heaven.

41. Redeeming principles must not be heir to the ills from which they seek to restore the sickly, fallen sufferer.

42. Means employed may serve as graduates, and when the end of their use is subserved, retire.

43. Cause must be superior to means, and to its undertaking, omnipotent.

44. Harmonial spiritualism claims no origin above nature.

45. The highest attainment of its superior qualities are therefore incomplete—need themselves perpetual correction.

46. The source, then, is defection.

47. Can the world be redeemed—perfected, by that which is also needy? and project itself through the cloudy obscurity over-hanging its sphere, and to a self-wrought inheritance, a dominion celestial, divine?

48. As well might the smitten tree and its blasted fruit, by dint of self-exertion impart to their own sickly, sinking nature the healthy sap, and unfold in perfect and luxurient growth, the choicest and most perfect harvest.

These suggestions are too self-evidently true to be easily overcome by the transcendental philosophy of the Nineteenth Century. The visionary tendency of the age may envelope the mind of millions in a fantastic halluncination; theorizers may project from their brains a kind of beatifying system, may build as sublimated zones, ethereal degrees that encompassing the earth, and people them with the spirits of the dead; they may reproduce, (as the savage does his hunting grounds in the land whither he journeys,) the earth-sphere with its conditions and uses,—still *principles* must endure. And when the dream is past, *mind* must revert to realities, for upon them it depends.

As orb-revolutions afford time for sleep, and the shadow-period induces the dreamy wanderings of the soul, even so there seems returning epochs, which beget a spiritual somnambulism, frought with fancy-pilgrimages to the kingdom of morpheus, a world of attenuated idealism.

CHAPTER IV.

MESMERISM AND PSYCHOLOGY, THE VENTRICLES OF HARMONIAL SPIRITUALISM.

Little need be said of the origin of animal magnetism, since no index to such an epoch has been discovered, save that which exists in the constitution of man. The only rational conclusion is, that whenever and wherever man has existed this principle has also existed; and that all attending phenomena, developed thereby, have been common with men, only, that the laws and means have not always been recognized as connected with the effects. What is now known as mesmerism, psychology, psychometry, biology, spirit-manifestation etc, were formerly known by different appellations. Such as necromancy, divination, magic, sooth-saying, charming, sorcery, etc.

Omitting the history of remote ages, we only pause to note, briefly, the development of the phenomena of the last century.

In "Stilling's Pneumatology," a work translated from the German, are many interesting illustrations—very many striking instances embracing magnetism and its demonstrations, trance conditions, spirit seeing, etc. And to conduct the mind gradually along this magnetic current to

the present expansion of the same manifestations, we indulge a few brief extracts from that work. "The science of animal magnetism," says Stilling, "which had occasionally manifested itself from the earliest ages, and was brought into system by Mesmer, between the years 1770 and 1780, but which, at the very outset, met with most profound contempt, in consequence of the most extravagant charlatanry, and the most shocking abuse which was made of it, was now investigated by very able, impartial, and candid naturalists—by men who really cannot be charged with the weakness of enthusiasm. . . . . .
To avoid all unnecessary prolixity, I will only here adduce such results of animal magnetism, as are certain and beyond a doubt. . . . .
But before I proceed further, I must give all my readers a serious caution: Animal magnetism is a very dangerous thing." "Pneumatology," pp. 27–8.

From the above, it appears that when Stilling wrote, near a century ago, the evils accruing from animal magnetism were somewhat, at least, understood. Well for the world if they had been, and were better known. If so, the cause, by many not discovered, of the most deplorable evils would be so revealed as to shock the sense of the much injured, by reason of a most diabolical use of insidious laws. "When an intelligent physician employs it for the cure of diseases," says Stilling, "there is no objection to it." Even so; but when *quacks* in medicine, and also the "affinitizing bands," who so benevolently (selfishly) pity those uncongenially united by the laws of matrimony,—when these employ it as a source of charming, it is disastrous to the social relations of life. It severs those pleasantly united, corrodes the conjugial element, dissipates the love of the "twain" that they are no more one flesh, and produces nameless results greatly to be lamented.

On p. 30, ibid, this author thus continues the subject of magnetism and its results:

"The history of the somnambulist of Lyons, says the journal of Paris, presents an assemblage of such striking facts, that we should be inclined to regard the whole as charlatanry and deceit, if credible eye-witnesses had not vouched for the truth of it. . . The catalepsy of a lady at Lyons, had been for some time the subject of conversation in that city; and M. Petetain had already published several very surprising facts relative to it, when Mr. Bellanche became desirous of becoming an eye-witness. He chose the moment, for visiting this lady, when she was approaching the crisis, (the time of magnetic sleep.) Upon this he approached the bed, in which he saw a female lying motionless, and who was, to all appearance, sunk into a profound sleep. He laid his hand, as he had been instructed, on the stomach of the somnambulist, and then began his interrogatories. The patient answered them all correctly. He then asked the sleeper if she could read the letter," (which he folded and laid on her stomach,) "to which she answered yes." According to the account, the somnambulist, clairvoyant, or medium, read to his satisfaction. The only difference between this case and the modern psychometric mode, is, the letter, now, is placed upon the cerebrum, over the perceptive faculties.

The medium at Lyons, during Mr. Ballanche's test, according to the account, read from a book through a wall. Can the mooted Poughkeepsie Seer do more? And how many of this developed age can equal even this case? Another instance related by Stillings was that of a somnambulist visited by Gmelin, who in search of mesmeric facts, in 1780, went to Carlsruhe and found that "what passed in the souls of those with whom she," (the somnambulist,) "was placed in connection could be read." For "she told him, distinctly, every thing that he imagined." p. 32, ibid.

"Another individual of great integrity," continues the author, p. 33, "and to whom I am much attached, told me that his wife had once a housekeeper, who had also been magnetized on account of illness, and had at length, during her magnetic sleep, attained an extraordinary degree of clearness of vision. In this state she had communicated remarkable and important discoveries concerning the invisible world. . . She brought intelligence from the invisible world, respecting certain important personages, enough to make the hearers' ears tingle. She once said to her master, in the crisis," (magnetic state,) "your brother has just expired at Magdeburg. No one knew anything of his illness, and, besides this, Magdeburg was many miles distant. A few days after, the news arrived of his death, which exactly agreed with the prediction."

These are cases where psychometry and spirit seeing was induced by animal magnetism. In 1848 the following similar case occurred in the town of Berlin, Rensselaer Co., N. Y.:

Mrs. Buton, who had long suffered from an extreme nervous debility, by the earnest solicitation of her friends, and as an experiment, was pathetised by the writer, then Pastor of a Baptist church in that town, of which the lady was a member. The object, at the time, was not so much to restore her lost health, as to quiet the agitated nervous system. From the effect of this pathetism, Mrs. Buton very frequently declared herself in the spirit world holding converse with the spirits of the dead, especially the spirit of her husband.

This occurred before the "spirit rapping" had emerged from Hydesdale, N. Y., and consequently before known of, by any one connected with the above incident.

Mrs. Buton revealed the characteristics of those referred to by Stilling, already noticed, and of those now known as spirit media. However, as she recovered her wasted strength, her disposition to spirit-seeing declined, and although still a resident of Berlin, N. Y., we have not heard that her mediumship has been revived.

In these cases, animal magnetism was the inducing cause of the spirit-seeing, and psychometric impressions, etc.

On page 41, of his work, Stilling thus philosophises:

"The causes from which a natural magnetic sleep may proceed are chiefly the following:—

"First: A lively and very irritable nervous system, and a vivid imagination appertaining to it, both of which are generally found united.

"Secondly: An incessant occupation of the soul with supernatural objects; for instance, when superstitious, ill-formed, simple people, are constantly thinking upon bewitchments and apparitions. Even if they be, at the same time, vile reprobate characters, they may at length be brought, by this means, into a real connection with evil spirits, and then sorcery is no longer an idle tale.

"Sensuous love, particularly in the female sex, is the most fertile source of magnetic fits, and hence arise horrible deceptions, particularly when religious feelings are intermixed with them. I am acquainted with many melancholy instances of this kind, of which, for the sake of persons still living, I will not now give publicity.

"A pious young woman visited the religious meetings which a pious but handsome *married* man held in his house. By degrees she fell in love with him; and, as an insuperable difficulty stood in the way of her attachment, her nerves succumbed in the conflict, and the poor unfortunate girl became a somnambulist," (a spirit-medium;) "at the commencement she uttered the most sublime and glorious truths in her fits; and she generally entered her crisis when present at these religious meetings. She predicted many things that were to happen in future, several of which were accomplished. She gained a number of followers. In her fits," (the spiritual state,) "she received information by degrees that the wife of the object of her affections was an abomination in the sight of God and angels; this was gradually insinuated with such Satanic cunning and hypocrisy, that the whole company, which consisted of several hundred persons, most devoutly believed it. The poor woman was, therefore, confined in a remote place, *by orders from the invisible world;* she lost her reason and died raving mad; and the widower then married the young woman, also by order from the spirit world."

Many instances of quite modern date, although their narration might vary somewhat in the minutiæ, are sufficiently analogous to indicate like causes. Neither will it answer to charge them altogether upon people of the lower and most indifferent classes—those who frantically receive and blindly obey the dictation of bigoted and unprogressed spirits. If our suggestion is questioned by the advocates of the "new philosophy," and the facts disputed, we can easily refer to some in high spiritual authority, who are considered "the Great" of this age, that have sailed in those seas, and returned with their booty.

Precedents are numerous illustrative of this principle, and the mania has already obtained to a much greater extent than the unnoticing public are prepared to admit. And there are more victims than supposed, by far, to this peace-destroying principle, this law of modern progression, this harmonizer of the race, adjuster of human relations, builder of the "spiritual temple," of the so called newly developed or greatly progressed moral and social rights! But we shall defer, at present, its full illustration by authentic facts. Nevertheless we are pledged to sustain the above by ample proof when dealing with that phase of Spiritualism—the social didactics of that school of philosophers, which is, perhaps, more active and efficient than any other now moulding the human mind: that which is moving in the element of thought, of mental and affectional principles; and by adaptation and practical exertion, is possessing the soul of the young.

CHAPTER V.

MESMERISM IN ASIA.

THE above extracts from Stilling's Pneumatology are sufficient to prove the existence and character of the manifestations of his age. And the following from "Buchanan's Journal of Man" will serve as the connecting link with modern demonstrations.

In an article by James Esdale, M. D., published in vol. 1. of the above named work, under the heading, "Mesmerism in Asia," we find the following:

"The people of this part of the world seem to be peculiarly sensitive to the mesmeric power; and as it has been observed that a depressed state of the nervous system favors its reception, we can understand why they, as a body, should be more easily affected than Europeans. Taking the population of Bengal generally, they are a feeble, ill-nourished race, remarkably deficient in nervous energy; and the natural debility of constitution being still further lowered by disease, will probably account for their being so readily subdued by mesmerism. Their mental constitution also favors us: we have none of the morbid irritability of nerves, and the mental impatience of the civilized man to contend against; both of which resist and neutralize the efforts of nature." If the heathen is the most befitting subject, and the nervous and mental activity of civilization is to be overcome by this practice, this law of nature, in order to its success; it follows that mesmerism first reduces the subject, as far as may be, to a heathen state, thence, perhaps, arises the cause why the refined modes of civilization, or the true Christian religion, are so directly assailed by a vast portion of the operators, and the sayings of the subjects. All familiar with these phenomena, know full well that mesmerism, and nature-worshiping spiritualism, if left to their own promptings, reduce the subjects to the most wild and barbarous demonstrations imaginable. And, indeed, to prevent such results in indiscriminate spirit-circles, requires the controlling power and discretion of some well balanced and properly cultivated mind in the external sphere. Still, although, as will be hereafter shown, the counsel and dictation of the spirits are acknowledged unworthy of human dependence, the public are advised of new and divine revelations by the spirits: of light from the spirit world. Thomas Paine, Voltaire, Volney, Bonaparte, Franklin, Washington, etc., etc., are declared to have, in great benevolence, descended to the plane of earth in order to elevate man from his ignorance, superstition, bigotry and false religions. Nevertheless, it is found to be important not to heed their teachings unless they accord with what man knows, with his sense! Thus the highly exalted spirits who have escaped the thraldom of mundane ignorance, and have progressed to the higher spheres, are to be, at last, dictated by those whom they in great love condescend to instruct! And man's undeveloped sense must decide upon the merit of the divine counsel! This would be like the Professor in mathematics, or any of the sciences, submitting his problem or principle to the judgment of the novice, and allowing him, while unlearned, to sit as judge upon the nature and utility of lessons given to the classes for their improvement.

How would it appear for the tyro to enter the classic library and cast out as useless those works of whose language and sentiment he had not the slightest knowledge? Or for the patient to decide the treatment of his disease for his physician? The inconsistency of like courses is too apparent to be misconceived. Nevertheless, it would be equally as consistent in the above cases, as for the manifestations of Heaven to be judged and received or rejected, by benighted human minds. If the manifestations are from God, for man's good, they are worthy of implicit confidence; and their requirements are always consistent and useful, hence they should be obeyed unreservedly; and if they are not of Heaven they should be rejected, for they seek the control of man. But the reverse is the counsel of spiritualists. And why? Simply because spiritualism cannot be relied upon. It must be nurtured, guided, helped and sustained by those to whom it is said to be unfolding by its superior influence, its knowledge of the spiritual worlds, to its sphere. Whoever submits to the dictum of the "spirits" is deemed, by the learned in those matters, "fanatic." The order of things is, then, by spiritualism, reversed, for the pupil becomes the teacher, or umpire over his exalted lessons, and the novice is the dictator. Day of progression! Day of wonders! But the author continues: "The success I have met with is mainly to be attributed, I believe, to my patients being the simple, unsophisticated children of nature; neither thinking, questioning, nor remonstrating, but submitting to my pleasure, without in the smallest degree understanding my object or intentions." A truthful acknowledgment! And what an honor to be a subject! "How far artificial"(civilized)"man may have forfeited his birthright, I have not yet had the means of knowing; but out of the small number of Europeans who have come under my observation, the majority have also succumbed to the influence; and if the proud sons of civilization will condescend to return for a moment to the feet of their mother nature, they also will probably benefit by her bounties." That is, if the masses will become the subjects of the few positive minds, the mesmerizers and psychologizers, and not knowing their motives, submit to their control, "without questioning or remonstrating," they will probably benefit by the bounties of nature. Civilization, then, is in the way of these teachers. We do not charge *all* with this motive, but the sequel proves that the "*interior element*," or the law of mesmerism, destroys self-control. Nor can it succeed without the unreserved submission of the mesmerized to its influence. The subject must, therefore, for the time being, at least, move blindly in the direction of the current. Thousands who are engaged in the manifestations are, no doubt, sincere; but the honest and pure-minded may be the subjects, unknowingly, of an element liable to be excited for a vile purpose. Would those negatively constituted, those exceedingly susceptible to the mesmeric influence, readily submit, or anxiously seek to be affected by that conquering subtle principle, if they understood the nature and power of the law to which they expose themselves? If mesmerism may be turned to good or evil, its determination must be in accordance with the quality of the motive power—the directing mind. If the prompting genius be evil inclined, the subject of the influence must succumb to the propensity of that controlling element. Who are the pure and good? Who sufficiently free from the ills of perverted nature to become the absolute dictators of a human soul? Who sufficiently wise to mould, by force of will, the character and therefore decide unreservedly, the destiny of another? Men may be mutual counselors, and mind needs instruction, but the author of the above extracts says the subject must unreservedly and without knowing the operator's motives, or questioning his procedure submit. And on page 261, he also declares, "that this agent may and will be turned to the most diabolical purposes, is most certain, if the public will not be at the trouble to think upon this subject and defend itself by common precautions."

What better authority than this need we? It is also *certain*, that when individuals have once submitted to that mysterious agent, they have no eyes to see or ears to hear, save those given by the controlling genius. Hence they must drift along its tide, and whoever admonishes them of their danger, is by them deemed their veriest foe. The charmer has full control of their sympathies, his visage is most fair and comely, but the true friends, the opposers of the usurper, appears haggard and frightful. "*O tempora, O mores.*"

This agent is that which unfolds the phenomena of mesmerism and psychology in all their forms and is also that by which the works of spiritualism are developed. Still, parents, guardians, companions and friends submit their greatest treasures to the fate of this current. This is the crucible in which fantastically glows the molten element of Anti-Christ. And as sure as the soul enters the affinitizing process, so sure it shall not return to its former state. Fearful adventure! Yet modern mind seems forming for the dread transition! Jesus alone can save thee, O reader! put thy soul in his charge, and live near the Cross, if thou wouldst escape the fearful consequences that await the end of these things. To those already beneath the charm, admonition is unavailing. Their sense is benumbed, their mind calloused. Blind infatuation seems to have possessed their souls. They laugh at counsel and wildly rush into the sweeping tide.

If the element is not capable of guiding, and yet to be developed it is necessary to yield to it unreservedly, where is the benefit, unless it be employed by the external magnetizer? and who shall be the judge of human wisdom suitable? God is infinitely wise, he offers counsel, whoso trusts him shall be saved. 'Tis better to forsake the creature and cleave unto the Creator: accept his word as the sure Word of Testimony.

On page 260 the writer thus continues his narrative:

"June 9, 1845.—I had to-day the honor of being introduced to one of the most famous magicians in Bengal, who enjoys a high reputation for his successful treatment of hysteria, and had been sent for to prescribe for my patient, (whose case will be afterward given,) but came too late; the success of my charm, Mesmerism, having left him nothing to do. Baboo Essanchunder Ghosaul, deputy magistrate of Houghly, at my request introduced me to him as a brother magician, who had studied the art of magic in different parts of the world, but particularly in Egypt, where I had learned the secrets of the great Sooleymann, from the Moollahs and Fuqueers, and that I had a great desire to know whether our charms were the same, as the hakeems of Europe held the wise men of the East in high estimation, knowing that all knowledge had come from that quarter. I proposed that we should show each other our respective charms, and, after much persuasion, he agreed to show me his process for assuaging pain. He sent for a brass pot containing water and a twig with two or three leaves upon it, and commenced muttering his charms, at arm's length from the patient. In a short time he dipped his fore-finger into the water, and with the help of his thumb, flirted it into the patient's face; he then took the leaves, and commenced stroking the person from the crown of the head to the toes with a slow drawing motion. The knuckles almost touched the body, and he said that he would continue the process for an hour, or longer, if necessary; and it convinced me that if these charmers ever do good by such means, it is by the Mesmeric influence, probably unknown to themselves. I said that I was convinced of the great efficacy of his charm, and would now show him mine; but that he would understand it better if I performed it on his own person. After some difficulty we got him to lie down, and, to give due solemnity to my proceedings, I chanted, as an invocation, the chorus of the "King of the Cannibal Islands!" I desired him to shut his eyes, and he clenched his eyelids firmly, that I might find no entrance to his brain by that inlet. In a quarter of an hour he jumped up, and said that he felt something coming over him, and wished to make his escape. He was over-persuaded to lie down again, however, and I soon saw the muscles around the eye begin to relax, and his face became perfectly smooth and calm. I was sure that I had caught my brother magician napping; but in a few minutes, he bolted up suddenly, clapped his hands to his head, cried he felt drunk, and nothing could induce him to lie down again. '*Abiit, excessit, evasit, erupit!*' Next day I saw him, and said, "Well, you were too strong for my charm last night; I could not put you to sleep!' 'O! yes, Sahib,' he answered, 'you did; I allow it; it is allowed that you put me to sleep.'

"A gentleman, whose case will be given hereafter, immediately recognized the identity of the two processes, and told me that he had been mesmerized, he knew, in a different part of the country, and with much relief, in a painful affection of the leg. In addition to the traction of the leaves, his mesmerizer had breathed carefully upon the pained part, just as my assistant had done when mesmerizing him locally for rheumatism. It thus appears that the beneficial effects of the Mesmeric process are unknown in this country, and the secret has probably descended from remote antiquity, in certain families or castes. Further on, when speaking of Somnambulism, a curious history will be given, which leads me to suspect that they knew the evil as well as the good of Mesmerism, and practised it for the most villainous purposes. The possible evil resulting from Mesmerism has been a favorite objection, even when the evidence of its existence and power could be no longer resisted."

Thus modern advocates of the system, prove it of long standing, even trace it to, and make it the same as ancient Magic. And the author of the foregoing remarks, indicates his knowledge of instances wherein somnambulism has been revealed in connection with mesmerism. Spiritualism it is well known unfolds from or by means of it. The only difference then, between the ancient and modern practices and manifestations, is in their modes. And with them there is a corresponding likeness. In former times the art of healing by the subtle agent was known; magnetized subjects became very sensitive to impressions, and in their trance conditions seemed to be conversant with the spirits of the dead. Mesmerism and psychology, therefore, are the connecting agents that unite the material with the spiritual. Or in other words, that which in the inferior plane is known as Mesmerism in its varied forms, when more sublimated, is either spiritualism, or the vehicle by which that still more subtle influence approaches the external. These are the principles engaged in spirit manifestations, and what now so much excites the more transcendental mind-element of this age is not a new development, an evidence of progression, but only the repetition of what has been from time immemorial.

History also reveals, that like phenomena have most obtained where civilization has the least influence. To this, as heretofore shown, the author of Mesmerism in Asia bears testimony. Rather, then, than such phenomena being an evidence of progression, they strongly indicate retrogression. The civilized man is not a fit subject, (so it is said,) but the unsophisticated, morbid and passive child of nature. To this conclusion the voice of these "isms," bears witness, also, for their loud acclaim is continually against whatever is established. They seek to demolish the temples hitherto erected by the hand of christian civilization, and to build their altars to nature and spirits, in the human heart, and their temples where affinities are as gods.

In some stages of the manifestations media have been developed by means of a manipulator, sometimes without any human agencies, but they are mostly spiritualized, (mesmerized) by the force of influence accumulated in circles, by the power of association. In such cases several persons who desire the demonstrations, join hands and concentrate their thoughts, silently invoking the spirits to develope some one or more of the group. The tendency of the mental current is to the negative point, hence the one most susceptible is liable soon to feel a peculiar change of nervous action. This is followed by some slight unnatural muscular movement or a torpid appearance, which attracts general attention. The thought induced in all minds by these demonstrations, is but one; the mind sphere feels an assurance that the desire has been regarded by the spirits, and that they have a medium in their midst. Whether aided from the "interior" or not the mesmeric power is now rapidly increased, and the subject secured. Personal ability—self-control, has been submitted to the invisible element, and a transition ensues; hence a spirit medium. Then the work of communicating with the dwellers in the invisible world is commenced. Repeated efforts of this kind finally render the subjects exceedingly sensitive to the influence, and they go forth as developed media.

As the subtle fluids are infused throughout gross substances, so this invisible principle, by its many means, steadily and surely, is working its way into the life principle, the heart of nations. And is manifesting itself in every conceivable form, from the cold and rigid state of the magnetizee, along the degrees of the rapping, seeing, writing, speaking, healing, and book making media of the spirit-mania.

Like the fire which unknown and unseen is charring the substance amid which it smolders, this is deadening the moral sensibility, and consuming the vital energies of the age. And even now strong parts of the edifice of civilization are weakened by its power. This is denied by many of the advocates of the "new philosophy," and men accept the denial as truth, even while in their ears echo the blasphemous denunciations of the christian religion and the strongholds of civilization. Civilization renders man an accountable being, and makes sacred beyond a name, the marriage covenant. But multitudes are boldly promulgating the doctrines of nonaccountability, that man is altogether a creature of circumstances, and to properly develop the being, they say, "let nature have her course." If man is controlled altogether by circumstances he *cannot be responsible for his actions.* What will follow such teachings? Or rather, what will not result from faith formed by such a creed? Another, and very active principle of the "ism," is that the prevailing law of matrimony is a source of human—of spiritual bondage, and should be very much modified, or entirely abolished. This is a most fatal blow aimed at the heart of family relations, at the great bond of civilization. Establish the above codes of the progressive school, then silence the religious press, prohibit the preaching of the gospel of Jesus; and do it by art, soothsaying, psychomancy, mesmerism, or by whatever means, and civilization is no more. That all persons engaged in the service of these elements are not understandingly or intentionally contributing to such results we do not doubt. Neither do we charge those principles working proper changes, changes in reality for the better, with like disastrous and inevitable consequences. But such we maintain is the soul, body and intended consummation of Harmonial Spiritualism, and all isms that adhere to the above-named sentiments. And we venture to affirm that by their works this charge can be fully demonstrated and proved, and in the Review of modern phenomena engage to make good these statements, by the facts unfolded from or appended to those principles of anti-civilization—of anti-Christ.

PART IV.

MODERN MANIFESTATIONS.

CHAPTER I.

MESMERIC PRODUCTIONS—A. J. DAVIS' DISCIPLES.

A FEW years previous to the introduction of the "Rochester Rappings," mesmerism had elicited some public attention and secured some able advocates and efficient operators. The most notable results, however, were the lectures of A. J. Davis, the Poughkeepsie magnetizee. These were delivered by him while in a magnetic state, induced by the manipulations of Dr. Lyon, and are now before the world, as "Nature's Divine Revelations," as shown in Vol. I. of this Work. Those lectures are evidently the great Scientific, Religious and Literary center of the "New Philosophy," and suggest whatever himself or any of the new School have been or are promulgating. Nor do the "spirits," said to be prompting that fraternity, add to those revelations. They are as a whole, comparable to an orb in whose sphere, the "spirits," media and philosophers, so numerous roam at ease. Their productions are essays, dissertations, poems, and rhapsodies upon sections of the radiations from that work. Their newness is but the re-expression, in a different form, of what Mr. Davis uttered while the subject of Dr. Lyon. Mr. Davis' relation to mesmerism, and the manifestations; and as the vocal organ of "interiorism" renders him, despite the desire and efforts of the many ambitious media and all opposition, the magnetic Chatechist of the age. When those lectures commenced, the popular spiritualism of these times was foreshadowed. And as every new religion, or new manifestation of principles or theory already known has its leader, even so did this. For reasons hereafter to be disclosed, it is important at this time to glance at the external agents of *Mesmeric Spiritualism*. For no slight review of this subject will meet the necessity of the case.

Mr. Davis, although only the medium of communications from the fountain, is before the world as the SEER, the great Apostle of the Nineteenth Century—the SUN of Earth's grand and final Epoch. As such his earliest supporters are his disciples. He evidently thus esteems them. Nor can time or circumstances change or in any way alter that relation. As such their names will be handed down to posterity.* For whatever they do, they are but working out the problem through him stated, and written upon

*Mr. Fishbough, according to present indications being the only exception.

the magic reflector of this mystic period. In descending to the minutiæ, and tracing this fountain throughout its ramifications, the Seer's original supporters will be found to have been first moved by that strange and thence mysterous inspiring wonder which enhaloed him in his magnetized state. The charm by which they were then entranced, and the impetus they then received, has been the power holding them as lesser floating bodies around Mr. Davis, the Center, and by which they have been primarily impelled along the current in which they are now drifting. If they may have wandered, they have never passed the boundaries of the "Davis-realm," and have been inevitably drawn back again. Whether, therefore, the Poughkeepsie Seer, infolds about himself substantial material, or is composed of, and encompassed by, an artificial combination of illusive parts, to these satelites he is *the substance, the power, the unfolding orb.*

However unpleasant these reflections may be, truth demands them. And were they omitted, the center of the newly constructed, or modernly arranged system of antiquated notions, would pass unnoticed, and the Review would be deficient in an important and essential point. It would have omitted the focal centre, the heart of the mystic automaton which arises and in its movements proposes to crush the *church of Christ* beneath its awful tread, and with its magic sabre, cut down the ranks that stand in defence of the Word of God. Nothing, therefore, can be understandingly investigated without reference to that external nucleus—Mr. Davis and his first disciples, the cabinet and ministers plenipotentiary of this magnetic kingdom, in whose centre he oscillates as a revolving mirror, while they as secondary reflectors, move in their respective orbits about him. The merits of this nervo-spiritual centre, its philosophy and religion, as well as its probable ultimation can be determined by reference to the discussion of Pantheism—Review of A. J. Davis. "ANTI-PANTHEIST," Vol. I. Nevertheless, however inconsiderable may be the true worth of the system, *this is its day*, and its sphere affects the human mind. It has arisen from the chaos of ancient ideas, somewhat blended with modern improvements.

Its appearance is like the Auroral luminations. It flashes upward its pale and transient light. Upon it the evening watchers gaze with wonder and fantastic admiration.

While it endures it is well to analyze it, and record its nature. From the verge of the shadowy dell of civilization that dim light may be discovered. Thither let us descend. Above us columns of Truth arise, and the canopy of the heavens gently smile upon the thatched bowers, that pending droop over the gloomy gorge. Let the mind first glancing, ascend the glory-crowned mountain of Light and Reason, that everlasting monument to eternal Truth, and then turning, look out upon the fathomless chasm below. Vast deep of false philosphy! of ethics most corrupt! In its nether regions, sunken and heavy, deadly magnetism hangs like a thick impenetrable cloud of night. From the hither side arise those false reflections which encompass the human circle of the "new philosophy." Above them move those spectral clouds which drift along the heavens and seem as manifestations of unkown realities. So perfect is the charm that the "group" behold the shadows as eternalized substances, and from them build ethereal zones, and people them with immortal races.

The above represents the new birth of that complicated system which has since extended its influence afar, and now threatens to involve the mind of the age in its deceptious mysteries.

About the time the "Revelations" were closed, a periodical advocating the new school, was commenced. The principal editor, we believe, was S. B. Brittan, formerly a Universalist preacher, who is now editor of the Spiritual Telegraph, published in New York, and devoted exclusively to spiritualism.

Thomas L. Harris, then pastor of a Universalist church in New York, resigned his charge and went forth under the auspices of Mr. Davis, as advocate of "Nature's Divine Revelations." He made a tour through Ohio, where he so presented the subject of the "Revelations," and so exalted the "Medium" thereof as to secure a respectable number of friends to the cause. These members of the group are named in this connection, for reasons that will hereafter be made apparent.

Those who composed that Center, from which has emerged so extensive a tide — the co-workers in a new enterprise — the advocates of a *Book*, the very culmination of all opposition to Theopneustic doctrines — the Bible and the religion of the Cross — proceeded for a season comparatively harmonious. But a storm awaited them; the auroral light was changed into a dark and fearful tempest, and when it burst upon them, it closed the "Univercœlum" and sundered to fragments the external germ of the new kingdom. Mr. Davis abandoned the absolute authors of his newly-formed being, his benefactors, those who had shielded him in his tender age from the withering blasts of the external world, and assumed an independent air, which he has since most admirably maintained. Mr. Fishbough, his amanuensis, and faithful friend, retired to his private closet, sensibly wronged. Mr. Harris commenced lecturing in a Hall in New York, to a company he denominated the "Independent Christian Society." And Mr. Brittan assumed the "professorship" of Psychology.

With fallen hopes and depressed spirits, these, and others of the group equally as disappointed, moved along without any especial aim, and with severed sympathies.

The external nucleus being broken and scattered, and the severed parts having become considerably antagonistic to each other, the system seemed to pause in a sort of disquieted, inefficient state. Mr. Davis, as before indicated, was however laboring to establish himself an independent clairvoyant. Mr. Harris was seeking to erect an opposite but independent "ism," under his own name and jurisdiction, while Mr. Fishbough applied to nature and reason for the solution of the philosophic question so strangely propounded through Mr. Davis, and which had, as he vainly supposed, been answered. Retired, and in search of true wisdom he struggled ardently to pierce the cloudy veil that encompassed the subject. Others not named, were also moving in various sections, but without any very satisfactory results, when lo, the spirit of the system burst from its smothered state in another and unexpected form.

CHAPTER II.

ORIGIN OF MODERN SPIRITUALISM.

At this time the Fox family, residing in Hydesdale, N. Y., were being annoyed with "the rappings." The echo reached the city, where the members of the old magnetic nucleus still resided; but from their recent failure in the works of the mysterious, those early advocates of the premonitory manifestations were little aroused, and perhaps less inclined to venture upon the unexplored waters of the newly discovered sea.

Finally, not only Hydesdale was affected by the strange visitant, but Rochester and Auburn, N. Y., and Stratford, Conn., became the sounding-board of spiritualism.

At length the heart-stricken band, one by one arose from their despondings, and paid their homage to the manifestations. Not, however, with united hearts, but in some instances with strong personal prejudices. Their sectional prepossessions were so active that some of those who composed the old coterie of the Poughkeepsie Seer, would not meet the Fox media in company, or announce appointments before their audiences for each other, without an apology, and even caution to the public.

Meanwhile the "Spiritual Telegraph" was commenced by Charles Partridge of New York, and the written productions of spiritualism began to multiply. The mania was spreading with unprecedented rapidity, and taking a strong hold upon the public mind, when the severed parts of the circle which had once united around Mr. Davis and his "Revelations," inclined to one common centre again. Although each was desirous of retaining his sectional identity, they, by a kind of intuition, began once more to blend in one common effort. Hence, though every one was determined to erect his own temple, they manifested a strong disposition to recline upon each other as mutual supporters in their conflict with the things that are.

Again, then, those who once joined hands around Mr. Davis, are seen mingling in one body. And now, although in their ramifications their theories vary somewhat, they are evidently, with the exception noticed, parts of a whole. They radiate in different directions, but from the same center receive the means of their reflections. And Mr. Davis is absolutely the main pillar of this new spiritual edifice. The old stock, therefore, the first supporters of "Nature's Divine Revelations," are absolutely the center components of the external manifestations, whence issues the fountain of magnetic spiritualism.

www.ingramcontent.com/pod-product-compliance
Lightning Source LLC
LaVergne TN
LVHW021221110826
845150LV00002B/209

9781425564551